BRINGING POWER TO JUSTICE?

STUDIES IN NATIONALISM AND ETHNIC CONFLICT
General Editors: Sid Noel, Richard Vernon

Studies in Nationalism and Ethnic Conflict examines the political dimensions of nationality in the contemporary world. The series includes both scholarly monographs and edited volumes that consider the varied sources and political expressions of national identities, the politics of multiple loyalty, the domestic and international effects of competing identities within a single state, and the causes of – and political responses to – conflict between ethnic and religious groups. The books are designed for use by university students, scholars, and interested general readers.

The editors welcome inquiries from authors. If you are in the process of completing a manuscript that you think might fit into the series, you are invited to contact them.

1 Nationalism and Minority Identities in Islamic Societies
Edited by Maya Shatzmiller

2 From Power Sharing to Democracy
Post-conflict Institutions in Ethnically Divided Societies
Edited by Sid Noel

3 Bringing Power to Justice?
The Prospects of the International Criminal Court
Edited by Joanna Harrington, Michael Milde, Richard Vernon

Bringing Power to Justice?

The Prospects of the International Criminal Court

Edited by
JOANNA HARRINGTON
MICHAEL MILDE
and
RICHARD VERNON

McGill-Queen's University Press
Montreal & Kingston · London · Ithaca

ISBN-13: 978-0-7735-2966-3 ISBN-10: 0-7735-2966-7 (cloth)
ISBN-13: 978-0-7735-2967-0 ISBN-10: 0-7735-2967-5 (paper)

Legal deposit second quarter 2006
Bibliothèque nationale du Québec

Printed in Canada on acid-free paper that is 100% ancient forest free (100% post-consumer recycled), processed chlorine free.

This book has been published with the help of a grant from the J.B. Smallman Publication Fund, Faculty of Social Science, The University of Western Ontario.

McGill-Queen's University Press acknowledges the support of the Canada Council for the Arts for our publishing program. We also acknowledge the financial support of the Government of Canada through the Book Publishing Industry Development Program (BPIDP) for our publishing activities.

Library and Archives Canada Cataloguing in Publication

Bringing power to justice? : the prospects of the International Criminal Court / edited by Joanna Harrington, Michael Milde, and Richard Vernon.
(Studies in nationalism and ethnic conflict)
Papers presented at a conference held, Mar. 22-23, 2003 at the University of Western Ontario, London, Ont.
Includes bibliographical references and index.

ISBN-13: 978-0-7735-2966-3 ISBN-10: 0-7735-2966-7 (cloth)
ISBN-13: 978-0-7735-2967-0 ISBN-10: 0-7735-2967-5 (pbk)

1. International Criminal Court-Congresses. I. Milde, Michael II. Vernon, Richard, 1945– III. Harrington, Joanna, 1968– IV. Series.
KZ6311.B75 2006 345'.01 C2005-906513-3

Typeset in Sabon 10.5/13
by Infoscan Collette, Quebec City

Contents

Acknowledgments

This book originates from a conference held at the University of Western Ontario in March 2003: we are grateful to all the participants, including those whose work could not be included in this volume. The conference was organized by the Nationalism and Ethnic Conflict Research Group of the University of Western Ontario, with the generous financial assistance of the Dean of the Faculty of Social Science at the University of Western Ontario and of the John Holmes Fund of the Department of Foreign Affairs and International Trade, Canada. We are also grateful for the assistance provided by Andrea Gonsalves in preparing the papers for publication.

The Editors

BRINGING POWER TO JUSTICE?

I

Introduction

JOANNA HARRINGTON, MICHAEL MILDE, and RICHARD VERNON

1. THE HISTORIC ROAD TO ROME

The world's first permanent international criminal tribunal for the prosecution and punishment of the world's most serious crimes became a reality on 1 July 2002. On this date, after attracting ratifications from roughly two-thirds of the world's states, the *Rome Statute (for the establishment) of the International Criminal Court*[1] came into force, triggering the treaty's provisions for the selection of the Court's eighteen judges and paving the way for operations to begin in 2003. At present, the International Criminal Court (ICC) has jurisdiction over individuals accused of committing genocide, crimes against humanity, and war crimes after 1 July 2002,[2] provided there are no national authorities able and willing to prosecute. Within its first year of operation, over five hundred communications urging investigations to begin were lodged with the ICC prosecutor,[3] and within two years, the first investigations had been launched.[4]

Negotiated at a UN Diplomatic Conference of Plenipotentiaries held in Rome in mid-1998, the ICC Statute marks the culmination of a long, somewhat frustrating, and sometimes dormant struggle for the establishment of such a court.[5] The idea of trying war crimes internationally has been discussed since the end of World War I when the Allied Powers sought to prosecute Kaiser Wilhelm II and members of the German armed forces before a special tribunal. Yet, despite the fact that the Treaty of Versailles had provided for such prosecutions, not one soldier was surrendered for trial and the kaiser himself escaped prosecution by securing asylum in the Netherlands. Only later was a compromise reached, resulting in a handful of alleged war criminals being tried nationally before the German Supreme Court in Leipzig.[6] Later, during the tenure of the League of Nations, a treaty was signed contemplating the establishment of an international court to try crimes of terrorism, but it never came into force, as it was ratified by only one state.[7]

After World War II, support for an international criminal court again resurfaced, but the Allies opted instead for the creation of a temporary "International Military Tribunal" in Nuremberg to try the major war criminals of Nazi Germany,[8] as well as a similar ad hoc tribunal in Tokyo to try those accused of war crimes in the Far East.[9] It was envisioned that these two tribunals would try specific individuals whose crimes were significant and had no particular geographic location, leaving lesser criminals to be tried by national military tribunals in the territory of the state where the crimes had allegedly been committed. The ad hoc tribunals were not, however, truly international, and the composition of the Nuremberg Tribunal in particular, with its staff of judges and prosecutors from only the four Allied Powers, fuelled complaints that such tribunals dispensed "victor's justice."

Nevertheless, within the UN, the idea of a more permanent international criminal court continued to hold some sway, gaining a brief mention in the *Genocide Convention* of 1948[10] and more substantial coverage in the early work program of the International Law Commission (ILC). Soon after its creation in 1947, the ILC was asked by the UN General Assembly to prepare a draft code of offences against the peace and security of mankind, incorporating the principles espoused at Nuremberg, and to study the desirability and possibility of establishing an international judicial organ for the trial of persons charged with genocide or other crimes. With respect to an international court, the ILC concluded that it was both desirable and possible to create one, and in 1950, the UN General Assembly established a Committee on International Criminal Jurisdiction to prepare a draft statute for such a court. This statute was submitted to the General Assembly for approval in 1952,[11] and again in 1954,[12] but it failed for two reasons. First, there was a lack of agreement between states as to the definition of aggression and, second, the emerging tensions of the Cold War blocked all further efforts to establish an international criminal court for the next three decades.[13]

Then, in 1989, a campaign was initiated by Trinidad and Tobago to establish an international criminal court to try those accused of international drug trafficking. Despite the backing of many Caribbean and Latin American states, support, however, was not forthcoming from many Western states. Nevertheless, the proposal revived interest in the concept of an international criminal court and the ILC was again mandated by the UN General Assembly to prepare a draft statute.

As the ILC was working, it became clear that the situation of mass killings, systematic detention, and "ethnic cleansing" in the former Yugoslavia required immediate action. On 22 February 1993, the UN Security Council adopted a resolution calling for the establishment of a third ad hoc international criminal tribunal, this time with jurisdiction for the prosecution of persons responsible for committing genocide, crimes against humanity, and war crimes in the territory of the former Yugoslavia since 1991. A subsequent report by the UN secretary general proffered a draft statute for the establishment of such a court, and on 25 May 1993, the UN Security Council adopted the statute without changes to establish the International Criminal Tribunal for the Former Yugoslavia (ICTY), using its powers to maintain or restore international peace or security under chapter VII of the UN Charter.[14]

This precedent was then followed in 1994 with the establishment of a fourth ad hoc tribunal by the UN Security Council to address the genocide that took place in Rwanda which claimed as many as 500,000 lives over a period of 100 days. Like the ICTY, the International Criminal Tribunal for Rwanda (ICTR) was established by resolution rather than treaty, and on a temporary basis. It has jurisdiction for the prosecution of persons responsible for genocide and other serious violations of international humanitarian law committed in the territory of Rwanda and neighbouring states from 1 January to 31 December 1994.[15]

These developments prompted further interest in the goal of establishing a permanent international criminal court, with attention turning to the draft statute finalized by the ILC in 1994.[16] The UN General Assembly established a Preparatory Committee (PrepCom), its membership open to all UN states, to review the ILC draft and to this end, meetings were held from 1996 to 1998. After the final PrepCom meeting was held in March 1998, a Diplomatic Conference was convened in June and July 1998, bringing together 160 states, and several hundred non-governmental organizations, to hammer out a final consensus on the treaty's text.[17] In the final result, 120 states voted in favour, 7 against (including the US),[18] and 21 abstained, marking the adoption of the ICC Statute as a milestone in the struggle to confront impunity with accountability for those who commit the most serious crimes.

It is at this stage, as we embark on a new phase in international criminal justice, that we ask what the prospects of the ICC are. In this book, we bring together assessments made from the perspectives of law, political science, and philosophy. This multidisciplinary approach is essential, in our view, for making both a realistic and comprehensive assessment at this point in time in the Court's evolution. The core of discussion has always been in legal theory and it will rightly continue to be there: but as the history of the Court's emergence clearly shows, both moral and political elements play a key role. On the one hand, the push to create the ICC has come from tremendous idealism, particularly on the part of NGOs, and from deep moral revulsion at the hideous cruelties perpetrated by states in the recent past. On the other hand, the process of establishing the Court has been consistently controlled and often thwarted by state interests, and will continue to be controlled – and perhaps thwarted – by the attitudes of major powers. Discussion therefore needs a moral dimension, as well as a legal one, in order to assess the Court's purposes, and a political dimension in order to assess its chances of success. All three dimensions find a place in this collection.

II. THE FUTURE PROSPECTS OF THE ICC

Based on the principle of complementarity, the goal of the ICC is to bolster the network of existing national courts of criminal jurisdiction in the prosecution of acts of genocide, crimes against humanity, and war crimes, stepping in only when national authorities are genuinely unable or unwilling to act.[19] Unlike the International Court of Justice (ICJ), which is also based in The Hague, the ICC will have jurisdiction over individuals rather than states, and only individuals who are either nationals of a state party, or who have committed crimes on the party's territory. The only exception to this rule would be for cases referred to the Court by the UN Security Council.[20] The Court's docket will be comprised of cases initiated by either the state parties, the UN Security Council, or the ICC's independent prosecutor, although the latter route requires judicial approval. It will also be a permanent international court, thereby serving as a hoped-for deterrent for the commission of future crimes.[21]

In addition to the requirements imposed by complementarity, the ICC is further obligated to restrict the use of its jurisdiction to cases of "sufficient gravity."[22] This suggests that the intention of the ICC, like its predecessors in Nuremberg and Tokyo, is to create an international tribunal in which to try major offenders – rather than minor ones – who have been charged with the commission of serious international crimes. This is the "big fish–little fish" dilemma in international criminal law and the current trial of "big fish" Slobodan Milosevic before the ICTY is clearly one that, as Professor Michael Scharf demonstrates in his contribution to this volume, will likely test the very mettle of the international criminal justice system. The trial provides us with a vivid foretaste of the problems that prosecutions before the ICC are likely to encounter.

Slobodan Milosevic is of course the former Serbian head of state facing indictments for crimes against humanity and violations of the laws and customs of war committed in Kosovo, and additional indictments for further crimes committed in Croatia and Bosnia. Long thought to be one of the key architects of the war in the Balkans, Milosevic also holds the dubious distinction of being the first head of state to stand trial before an international criminal tribunal.[23] And, as Scharf points out, his trial may well prove to be the most challenging.

Given the frailty of peace in the Balkans, it is hoped that the successful prosecution of Milosevic will contribute to a more permanent reconciliation of long-held grievances in the region. Those who have suffered at the hands of Milosevic want to see their account of history tried and tested under cross-examination and then put on record, with a final result in favour of conviction. But as Scharf aptly demonstrates in his discussion of the trial, these efforts will matter little if the tribunal, and through it, the international community, cannot counter the perceptions of unfairness that have arisen, regardless of whether in fact those perceptions represent truth.

Yet, if we remain committed to the Nuremberg principle of holding individuals, rather than states, responsible internationally for their crimes, all the tribunal can do is hope that in the long run the final record will speak for itself. This may, however, be a long time coming. The Milosevic trial may well take up to the end of the decade to close, and if Scharf is correct, it will take a full generation after that for the final record to have its intended impact on those with sympathies for his cause.

The Milosevic trial also marks a turning point in the debate within the international community concerning the propriety of trying a head of state or other senior state official before a foreign criminal court. As Dapo Akande explains in his contribution to this volume, international law has traditionally granted immunity to a state, and to certain individuals representing that state, from all forms of legal process in a foreign state, including the national jurisdiction of that state's criminal courts. This rule of state immunity is said to flow from the recognition that all states hold equal status within the international community and must therefore respect each other's sovereign independence and refrain from interfering in each other's internal affairs.[24] Since the state is an abstract concept, the immunity also benefits the individual officials, including the head of the state, who personify the state when abroad, with the immunity rule serving essentially as a procedural bar to the commencement of legal proceedings in a foreign state. While initially an absolute bar to jurisdiction,[25] the rule has since evolved to permit some exceptions, such as when the subject matter relates to a state's commercial dealings.[26]

With respect to the criminal prosecution of individual officials, international law has long recognized the application of two forms of immunity. The first is personal immunity, or immunity *ratione personae*, which attaches to the particular office of certain state officials, such as the head of the government, and provides an absolute bar to any criminal prosecution of that official in another state while that official remains in office. This means that a foreign state will be held in violation of international law if it attempts to prosecute a sitting head of state or the foreign minister of another state, an obstacle that may be overcome by waiting until the individual no longer holds office.[27] State officials may, however, enjoy another form of immunity, known as functional immunity, or immunity *ratione materiae*, which attaches to the official acts themselves and can be relied upon even when the official has left office.

The rationale for such an immunity is that there are some acts for which the official should not be held responsible since the acts are in effect those of the state, and while it is more often applied in practice to civil cases, it is, as Akande explains, nonetheless available for criminal matters.

The more difficult question, however, is whether either immunity can apply when the crimes alleged to have been committed are crimes now internationally recognized as universally abhorrent, such as the crime of genocide, war crimes, and crimes against humanity. Will international law still grant immunity from arrest and prosecution when the crimes alleged to have been committed by a state official are international crimes? Given the renewed interest in prosecuting such crimes before either foreign domestic courts or international tribunals such as the ICC, the question is far from moot and, as rightly recognized by Akande, a full answer must consider both the customary international law position and the specific rules adopted by states for the ICC.

In the case of Milosevic, no rule of immunity bars his prosecution as his trial is taking place before a tribunal created by the UN Security Council, and Council decisions, including those removing any applicable rule of immunity, are binding on all UN member states. The position, however, is different with respect to a treaty-based court, such as the ICC, where only those states that have consented to the terms of the treaty, including its provisions on immunity, have consented to the removal of immunity. Akande's contribution thus provides a detailed discussion of the provisions of the ICC Statute concerning immunity, and recognizes also that the current position on immunity under customary international law remains relevant to the ICC, particularly if the Court wants to prosecute the state official of a non-party state. Moreover, as Akande argues, the application of the customary immunity rule within a foreign state's national jurisdiction also remains relevant since the ICC has no independent power of arrest and must therefore rely on the absence of immunity to secure the arrest and surrender of a wanted state official from the national jurisdiction to the Court.

III. SUPPORTERS AND CRITICS

The advent of the ICC has led to radically opposed reactions and predictions. On the one hand, human rights advocates welcome the

Court as another important component of a legal regime that has gradually been taking shape over two generations. British lawyer Geoffrey Robertson, for example, in a 1999 book that has been called "a crusading tract, or a statement of faith,"[28] presents the Court in terms of "a great post-war dream."[29] Its introduction owed much to the passionate advocacy of "hundreds of non-governmental organizations and professional associations, demonstrating the extent to which this mass movement has come to influence 'like-minded' democracies," a new global constituency that has become a force to be reckoned with.[30] Of course, its achievement thus far remains incomplete, for the Court now in existence, according to Robertson, is insufficiently independent of superpower influence, and its mandate reflects a world that is still too attached to the principle of sovereignty and to a fondness for diplomacy over law. Nevertheless, for all its flaws, the Court is another move in the long struggle to "unlock the closed door of state sovereignty"[31] and to hold state leaders accountable for abusing their subjects' rights.

For the opposite view of recent events, we can do no better than turn to former US secretary of state Henry Kissinger. While visiting Paris in the spring of 2001, Dr Kissinger was served with a summons to give evidence in a case brought in a French court on behalf of the victims of Operation Condor, the terror campaign carried out in several Latin American states during the 1970s, a campaign which, as some believe, depended on Kissinger's blessing.[32] Later that year, Kissinger's view of the matter appeared in an article in the influential journal *Foreign Affairs*.[33] "In less than a decade," wrote Kissinger, "an unprecedented movement has emerged to submit international politics to judicial procedures."[34] While it is quite right, he believes, that steps should be taken to bring legal norms to bear on human rights violations and the like, the movement contains a danger, that is, the danger of "substituting the tyranny of judges for that of governments."[35] Referring particularly to the case of General Pinochet, Kissinger draws attention to a number of issues that may arise when the actions of one state become criminally punishable by the judges of another. Setting aside here his own interpretation of Chilean political history, three main issues are offered. First, the practice would deny appropriate space for domestic processes of reconciliation, which must have an opportunity to occur without interference from abroad.[36] Second, the practice would allow parties to any severe conflict to project their disputes from the political and military planes to the judicial one. Palestinians and Israelis, for example, could both seek to have each others' leaders charged with criminal offences, thereby turning "a doctrine designed to transcend the political process ... into a means to pursue political enemies."[37] Thus, the attempt to judicialize politics would lead to the politicization of law. Third, there is the question of arbitrariness and selectivity. One need not accept Kissinger's view that contempt for Pinochet is merely – as he implies – "fashionable" to see his point that the transnational prosecution of state crimes is likely to be much less even-handed than one expects the domestic equivalent to be. A domestic system that was selective to that extent would violate the principle that all are equally entitled to the protection of law.[38]

Kissinger acknowledges, however, that there is less to object to in the creation of a standing court than in giving transnational jurisdiction to national judges. He even holds out the prospect of an eventual improved ICC, one that will have been modified to meet legitimate US concerns. We should note, though, that those concerns are very substantial and far-reaching, for they are concerns about unacceptably "assigning the ultimate dilemmas of international politics to unelected jurists – and to an international judiciary at that."[39] What is unacceptable about this is that the crimes falling to the Court's jurisdiction are "vague" and therefore open to politicized interpretation, and they are subject also to political pressure for the widest possible interpretation. The central flaw is thus the large scope of prosecutorial discretion. The Court's prosecutor may indict "subject to review only by a [pre-trial] panel of three judges," and while indictments can be quashed by the UN Security Council such quashing is subject to veto, thus enabling the prosecutor to proceed with the support of any one member of the council.[40] (The contrast between this and Geoffrey Robertson's view that the Court is unduly hamstrung by superpowers is striking.) Finally, backtracking somewhat on his initial suggestion that a better ICC might be evolved, Kissinger proposes that the UN adopt and extend the practice of special ad hoc tribunals on the Yugoslav and Rwandan model. Although the point is left unstated, this would of course restore the full force of the US veto, or the veto of any permanent member of the UN Security Council, thus restoring the supremacy of politics over law.

The welcoming and sceptical views of international jurisdiction are often categorized, respectively, as "European" and "American" positions. Whether or not the labelling accurately captures exactly who holds which approach, the two views are thought to reflect a fundamental difference in ideas of world politics. The difference is provocatively explored in "Power and Weakness," a wide-ranging article by Robert Kagan.[41] Kagan traces two contrasting approaches to international institutions such as the ICC, approaches which he argues stem from, first, different strategic situations, and, second, different ideational matrices; they should not be attributed to the political preferences of current office-holders. First, different strategic situations arise from very different levels of military preparedness. The well-armed state is naturally more likely to favour a military confrontation that it can win than a juridical contest in which its power counts for nothing. Second, turning their collective back decisively on their own corpse-strewn past, "Europeans," drawing on their own post–World War II experience, now imagine a "Kantian" rather than a "Hobbesian" world, that is, a state system that recognizes the supremacy of cosmopolitan law rather than ultimately uninhibited sovereignty. So in both respects Europeans are distanced from the US view; but in defence of the US view, Kagan reminds us that in both respects the European approach conceals its own debt to US power: European states could reduce their defence spending only because they could shelter under the US umbrella, and they could become "Kantians" only because the US was still willing to confront the "Hobbesian" reality and take on rogue states.

Be all that as it may, it may be the case that "European" hopes and "American" fears buy into a false contrast. David Wippman's contribution to this volume argues that they do exactly that. "The debate over the ICC," he writes, "is an exemplar of a larger debate concerning the proper role of international law and international institutions in international affairs."[42] Nevertheless, he argues, some of the large issues must give way to a careful, detailed analysis of the actual powers and likely prospects of the Court. Its resources – in terms of time, in particular, and in terms of enforcement jurisdiction – are very limited, and it is not within its effective power to prosecute more than a tiny handful of future perpetrators. This of course greatly hampers its ability to put an end to "the culture of impunity" as its supporters wish it to do; and it also greatly limits any deterrent effect that one might suppose it to have. Some supporters stress, rather, its educative value; but this, too, is problematic, given that the Court will be injected into violently polarized disputes which will make the appearance of impartiality hard to sustain. On the other hand, some fears – particularly on the part of the US administration and some members of Congress – are equally unrealistic. The risk that the Court's prosecutor may run out of control is more theoretical than real. The level of professionalism is high, and the majority of states comprising the Assembly of States Parties share the same democratic values as the US. Moreover, the Court's hands will be more than full with cases of manifestly gross human rights abuses, and it is unlikely to engage in adventurous prosecutions turning on disputed questions of strategic conduct. On balance, Wippman believes, the case for the Court may be positive: but there is nothing to gain, and quite a bit to lose, by exaggerating its potential.

At the same time, there can be little doubt that the standing of the Court, and its general effectiveness, would be greatly enhanced if the US were to ratify the ICC Statute. Shades of America's failure to join the League of Nations following World War I continue to haunt many analyses and evaluations of the Court's potential. But is there an argument that might convince the world's dominant political, economic, and military power to change its mind?

Alex Tuckness develops an argument that is founded on the ideal of impartiality. This may appear to be an unpromising line, since explanations of US resistance to the Court are generally predicated on the assumption that it is not in the political self-interest of the US to submit any part of its jurisdiction to an extra-national institution. Tuckness argues that even if this turns out to be the case, the US may have a moral obligation to acknowledge the Court. And furthermore, properly understood, acceptance of this obligation is required for the US to be consistent with its expressed international commitments.

Tuckness's strategy starts with the aknowledgment that there may well be a conflict between self-interest and impartiality. "Suppose for the sake of argument that it is *not* in the self-interest, narrowly defined, of the US to join the ICC, but that the ICC regime *is* superior to the US alternative if we assess the two options from the perspective of an impartial observer."[43] The task is then to show, first, that the impartial observer really would prefer the ICC regime to the US alternative and, second, that the US has internally effective moral grounds to agree with the impartial observer. Currently, Tuckness suggests, the US alternative can reasonably be interpreted to be the principle that "each state should be free to pursue justice in war crimes prosecutions and trials according to its own understanding."[44] But, as Tuckness points out, this is a principle that only very powerful states would adopt. And it also creates a situation in which each state is responsible for judging its own government, functionaries, and military. In so doing, it runs counter to one of the most basic principles of justice, one that is widely accepted within the US legal and political culture, namely that one should not be permitted to act as judge in one's own case. An impartial observer would thus have good reason to prefer the ICC alternative.

A supporter of the US principle might object that the ICC regime constitutes an assault on the concept of state sovereignty because it allows supra- and extra-national institutions to exercise authority in the domestic affairs of participating states. And, the argument goes, state sovereignty is so essential to the preservation of international order and stability that it cannot be compromised for any cause, no matter how noble. But, as Tuckness notes, this objection is not available to the US, which has shown a willingness to sacrifice state sovereignty for the sake of defending certain fundamental rights. Interventions in the former Yugoslavia and in Iraq are the most recent examples of this commitment. Internal consistency thus requires the US to submit its actions (and the actions of its agents, political and military) to external scrutiny on the basis of these same fundamental principles. With appropriate safeguards in place to ensure that the US is not unfairly persecuted in the international adjudicative process, Tuckness concludes that the US has a moral obligation to endorse the ICC.

IV. ISSUES OF JUSTICE

At the most basic level, the role of the ICC is to bring retribution to state agents who would otherwise escape prosecution. In the approving view of its advocates, it is to "put an end to the culture of impunity," while in Kissinger's more jaundiced description, it rests on "the notion that heads of state and senior public officials should have the same standing as outlaws."[45] One important justification for such a retributive project relies on the notion of the rightness of the act of punishment as such. It is an affirmation, as Jean Hampton wrote, of the worth of the victim.[46] The perpetrator, in this model, implicitly claimed a privilege which defined the victim's worth as of no account: to punish the perpetrator is to formally discredit his or her "false claim to superiority" by exercising "a second act of mastery" that negates the original false claim.[47] There can be no doubt that some kind of belief based in retribution underlies the demand for international criminal prosecution. Agents of states, by virtue of the massive coercive powers at their disposal, commit deeds many times more horrible than ordinary criminals do; it is unconscionable that they should escape punishment when ordinary criminals are called to account; they must not be allowed to slip through the retributive net. So, somewhat like pirates in the early history of modern international law, they are "enemies of humanity," and are subject to its punishment because they escape the punishment of states.

In the case of domestic justice, the retributivist view has often been challenged, and from various angles. One angle, that of "restorative justice," is developed by Elizabeth Spelman in her book *Repair*.[48] Rather than seek an abstract "negation" or cancellation of the kind that Hampton proposes, Spelman argues that we should focus on the practical making-good of damage: on making good the damage to the victim, and also on making good the future relations between victim and perpetrator so that the possibility of coexistence is restored. The restorative justice paradigm has made headway particularly in programs for the treatment of young offenders. Such an approach finds its larger equivalent in the idea that devices such as truth commissions, rather than criminal trials, are the better response to mass atrocity.[49] Their superiority is three-fold. They are better suited to the revelatory telling of stories, something which the adversarial form and evidentiary requirements of trials impede; and they are better suited as responses to violence on a scale which defeats the capacity of the criminal process; and they may lead to more complex kinds of understanding than binary judgments of guilt/innocence permit. The chapters in this volume by Tracy Isaacs, Catherine Lu, and Darryl Robinson illuminate this issue in different ways.

Criminal trials may be justified in other than the Hamptonian manner. They are perhaps most commonly justified, of course, in terms of their deterrent value (a notion which Wippman discusses in his contribution to this volume). And at least since Nuremberg, it has also been argued that trials can contribute to restoration by individualizing guilt: the conviction of leaders may lift the burden of collective guilt from a whole society and thus contribute to its reconciliation with victim groups. Perhaps the first issue that needs to be addressed in this regard is how the scope of the concept of responsibility should be understood. As Isaacs points out in considering the crime of genocide, "an individual agent cannot, except in extraordinary circumstances, perpetrate a genocide single-handedly. It usually involves a number, and in some cases, such as the 1994 Rwandan genocide, an extraordinarily large number, of perpetrators."[50] How does one assess and evaluate the participation of all of these actors?

Isaacs distinguishes between causal responsibility and moral responsibility for an act. Not everyone who is morally responsible for a genocide needs to be causally responsible (in the sense of having carried out mass killings). Often, and perhaps typically, leaders of states do not personally engage in any direct killing. But we want to hold them responsible, and perhaps assign them a larger share of the moral responsibility. To ground this intuition, Isaacs draws upon the theory of action developed by theorists such as Donald Davidson.[51] The leading idea here is that actions can be, quite properly, classified under a variety of descriptions. So, an arm moving can also be the swinging of a machete, which can also be an act of murder, which can also be a contribution to genocide. And movement of the lips can also be a speech, which can also be an incitement to murder, and then also a contribution to genocide. Our assignment of responsibility will depend on the accuracy and legitimacy of these various ascriptions and the relative moral weight that we give to them.

Isaacs considers three models for apportioning responsibility. The first holds individuals responsible only for their actions and the consequences of their actions. The second model, developed by Larry May,[52] suggests that it is possible to hold a collective entity responsible for genocide, such as a state, and then single out the political leaders of the state as bearing a greater share of the responsibility for that action. The third model, taken from Christopher Kutz, develops the idea of complicity in collective action: "The Complicity Principle: (Basis) I am accountable [responsible] for what others do when I intentionally participate in the wrong or harm they cause. (Object) I am accountable [responsible] for the harm or wrong we do together, independently of the actual difference I make."[53] On this view, all of the actors are equally responsible for a collective action such as genocide.

Isaacs acknowledges that each of these models has its merits: each captures some part of our intuition regarding culpability. But ultimately Isaacs argues in favour of a suitably modified version of the first model, one that allows for the possibility of individual participation in collective action via the notion of contributing to an action that could not be carried out individually. On this view, individuals are responsible for their share or contribution. And the determination of what their share is (and what it is a share of) will then form the basis on which their action can be assessed morally and/or legally.

Catherine Lu's contribution to this volume enlarges our understanding of the ways in which trials, though retributive in form, may nevertheless have a forward-looking effect in terms of "regeneration." While there are various severe constraints on the powers of the ICC, these need not detract from its moral authority. The Court's significance may primarily lie in its giving institutionalized prominence to a cosmopolitan morality – one founded on a sense of shared human vulnerability – that will eventually affect the behaviour of states. Its work in the prosecution and punishment of international crime should be understood as "a beginning, opening the door to further avenues of investigation into the responsibility of other individuals, and of institutions such as governments, banks, churches, militaries, judiciaries, international organizations and other interested parties."[54] Its fact-finding work will challenge "the truthfulness and moral validity" of identity-constituting myths that sustain continued conflict. Somewhat like a truth commission, its most important role may be to establish a public record that encourages the "self-reflection" needed in the process of moral rebuilding; in this respect, we should see the Court as only one among several initiatives – which may also include truth commissions – that the process of regeneration requires.

Darryl Robinson's contribution, however, draws a somewhat sharper contrast between the work of courts and of truth commissions, and draws attention to some of the perceived difficulties in using both. In particular, non-judicial responses to atrocity (such as truth commissions, negotiated settlements, amnesties, and the like) give up a demand that, from a retributive point of view, is nothing less than essential – the punishment of guilt. Adopting non-punitive solutions may in fact place transitional states in violation of their duty to punish international crimes, yet such solutions may be virtually unavoidable from a political point of view. Part of the answer to this dilemma may lie in a morally sustainable distinction between the liability of leaders and that of followers; a distinction that is effectively being attempted in a "two-track" approach in Sierra Leone.[55] Provided that those who plotted genocide and incited violence, abusing their official positions of authority, are punished, it may be acceptable to adopt a regime of confession and apology, and perhaps of reparation, for those who merely followed. Beyond that, we will need to look carefully at the proposed non-punitive settlement in detail, and whether or not we find it acceptable will depend on a variety of contextual and institutional factors: Is it democratically supported? Is the punitive alternative genuinely unavailable? How effective will enquiry be? Will victims be compensated? While there is "no intrinsic tension" between the goals of courts and of truth commissions, the two can complement each other only if the retributive program is applied without rigidity.

But there exists another angle of critique, one that is familiar in discussions of retributive justice in the domestic context. Employing its own conventions of understanding in relation to causality, responsibility, and blameworthiness, the criminal justice system assesses individual guilt in the narrow context of the performance of deliberate acts. It closes its eyes to the larger contexts of power relations, for example those inscribed in the contexts of class, ethnicity, and gender. To close one's eyes to the deeply pervasive effects of such things, however, is surely to vitiate one's determination of causality and blame.

This line of criticism also finds an important application in the international context, as Antonio Franceschet's contribution to this volume demonstrates. Franceschet distinguishes three approaches to international order. A "legalist" model of international justice, exemplified above all in the ICC, is certainly an advance on the "Westphalian" model; for the goal of protecting human rights universally challenges traditional ideas of sovereignty to the extent that these ideas serve to shield gross abuses. Moreover, in offering a measure of protection against abusive states, international "legalistic" justice may contribute to the effective emergence of oppositional politics in oppressive regimes. But the fact remains that the model of justice that it contains is a limited one.

A more critical model presses the claim of substantive equality, and in doing so it discloses the ways in which the institutions of Liberal legalism are complicit in a system of global economic and political inequality. As in the case of domestic criminal prosecution, the story needs to be taken several stages back. Behind the crime there is a background of poverty, oppression, and dislocation that the legal model ignores. Moreover, in focusing narrowly on only one kind of damage, the legal model leaves out of its account the ravages caused by economic agents in the global economy. In the aftermath of 11 September 2001, an objection was often levelled at this line of critique: that the perpetrators of international crimes rarely if ever come from the most severely ravaged nations in the world. Rather, they tend to come from nations whose aggregate wealth is quite high, but within which the distribution of wealth is unequal, and the distribution of power even more so. But this hardly defeats Franceschet's point, for the distribution of wealth and power in such nations could not in some cases have come about, and in other cases could not be sustained, without the self-interested support of Western powers. So, when a court focuses on the version of responsibility and guilt which comes within its remit and the scope of its methods, it will leave out of account a larger story of causal responsibility and moral guilt, a story about how other powers have in one way or another imposed their will on, and obstructed political development within, the countries in which international crimes are typically committed, or from which crimes against the citizens of other countries are typically launched. Clearly this critique may have more potential force in some cases than in others. But in general it reminds us of the importance of attending to the demands of distributive justice in assessing retributive institutions.

CONCLUSION

Above, we noted the importance of taking different disciplinary perspectives into account. The chapters in this collection also demonstrate that assessing the prospects of the ICC calls for discussion at very different levels of generality – indeed, we can question the very idea of the adequacy of retributive justice, as does Franceschet. We also have to think about the place of retributive processes within the larger scheme of transitional justice, which, as many scholars believe, may need to place greater weight on processes of restoration and reconciliation. Inseparable from that issue is the question of individual responsibility within collective action, a question that in turn calls not only for conceptual clarity but also for treatment in terms that take into account important legal precedent. Then there is the matter of the policies and practices of individual states, especially of powerful states, and the norms and other considerations that enter into their political choices. Finally, there are the dynamics of the Court's processes, its administration and financing, and the dynamics of trials that have quite unusual features as well as a complex political impact. The most abstract and the most concrete issues have a way of implicating each other mutually, and this book is an attempt to stimulate the many-levelled discussion that the arrival of the ICC calls for.

NOTES

1 Adopted 17 July 1998, UN Doc. A/CONF. 183/9, 2187 UNTS 90, reprinted in *International Legal Materials* 37, no. 5 (1998): 1002 [hereinafter ICC Statute]. The official ICC Web site is at <http://www.icc-cpi.int>.

2 Article 5 of the ICC Statute also indicates that once the state parties agree on a definition of the crime of aggression, the ICC will have jurisdiction over this crime as well.

3 "Press Conference of the Prosecutor – Communications," 24 July 2003, available online at <http://www.icc-cpi.int/press/pressreleases/68.html>.

4 On 23 July 2004, the chief prosecutor announced his decision to investigate grave crimes allegedly committed on the territory of the Democratic Republic of Congo since 1 July 2002. A short time later, a second investigation was opened for the situation in Northern Uganda. Press releases confirming the opening of these investigations are available from the ICC Web site: <http://www.icc-cpi.int/newspoint/pressreleases.html>.

5 See further, M. Cherif Bassiouni, "From Versailles to Rwanda in Seventy-Five Years: The Need to Establish a Permanent International Criminal Court," *Harvard Human Rights Journal* 10, no. 1 (1997): 11–62 and Sharon A. Williams, "The Rome Statute on the International Criminal Court: From 1947–2000 and Beyond," *Osgoode Hall Law Journal* 38, no. 2 (2000): 297–330. See also M. Cherif Bassiouni, ed., *The Statute of the International Criminal Court: A Documentary History* (Ardsley, NY: Transnational

Publishers, 1998) and Benjamin B. Ferencz, *An International Criminal Court: A Step Toward World Peace: A Documentary History and Analysis* (Dobbs Ferry, NY: Oceana Publications, 1990).

6 Two of the most well known of the Leipzig trials are the Dover Castle and Llandovery Castle cases on the deliberate sinking of two Allied hospital ships by German U-boats in 1917. These cases are reported in *American Journal of International Law* 16, no. 4 (1922): 704–8 and 708–24, respectively.

7 *Convention for the Prevention and Punishment of Terrorism*, adopted 16 November 1937, reprinted in M.O. Hudson, ed., *International Legislation*, vol. 7 (Dobbs Ferry, NY: Oceana Publications, 1972), 862. The one state was India.

8 See *Agreement for the Prosecution and Punishment of the Major War Criminals of the European Axis*, adopted 8 August 1945, 82 UNTS 279 and the *Protocol to the Agreement and Charter*, adopted 6 October 1945, 59 Stat. 1586.

9 See *Charter of the International Military Tribunal for the Far East*, adopted 19 January 1946, amended 26 April 1946, TIAS 1589.

10 Article VI of the *Convention on the Prevention and Punishment of the Crime of Genocide*, adopted 9 December 1948, 78 UNTS 277, provides that "persons charged with genocide ... shall be tried by a competent tribunal of the State in the territory of which the act was committed, or by such international penal tribunal as may have jurisdiction." A similar provision can be found in article V of the *International Convention on the Suppression and Punishment of the Crime of Apartheid*, adopted 30 November 1973, 1015 UNTS 243.

11 *Report of the Committee on International Criminal Court Jurisdiction*, UN Doc. A/2135 (1952).

12 *Report of the Committee on International Criminal Jurisdiction*, UN Doc. A/2645 (1954).

13 The ILC was asked to return to its work on drafting a code of crimes in December 1981: GA Res. 36/106 (1981).

14 See SC Res. 827, UN SCOR, 48th Sess., Res. & Dec., UN Doc. S/INF/49 (1993), at 29, reprinted in *International Legal Materials* 32, no. 4 (1993): 1203. Further details on the work of the ICTY can be found at <http://www.un.org/icty/index.html>.

15 See SC Res. 955, UN SCOR, 49th Sess., Res. & Dec., UN Doc. S/INF/50 (1994), at 15, reprinted in *International Legal Materials* 33, no. 6 (1994): 1602–13. Further details on the work of the ICTR can be found at <http://www.ictr.org>.

16 See further, James Crawford, "The ILC's Draft Statute for an International Criminal Tribunal," *American Journal of International Law* 88, no. 1 (1994): 140–52.

17 See further, M. Cherif Bassiouni, "Negotiating the Treaty of Rome on the Establishment of an International Criminal Court," *Cornell International Law Journal* 32, no. 3 (1999): 443–69, and Philippe Kirsch and John Holmes, "The Rome Conference on an International Criminal Court: The Negotiating Process," *American Journal of International Law* 93, no. 1 (1999): 2–12. For a detailed history, see Roy S. Lee,ed., *The International Criminal Court: The Making of the Rome Statute: Issues, Negotiations, Results* (The Hague: Kluwer Law International, 1999).

18 The US shared company with China, Libya, Iran, Iraq, Israel and Sudan: Monroe Leigh, "The United States and the Statute of Rome," *American Journal of International Law* 95, no. 1 (2001): 124–31, 124. See also David J. Scheffer, "The United States and the International Criminal Court," *American Journal of International Law* 93, no. 1 (1999): 12–22.

19 ICC Statute, *supra* n 1, preamble and arts 1 and 17.

20 It is also possible for a non-party state to make a declaration recognizing the Court's jurisdiction in a specific case.

21 See, however, David Wippman, "Atrocities, Deterrence, and the Limits of International Justice," *Fordham International Law Journal* 23, no. 2 (1999): 473–488, and his contribution in this volume, for the view that the deterrent effect is likely to be modest and incremental, rather than dramatic and transformative.

22 ICC Statute, *supra* note 1, art. 17.

23 While Milosevic was the first head of state to stand trial, Jean Kambanda, the prime minister of the interim government of Rwanda from 8 April 1994 to 17 July 1994 was the first head of a government to be tried. Kambanda was brought before the Trial Chamber of the International Criminal Tribunal for Rwanda in 1998. He plead guilty to six charges of genocide and crimes against humanity, and is currently serving a life sentence. See further <http://www.ictr.org/ENGLISH/cases/Kambanda/index.htm>.

24 See further, Hazel Fox, *The Law of State Immunity* (Oxford: Oxford UP, 2002), 23–39.

25 The Anglo-American embrace of absolute immunity dates back to *The Schooner Exchange* v. *McFaddon*, 11 US 116 (1812) and *The Parlement Belge* (1879–90) 5 Prob Div 197 (CA).

26 Fox, *supra* n24, 272–322.

27 See further, *Arrest Warrant of 11 April 2000 Case (Democratic Republic of Congo* v. *Belgium)*, judgment of 14 February 2002, (International Court of Justice), reprinted in *International Legal Materials* 41, no. 3 (2002): 536–653.

28 A.W.B Simpson, "Rights Talk, Rights Acts," *Times Literary Supplement*, 27 August 1999, 9.

29 Geoffrey Robertson, *Crimes Against Humanity* (London: Allen Lane, 1999), 341.
30 Ibid., 340.
31 Ibid., 375.
32 Mallory Conklin, "Kissinger at the Ritz," on-line: Parisiana <http://www.parisiana.com/article.php3?id_article=41>.
33 Henry A. Kissinger, "The Pitfalls of Universal Jurisdiction," *Foreign Affairs* 80, no. 4 (2001): 86–96.
34 Ibid., 86.
35 Ibid.
36 Kissinger uses the example of Spain, where it was decided to not pursue the crimes of the Franco regime after General Franco's death. In "Holding Francoists Accountable," a paper delivered at the conference "Bringing Power to Justice," University of Western Ontario, 22–23 March 2003, Mireya Folch-Serra described current regrets about this decision.
37 Kissinger, *supra* n33, 92.
38 See Trudy Govier, "Prosecuting Crimes against Humanity: Rule of Law and the Selectivity Argument," in *Crime against Humanity*, ed. Charles Jones, (forthcoming).
39 Kissinger, *supra* n33, 93.
40 Ibid., 93–5.
41 Robert Kagan, "Power and Weakness," *Policy Review* June/July 2002, no. 113: 3–28.
42 *Infra* 130.
43 *Infra* 141.
44 *Infra* 145.
45 *Supra* nn33, 87.
46 Jeffrie Murphy and Jean Hampton, *Forgiveness and Mercy* (Cambridge: Cambridge UP, 1998), 127.
47 Ibid., 129.
48 Elizabeth Spelman, *Repair: The Impulse to Restore in a Fragile World* (Boston: Beacon Press, 2003).
49 Martha Minow, *Between Vengeance and Forgiveness* (Boston: Beacon Press, 1998).
50 *Infra* 167.
51 Donald Davidson, *Essays on Actions and Events* (Oxford: Clarendon Press, 1980).
52 Larry May, *Crimes against Humanity: A Normative Account* (Cambridge: Cambridge UP, 2005).
53 Christopher Kutz, *Complicity: Ethics and Law for a Collective Age* (Cambridge: Cambridge UP, 2000), 122.

54 *Infra* 201.

55 A Truth and Reconciliation Commission for Sierra Leone was created as a result of the Lomé Peace Agreement of 1999, which brought an end to the nine-year civil war. It was established by legislation enacted in February 2000, but a short time later a proposal for a hybrid tribunal – comprised of international and national judges and prosecutors – was put forward to prosecute those who were most responsible for past human rights violations. The Special Court for Sierra Leone was established in 2002 through a special agreement between the UN and Sierra Leone. Its jurisdiction overlaps with the temporal jurisdiction of the commission. The court's Web site is at <http://www.sc-sl.org>.

2

The Legacy of the Milosevic Trial

MICHAEL P. SCHARF♣

Slobodan Milosevic, a.k.a. the "Butcher of the Balkans." From 1991 to 1999 his Serb troops and Bosnian Serb proxies fought four brutal Balkan wars. Hundreds of thousands died, most of them innocent civilians, and millions were displaced. Milosevic saw himself as a modern-day Abe Lincoln, employing force in a valiant effort to hold his crumbling Yugoslavia together. He now stands accused of the most serious crimes known to mankind – grave breaches of the Geneva Conventions, crimes against humanity, and genocide.

On 12 February 2002, the former Serb leader became the first head of state ever to face trial before an international criminal tribunal.[1] With the combative Milosevic acting as his own lawyer, a legal battle of epic proportions is being waged at the UN Security Council–created tribunal in The Hague known as the International Criminal Tribunal for the Former Yugoslavia (the "Yugoslavia Tribunal").[2] It is often said that while courts try cases, cases also try courts. This has proven to be particularly true with respect to the Milosevic trial, since Milosevic's primary strategy has been to challenge the Yugoslavia Tribunal's legitimacy and impartiality, rather than to seek an acquittal through conventional tactics.

Will history remember Milosevic as a victim of victor's justice – a scapegoat tried in a show trial before a one-sided court? Or will the Milosevic trial be seen as fair and free of political influence, and its judgment supported by credible evidence? Written at the midpoint in the Milosevic trial (which is expected to last through 2005), this essay seeks to answer these questions through an examination of the proceedings to date and by drawing comparisons to the post–World War II Nuremberg trials for historic perspective.

Although the Yugoslavia Tribunal has tried two dozen other indicted war criminals, *Prosecutor* v. *Slobodan Milosevic* is clearly the trial for which the ad hoc court was created. Thus, the answer to these questions may dictate the ultimate success or failure of the tribunal itself as a mechanism for restoring peace in the Balkans. More broadly, the Milosevic trial is of keen interest to those seeking to bring other rogue leaders, such as Saddam Hussein of Iraq and Charles Taylor of Liberia, to the bar of international justice.

If viewed as legitimate, the Milosevic trial could potentially serve several important functions in the Balkan peace process. By pinning prime responsibility on Milosevic and disclosing the way the Yugoslav people were manipulated by their leaders into committing acts of savagery on a mass scale, the trial would help break the cycle of violence that has long plagued the Balkans. While this would not completely absolve the underlings for their acts, it would make it easier for victims to eventually forgive, or at least reconcile with, former neighbours who had been caught up in the institutionalized violence. This would also promote a political catharsis in Serbia, enabling the new leadership to distance itself from the discredited nationalistic policies of the past. The historic record generated from the trial would educate the Serb people, long subject to Milosevic's propaganda, about what really happened in Kosovo, Croatia, and Bosnia, and help ensure that such horrific acts are not repeated in the future. Finally, the trial would prove that international tribunals are capable of fairly and effectively trying former leaders accused of the gravest crimes known to humankind.

On the other hand, a trial seen as victor's justice would undermine the goal of fostering reconciliation between the ethnic groups living in the former Yugoslavia. The historic record developed by the trial would forever be questioned. The trial would add to the Serb martyrdom complex, amounting to another grievance requiring vengeance. And the judicial precedent would be tainted. For any real advance to be made in the long march toward the establishment of a permanent international criminal court, Milosevic's trial must be seen to be more about real justice, than realpolitik.

I. THE PERILS OF PERMITTING SELF-REPRESENTATION

In accordance with the rule prevailing in most common law countries, a defendant is generally permitted to decline appointed counsel and represent himself if he is determined to be of sound mind.[3] No decision would have a more profound effect on the course of the Milosevic trial than the ruling of the Yugoslavia Tribunal's Trial Chamber permitting Milosevic to act as his own counsel during the proceedings.[4]

First of all, the tribunal's ruling significantly affected the length of the trial, as well as the volume of testimony the prosecution could present. Because the sixty-one-year-old Milosevic has extremely high blood pressure (240 over 120) and a severe heart condition, the tribunal cut the number of days per week for the trial from five to three, the daily maximum number of hours for the trial from eight to four, and on several occasions adjourned for two- to three-week periods to allow Milosevic to regain his strength. In the midst of these delays, one of the three judges presiding over the Milosevic case, Judge Richard May of the United Kingdom, died of cancer and a replacement judge had to be appointed halfway through the trial.[5]

Despite these accommodations, the committee for Milosevic's defence, known as Slobda, accuses the court of "attempted murder."[6] His health problems have boosted Milosevic's underdog appeal back home in Serbia. Moreover, the one thing the tribunal wants to avoid more than anything else is having Milosevic expire during the trial. His death would literally erase history from being recorded since under the tribunal's precedent, a judgment cannot be rendered if the defendant is not alive at the time it is issued.[7] In an effort to try to keep the trial on track to finish in 2005, the tribunal has ordered the prosecution to pare down its witnesses, "to the point where prosecutors claim their case is being emasculated."[8]

In addition, the decision to allow Milosevic to defend himself enabled him to generate the illusion that he was a solitary individual pitted against an army of foreign lawyers and investigators. Day after day he sits alone in the courtroom behind a row of conspicuously empty desks that would ordinarily be occupied by the defence team. According to a Serb who has watched the trial proceedings on television in Belgrade – to get a flavour for how this plays back in Serbia – "We cheer when he outsmarts the prosecutors. When he's defending himself all alone against the world."[9]

In reality, Milosevic, himself a lawyer who graduated near the top of his class from the prestigious University of Belgrade School of Law, has had a squadron of legal counsels assisting him from behind the scenes, including some of the world's most distinguished trial attorneys. Heading Milosevic's legal team are Ramsey Clark, a former US attorney general, and Jacques Verges, the French lawyer who defended Gestapo chief Klaus Barbie. Under their direction, and with funding from a network of Milosevic defence committees in Serbia, the US, Britain, Russia, and France, lawyers and supporters of Milosevic dig up files and background on witnesses who are about to appear in court.[10] Armed with this material, Milosevic often seems better informed than the prosecution, which is convinced that he has a stash of secret police and army files that he has refused to produce in contravention to the tribunal's rules. Prosecutors also believe that Milosevic supporters in Serbia have withheld official documents and discouraged witnesses from giving evidence.[11]

Yet, the most significant ramification of the tribunal's ruling is that it gave Milosevic the chance to make unfettered speeches throughout the trial and to attack the legitimacy of the tribunal at every turn. In contrast, a defendant is ordinarily able to address the court only when he takes the stand to give testimony during the defence's case-in-chief. In the usual case, the defendant is limited to giving evidence that is relevant to the charges, and he is subject to cross-examination by the prosecution.

By acting as his own counsel, Milosevic was able to begin his case with eleven hours of opening argument, which included a Hollywood-quality video and slide show presentation showing the destruction wrought by the 1999 NATO bombing campaign. The lead prosecution attorney, Geoffrey Nice, had shown some of the prosecution's own photos of victims of Serb atrocities during his opening, but they were not nearly as numerous or as gruesome as those Milosevic presented, prompting the *New Yorker* to conclude, "Horror for horror, [Nice] was outdone by Milosevic."[12] Milosevic made a similarly compelling presentation on 26 September 2002, at the start of the second phase of the prosecution's case, involving the war with Croatia and Bosnia.

Bending over backwards to maintain the appearance of fairness, the tribunal's judges have allowed Milosevic to treat the witnesses, prosecutors, and themselves in a manner that would earn ordinary defence counsel expulsion from the courtroom. In addition to regularly making disparaging remarks about the tribunal and repeatedly browbeating witnesses, Milosevic pontificates at length during cross-examination of every prosecution witness. While the tribunal at first gave Milosevic substantial leeway, the judges began to express impatience with Milosevic's "political points." On numerous occasions, the tribunal's presiding judge has warned: "Mr. Milosevic, you are making speeches again. You're supposed to be asking questions and not making denigrating comments about the witnesses."[13] But the lawyer-defendant Milosevic, who spends his nights at the tribunal's detention centre, has no incentive to heed the judges' admonitions.

Summing up the impact of Milosevic's trial performance, one former employee of the tribunal has stated: "You can't help falling under his spell. He's very sharp and he's funny. It's sick, I know, given what he's there for, but he's so cynical and quick that he's had the courtroom in fits of laughter at times."[14] As long as it continues to prove its case, the prosecution team does not seem concerned about the effect of Milosevic's performance on those who watch the daily broadcasts of the proceedings, which are beamed into Serbia by the US Agency for International Development. Yet, according to Serbian Prime Minister Zoran Djindjic, now deceased, "The prosecution says 'What we care about is the law, and the fact that Milosevic has hundreds of hours to promote his politics is not our problem.' That's naïve."[15]

The judges presiding over the Milosevic case initially felt that they had no choice but to permit Milosevic to go on representing himself, despite the disruptions this was causing, because article 21(4)(d) of the tribunal's statute provides that the defendant has the right "to defend himself in person or through legal assistance of his own choosing." Shortly after Judge May was replaced by Scottish judge Iain Bonomy, however, the Milosevic bench decided to revisit its earlier ruling. On 22 September 2004, with the Milosevic trial about to begin the defence phase, the Trial Chamber ruled that in light of the disruptions caused by self-representation, Milosevic would have to work through counsel for the remainder of the trial.[16]

But Milosevic still had another card to play. Following the Trial Chamber's decision of 22 September 2004, Milosevic refused to cooperate in any way with assigned counsel. Believing that they could not adequately represent the defendant without such cooperation, assigned counsel brought an interlocutory appeal to the Yugoslavia Tribunal's Appeals Chamber. On 1 November 2004, the Appeals Chamber issued its decision.[17]

The Appeals Chamber agreed with the Trial Chamber's decision of 22 September 2004 that the right of self-representation was subject to limitations. According to the Appeals Chamber, the test to be applied is that "the right may be curtailed on the grounds that a defendant's self-representation is substantially and persistently obstructing the proper and expeditious conduct of his trial."[18] Applying this test, the Appeals Chamber concluded that the Trial Chamber had not abused its discretion in deciding to restrict Milosevic's right to self-representation.[19]

However, the Appeals Chamber felt that the Trial Chamber's order requiring Milosevic to act through appointed counsel went too far, and that the proportionality principle required that a more "carefully calibrated set of restrictions" be imposed on Milosevic's trial participation.[20] Under these, when he is physically able to do so, Milosevic must be permitted to take the lead in presenting his case – choosing which witnesses to present, questioning those witnesses, and giving the closing statement, and making the basic strategic decisions about the presentation of his defence.[21] According to the Appeals Chamber, "if Milosevic's health problems resurface with sufficient gravity, however, the presence of Assigned Counsel will enable the trial to continue even if Milosevic is temporarily unable to participate."[22]

The Appeals Chamber decision had the benefit of enabling the Milosevic trial to proceed with the cooperation of the defendant, while at the same time keeping counsel available in case things started to go wrong. From a short-term practical perspective, the decision was inspired; from a longer-term and wider perspective, it may turn out to have troubling consequences. This is because the Appeals Chamber decision focused only on Milosevic's health as the source of disruption justifying restriction on his right of self-representation. Notwithstanding the arguments of the prosecution, the Appeals Chamber did not find that Milosevic's trial tactics and in-court behaviour rose to the level of "substantial and persistent" disruption that justifies appointment of defence counsel.

The stringent "substantial and persistent disruption" test formulated by the Appeals Chamber will likely make it more difficult for judges to maintain decorum in future war crimes trials. In particular, Saddam Hussein, whose war crimes trial is set to begin in 2005, will be able to argue that he, too, has a right to represent himself before the Iraqi Special Tribunal, since that tribunal's statute contains the same language on self-representation as the statute of the Yugoslavia Tribunal. If Hussein were allowed to follow Milosevic's playbook – using the unique opportunity of self-representation to launch daily attacks against the legitimacy of the proceedings – this would seriously undermine the goal of fostering reconciliation between the Iraqi Kurds, Shiites, and Sunnis; the historic record developed by such a trial would be open to question; and the trial could transform Hussein and his subordinates into martyrs, potentially fueling violent opposition to the new Iraqi government.

II. REAL JUSTICE OR *REALPOLITIK*?

A. *Challenges to the Legitimacy of the Yugoslavia Tribunal*

Beginning at his arraignment before the Yugoslavia Tribunal on 3 July 2001, Milosevic launched his challenge to the validity of the UN Security Council–created court. "You are not a judicial institution; you are a political tool," Milosevic told the panel of three judges.[23] Drawing on the commonly accepted notion that the post–World War II Nuremberg Trials were tainted by victor's justice, one of Milosevic's behind-the-scenes lawyers, former US attorney general Ramsey Clark, publicly circulated a draft brief (which included Milosevic's handwritten notations), whose sole purpose appeared to be to discredit the tribunal.

While the Nuremberg Charter precluded challenges to the legitimacy of the Nuremberg Tribunal itself, the Yugoslavia Tribunal considered the question in its first case in 1995.[24] The tribunal ruled that, although its creation by the UN Security Council was without precedent, it was a valid product of the council given its broad powers to take action to maintain international peace and security.[25] But, as Milosevic himself has pointed out, the judges that made that decision could not be seriously expected to decide the issue impartially, given that their incredibly prestigious $150,000 US per year jobs (tax free) would have been instantly extinguished if they had decided otherwise.

Having rendered that decision, the Yugoslavia Tribunal has declined to revisit the question in the Milosevic trial. In response to Milosevic's challenges to the tribunal's legitimacy at a pre-trial hearing in August 2001, Presiding Judge Richard May responded,

"Mr. Milosevic, we are not going to listen to these political arguments." While this might seem unduly harsh, it is a bit late in the day for Milosevic to be challenging the tribunal on this ground, given that he recognized the legitimacy of the tribunal when he signed the Dayton Accords in 1995, which require the parties to cooperate with the tribunal.[26] Any doubt should have been erased when Milosevic authorized the transfer of Drazen Erdemovic for prosecution before the tribunal for the part the young Serb soldier played in the massacres at Srebrenica.

Having failed to convince the Yugoslavia Tribunal to reconsider this issue, Milosevic attempted to attack the legitimacy of the tribunal in The Hague District Court. But the Dutch court declared itself incompetent to consider the question.[27] He then took his case to the European Court of Human Rights, which ruled that it lacked jurisdiction to consider the claim since Milosevic had failed to exhaust domestic remedies by neglecting to appeal The Hague District Court decision to the Dutch Court of Appeals prior to filing his claim with the European Court of Human Rights.[28] That Milosevic's high-powered legal team would unintentionally make such a novice legal mistake is hard to believe. It is more likely that they desired this outcome so that Milosevic could make the political argument that he was being railroaded at The Hague.

B. *Victor's Justice*

To the extent Milosevic's goal is not to obtain a dismissal or acquittal but to publicly discredit the tribunal, he is having a greater degree of success with his argument that the Yugoslavia Tribunal, like Nuremberg, represents victor's justice.

In contrast to Nuremberg, however, the Yugoslavia Tribunal was created neither by the victors nor by the parties involved in the conflict, but rather by the UN, representing the international community of states. The judges of the Yugoslavia Tribunal come from all parts of the world, and are elected by the UN General Assembly, in which each of the world's 191 countries gets an equal vote. Moreover, the message of the Yugoslavia Tribunal's indictments, prosecutions, and convictions to date of Muslims and Croats, as well as Serbs, has been that a war crime is a war crime, whoever it is committed by. The tribunal has self-consciously taken no sides.

On the other hand, Milosevic has pointed out that the decision to establish the Yugoslavia Tribunal was made by the UN Security Council, which cannot truly be characterized as a neutral third party; rather, it has itself become deeply involved and taken sides in the Balkan conflict. The Security Council has, for example, imposed sanctions on Milosevic's Serbia, which it felt was most responsible for the conflict and atrocities. Throughout the conflict, the UN Security Council had been quite vocal in its condemnation of Serb atrocities, but its criticisms of those committed by Muslims and Croats were comparatively muted. And most problematic of all, three of the Permanent Members of the Council – the US, France, and the UK – led the seventy-eight-day bombing campaign against Milosevic and Serbia in 1999. Moreover, as Milosevic has repeatedly observed, NATO cruise missiles specifically targeted Milosevic's residence in an effort to kill him and his family.

While both the prosecutor and the judicial chambers of the Yugoslavia Tribunal were conceived to be independent from the UN Security Council, one cannot ignore the fact that the Tribunal's Statute provides that the tribunal's prosecutor is selected by the UN Security Council.[29] The judges are selected by the UN General Assembly from a short list proposed by the Security Council, and they have to stand for re-election after a four-year term.[30] Moreover, the operation of the Yugoslavia Tribunal has been dependent on hundreds of millions of dollars of contributions from the US and its Western allies. In addition, at the time, many of the members of the staff of the Office of the Prosecutor were on loan from NATO countries.

Although a creature of the UN, the Yugoslavia Tribunal has, according to its former president, Antonio Cassese, tended to "take into account the exigencies and tempo of the international community." Milosevic has suggested that this means that the Tribunal has yielded to the objectives of the US and other NATO powers, without whose financial and military support the tribunal could not function. Thus, it should come as little surprise that in a survey conducted in May 2002 by the US polling firm Greenberg, Quinlan and Rossner for the National Democratic Institute for International Affairs, 80 per cent of 1,300 Serbs said they believed the tribunal prosecutes Serbs more vigorously than it does non-Serbs, while 57 per cent said they were convinced the tribunal was unjust.[31]

C. *The Timing of the Indictment*

For evidence of the political influence of the US on the Yugoslavia Tribunal, Milosevic has pointed to the suspicious timing of his indictment. It was issued on 22 May 1999, sixty days into the seventy-eight-day NATO bombing campaign against Serbia. The indictment came down at a crucial time when popular support for the intervention was waning in several NATO countries in the face of intense press criticism of NATO's use of cluster bombs and depleted uranium munitions; its attacks on civilian trains, truck convoys, and media centres; and the accidental bombings of the Chinese embassy in Belgrade and the territory of neighbouring Bulgaria. If this forced a premature end to the bombing campaign, American officials feared that it might irrevocably damage the credibility of NATO, potentially leading to its demise.

After years of pressuring the tribunal's prosecutor not to indict the Serb leader whose cooperation was seen as essential for the Balkan peace process, suddenly the US was pressing for the immediate issuance of charges against Milosevic, knowing that such action would bolster the political will of the NATO countries to continue the bombing campaign, and ultimately force Milosevic to accept NATO's terms for Kosovo. And, after years of refusing to turn over sensitive intelligence data to the Yugoslavia Tribunal in order to protect "sources and methods," the US and Britain were hurriedly handing over reams of satellite imagery, telephone intercepts, and other top-secret information to help the prosecutor make the case against Milosevic.

Finally, from the standpoint of perceptions, it did not help that the tribunal's chief prosecutor, Louise Arbour, was appointed to the Supreme Court of Canada just two weeks after issuing the Milosevic indictment. This gave Milosevic supporters ammunition to argue that Prosecutor Arbour got her dream job in return for rushing forward with the Milosevic indictment.

D. *The Manner of Milosevic's Transfer to The Hague*

The newly-elected president of the Federal Republic of Yugoslavia, Vojislav Kostunica, backed up by a federal court ruling, refused to permit the extradition of Milosevic to The Hague. But in a late night move that caught everyone off guard, Kostunica's political rival, Prime Minister Zoran Djindjic, instructed the Serb police under his command to secretly take Milosevic to an American air base in Tuzla, Bosnia, from which Milosevic was transferred by military jet to The Hague on 28 July 2001. In announcing the action in defiance of the Supreme Court's order, Djindjic said that he had been forced to take a "difficult but morally correct" decision to protect the interests of Serbia – that is, the US and its European allies were promising $1.28 billion US in aid in return for the surrender of Milosevic. This led Serb newspaper headlines to proclaim that Milosevic had become "Serbia's most valuable export commodity."[32] Immediately thereafter, a furious Kostunica protested that the extradition of Milosevic was "illegal and unconstitutional."

Meanwhile, on board the flight to The Hague, Milosevic reportedly told the tribunal officials who read him his rights: "You are kidnapping me, and you will answer for your crimes." In the analogous cases of *Stocké* v. *Germany*[33] and *Bozano* v. *France*,[34] the European Court of Human Rights had held that luring or abduction in violation of established extradition procedures is a human rights violation for which dismissal is the appropriate remedy. But the Yugoslavia Tribunal rejected the argument in the *Nicolic Case*, in which it held that dismissal was only appropriate in a case of irregular surrender where "the rights of the accused were egregiously violated in the process" of his arrest and transfer, for example where he has been "subject to inhuman, cruel or degrading treatment, or torture, before being handed over to the Tribunal."[35] Whatever the technical legal merits of his argument, politically, the timing of Milosevic's irregular surrender could not be worse for the Yugoslavia Tribunal. He arrived at the tribunal on St. Vitus Day, the solemn holiday commemorating the historic Serb defeat to the Ottoman Turks at the battle of Kosovo Polje in 1389, which figures so prominently in the Serb mythology of victimization.

E. Unclean Hands

To further illustrate the tribunal's politicization, Milosevic has tried to force the Yugoslavia Tribunal to face the "*tu quoque*" argument (literally meaning "you also"). The argument had some success at Nuremberg with respect to the charge of waging unrestricted submarine warfare levied against German grand admiral Karl Doenitz.

In light of an affidavit obtained by Doenitz's lawyer from US admiral Chester Nimitz, indicating that the US Navy had used the same tactic in the Pacific, the Nuremberg Tribunal acquitted Doenitz of the charge.[36]

Drawing on the Nuremberg precedent, Milosevic first complained that Franjo Tudjman, the former leader of Croatia, was never indicted by the Yugoslavia Tribunal for the mass atrocities that Croatian troops committed against the Serbs in retaking Serb-controlled areas of eastern Croatia. In fact, Tudjman was welcomed to the US for cancer treatment at the Walter Reed Hospital in Washington, DC, a few months before his death in 1999.

Next, Milosevic has repeatedly raised the issue of NATO war crimes. When Human Rights Watch and several other NGOs urged the tribunal to investigate the possibility that NATO had committed war crimes during the 1999 intervention, the then prosecutor, Louise Arbour (from Canada, a NATO country), assigned the task to her legal adviser, William Fenrick. Fenrick is an ex-NATO lawyer who went to the Yugoslavia Tribunal directly from his post as director of law for operations and training in the Canadian Department of Defence. Not surprisingly, Fenrick's report, which was released in June 2000, concluded that NATO had committed no indictable offences.[37] But critics have been quick to seize upon the clause of the report that notes that the review of NATO's actions relied primarily on public documents produced by NATO, and that the authors of the report "tended to assume that the NATO and NATO countries' press statements are generally reliable and that explanations have been honestly given."[38]

Finally, Milosevic has suggested that the Bush administration's opposition to a permanent International Criminal Court has undermined its moral right to participate in any way in the trial of Milosevic.[39] According to US officials, such international tribunals are prone to politicization – the very argument that Milosevic has made about the Yugoslavia Tribunal.

There are four answers to Milosevic's *tu quoque* challenge, which the prosecution will presumably make during its closing argument. First, whatever Franjo Tudjman and NATO have done, their actions do not excuse what Milosevic did. Second, the tribunal's prosecutor at the time of the Milosevic indictment, Louise Arbour, has stated that she was about to issue an indictment for Franjo Tudjman just before the Croatian president passed away, demonstrating that the tribunal was striving to be evenhanded. Third, whether or not one believes NATO violated the laws of war during the 1999 bombing campaign, NATO did not systematically set out to kill and torture civilians on a mass scale – the crimes of which Milosevic has been accused. The alleged NATO offences are just not in the same league as those which Milosevic is charged with. And fourth, while these arguments might suggest that the tribunal's prosecutors may have been out to get Milosevic, selective prosecution is never a valid defence, even in domestic trials. Milosevic's ultimate fate is in the hands of the tribunal's judges, not its prosecutor. As long as the bench is impartial, and the procedures are equitable, the trial of Milosevic should be considered credible.

F. Composition of the Bench

Unlike most domestic systems, the Yugoslavia Tribunal's judges are not randomly assigned to cases by lot. Given that the pool of the tribunal's judges that were available for the Milosevic trial included citizens from several countries that had no stake in the Balkan conflict, the jurist picked by Judge Jorda of France, the tribunal's president, to preside over the Milosevic case represented a most unfortunate selection. The problem is that the judge selected to head the panel, Richard May, hailed from the UK, one of the NATO countries that led the 1999 intervention against Serbia.

Judge Jorda selected Richard May for the job because he was widely viewed as the best trial judge among the tribunal's judges, a man uniquely capable of keeping Milosevic in line and the trial moving smoothly forward. Perhaps this distinguished jurist could not be expected to recuse himself from presiding over the Milosevic trial because that would be an admission of his bias, and would subvert the credibility of the tribunal as a whole. Indeed, in none of the two dozen cases tried before the Yugoslavia Tribunal and its sister institution, the International Criminal Tribunal for Rwanda, has a judge recused him or herself, despite numerous attempts by defendants to obtain recusal. And yet, however fair and impartial Judge May might actually have been, one can certainly understand why many Serbs feel the "fix is in" as long as a British judge presides. When Judge May died in March 2004, the tribunal had an opportunity to ameliorate the situation by appointing a judge from a more neutral country to fill his slot. Instead, Judge May's countryman, Lord Iain Bonomy of Scotland was selected for the task. In this regard, Osgoode Hall law professor Michael Mandel maintains that "Milosevic has about as much chance of getting a fair trial from this court as he had of defeating NATO in an air war."[40]

G. Fairness of the Procedures

In addition to an impartial bench, the validity of the trial depends on the court allowing Milosevic the equality of arms and fair procedures which the defendants at Nuremberg did not receive. While the prosecution has brought the president of Croatia, as well as several international figures – such as US general Wesley Clark – to The Hague to testify against Milosevic, the defendant has been rebuffed in his initial efforts to obtain the testimony of former US president Bill Clinton, British prime minister Tony Blair, US secretary of state Madeleine Albright, and US special envoy Richard Holbrooke.[41] The tribunal has also declined to grant Milosevic's request that the tribunal issue an order to the secret services of Britain, the US, France, and Germany, demanding that they disclose relevant documents.[42]

Milosevic's strategy as the trial enters the defence phase will be to call such officials to the stand and say to them point blank: "You embraced me as a crucial element in the peace negotiations. After the conclusion of the Dayton Accords, I was mentioned as a leading candidate for the Nobel Peace Prize. How can you now argue that I am responsible for crimes in Croatia and Bosnia of which you were perfectly aware at the time of Dayton?"

With respect to the charges concerning Kosovo, Milosevic will seek to compare his actions with the post–11 September 2001 American war on terrorism and its efforts to drive the Taliban and al-Qaeda from Afghanistan. As late as February 1998, the US, and other members of the so-called "Contact Group" (France, the UK, Germany, Italy, and Russia) were calling the Kosovo Liberation Army a "terrorist group," and condemning the organization's violent actions.[43] Milosevic will want to call Western leaders to testify about the basis for the terrorist designation, which served as the bedrock of his public justification for the use of force in Kosovo.

Unlike a domestic court, the Yugoslavia Tribunal does not have the power to subpoena persons who are no longer in government. If the former officials listed above refuse to appear as witnesses, which is likely to be the case, then Milosevic can make a compelling case to the public that he was in fact denied a fair trial after all.

Another development that has given Milosevic ammunition to argue that the process at The Hague is less than fair occurred when the tribunal's appointed amicus curiae counsel, Michail Wladimiroff, told the press halfway through the trial that Milosevic's chances of acquittal "were negligible." Milosevic charged that by giving such an assessment, Wladimiroff – who had been appointed by the tribunal over Milosevic's objections precisely to ensure that Milosevic received a fair trial – had instead prejudged the tribunal's verdict.[44] The Trial Chamber reluctantly agreed. "The statements taken as a whole would, in the Chamber's view, give rise to a reasonable perception of bias on the part of the *amicus curiae*," Judge May said in the decision to remove Wladimiroff from the case.[45] But by that time the damage to the tribunal's integrity had already been done.

A final area in which the Yugoslavia Tribunal does not receive high marks for fairness involved the tribunal's handling of the death of presiding Judge Richard May halfway through the Milosevic trial. Unlike the Nuremberg Tribunal or the new International Criminal Court, the Yugoslavia Tribunal did not initially appoint an alternate judge to observe the Milosevic trial and stand ready to step in if something happened to one of the three members of the bench. The reason for this was simply to save money. But given the expected length of the trial, the importance of the defendant, and the age of the judges, the lack of an alternate judge was inexcusable.

Judge Bonomy replaced the ailing Judge May at the end of the prosecution's case-in-chief in March 2004.[46] In a domestic case, this would have been grounds for a retrial or dismissal, but the Milosevic trial pressed on. To accomplish this, the Yugoslavia Tribunal had to amend Rule 15(E) of its Rules of Procedure, which had previously provided that in the event that a judge had to be replaced in the middle of the trial, there would have to be a retrial unless the defendant consented to continue the proceedings from that point with the new judge.[47] This action gave Milosevic's supporters the grounds to complain that the Yugoslavia Tribunal was changing the ground rules in the middle of the trial.

Judge Bonomy's first judicial act was to help decide whether to grant the motion to acquit for insufficiency of evidence, which was filed by the amicus counsel. While the prosecution had shown plenty of evidence of war crimes and crimes against humanity in Bosnia, Croatia, and Kosovo, many legal experts and trial observers opined that the prosecution had failed to prove the charge of genocide in Bosnia.[48] The remaining Milosevic Trial Chamber judges (Patrick Robinson of Jamaica and O-Gon Kwon of South Korea) split their vote on the issue (Judge O-Gon Kwon voting for acquittal), with the deciding vote cast by the replacement judge who had not been present for a single day of the trial up to that point.[49]

CONCLUSION: THE IMPACT ON PEACE AND RECONCILIATION IN THE BALKANS

The Milosevic trial was far from perfect. But international law does not guarantee a defendant the right to a textbook trial, only a fair trial; and taken individually, none of the missteps of which Milosevic complains constitute a violation of the rights of the defendant as guaranteed by the International Covenant on Civil and Political Rights and the ICTY Statute.

Meanwhile, witness by witness, document by document, the prosecution managed to construct a formidable case against Milosevic at The Hague. Convinced that exposure to the Milosevic trial would have a cathartic effect on the Serb population, the US Agency for International Development shelled out $24,000 US a month to broadcast the trial proceedings throughout Serbia.[50] As noted in the *New Yorker*, "during the trial's first couple of weeks, five channels carried the proceedings live, and more than half of all [Serbian] households were tuned in."[51] At the trial's midpoint, the trial proceedings are still shown for up to five hours each day on Station B92, where it receives the network's biggest market share (on average 27 per cent).

Perhaps the trial broadcasts would have achieved the hoped for effect if Milosevic had accepted to play by the rules (that is, if he had let a lawyer defend him in the conventional manner). While his defence strategy is unlikely to win him an acquittal, it has been described by a Balkans expert as "brilliantly cunning, designed to play on Serbia's psychological vulnerabilities and continued Serb resentment of the 1999 NATO bombing."[52]

To the extent that it is aimed not at the court of law, but the court of public opinion back home in Serbia, Milosevic's strategy has been quite successful. His approval rating in Serbia doubled during the first weeks of his trial.[53] A poll taken at the midpoint of the trial found that 39 per cent of the Serb population rated Milosevic's trial performance "superior" while less than 25 per cent felt that he was getting a fair trial, and only 33 per cent thought that he was actually responsible for war crimes.[54] Milosevic has gone from the most reviled individual in Serbia to number four on the list of most admired Serbs, and in December 2003, Milosevic easily won a seat in the Serb parliament in a nationwide election.

Does its lack of legitimacy in the eyes of the Serbian people mean that the Milosevic trial will fail to achieve the goals of denying collective guilt by establishing individual responsibility, of enabling the dismantlement of institutions responsible for perpetuating the commission of atrocities, of establishing an accurate historical record, of providing a cathartic process for victims, and of deterring further instances of violence in the Balkans as well as deterring atrocities in similar conflicts elsewhere? To answer this question, one might turn to the precedent of the Nuremberg Tribunal. Like the Yugoslavia Tribunal, the Nuremberg Tribunal was accused of victor's justice and unfair proceedings. As the Yugoslavia Tribunal has done with Milosevic, the Nuremberg Tribunal permitted Nazi leader Hermann Goering relatively free reign in his testimony. Like Milosevic, the unrepentant Goering repeatedly attacked the validity of the proceedings, indulged in propaganda, and attempted to justify his policies and actions as Hitler's Reich Marshal. Indeed, history records that Goering got the better of the lead Nuremberg prosecutor, Justice Robert Jackson of the US Supreme Court, during a cross-examination that went on for two days in 1946.[55]

One of the modern myths of Nuremberg is that the German people immediately accepted the legitimacy of the Nuremberg Tribunal and its judgment. It is generally believed that few Germans questioned the validity of the findings of the Nuremberg Tribunal because the defendants were convicted on the strength of their own meticulously kept documents. Likewise, diplomats hope that if the prosecutor for the Yugoslavia Tribunal is able to prove the case against Milosevic with compelling evidence, Milosevic will fail in his effort to convince the people of Serbia that his trial represents a denial of justice.

Yet, such aspirations for the Milosevic trial were based on an inaccurate reading of history. Opinion polls conducted by the US Department of State from 1946 through 1958 indicated that a large majority of West Germans considered the Nuremberg proceedings to be nothing but a show trial, representing victor's justice rather than real justice.[56] By 1953, the State Department had concluded that the trials conducted at Nuremberg and under Control Council Law No. 10 had failed to "re-educate" West Germans. According to a declassified 1953 State Department report: "From the political point of view, the crux of the war criminals problem in Germany is the refusal of a large number of Germans to accept the principles underlying the [Nuremberg] trials or the findings of the trials ... In spite of all [that] the Western powers have said to the contrary, the trials are generally portrayed as acts of political retribution without firm legal basis."[57]

Two generations later, however, the German people largely speak of the Nuremberg Tribunal with respect,[58] and Germany is one of the foremost advocates of the permanent International Criminal Court, a modern day Nuremberg Tribunal. Perhaps this suggests that no matter the strength of the evidence, the Serb people should not be expected to immediately embrace the findings of the Yugoslavia Tribunal in the Milosevic case, and that the question of its success must await the judgment of future generations.

NOTES

♣ From 1989 to 1993, Professor Scharf served as the US State Department lawyer responsible for issues relating to international war crimes trials. This essay is an expanded and updated version of "Real Justice or Realpolitik: Can Milosevic Get a Fair Trial?" in Michael P. Scharf and William A. Schabas, *Slobodan Milosevic on Trial: A Companion* (New York: Continuum Publishing, 2002), 97–111.

1 A copy of the initial indictment issued in May 1999 concerning charges of crimes against humanity and violations of the laws and customs of war in Kosovo, as well as the additional indictments issued in 2001 relating to crimes in Croatia and Bosnia, can be found on the Tribunal's Web site at <http://www.un.org/icty/ind-e.htm>. The three indictments were joined on 1 February 2002, following a decision by the tribunal's appeals chamber. The trial on the three joined indictments began on 12 February 2002 as Case No. IT-02-54. Transcripts from the trial proceedings are also available via links from the above Web site.

2 The Yugoslavia Tribunal was established pursuant to UN Security Council resolution 808 of 22 February 1993 and resolution 827 of 25 May 1993. For a detailed account of the tribunal's creation, see Michael P. Scharf, *Balkan Justice: The Story Behind the First International War Crimes Trial since Nuremberg* (Durham, NC: Carolina Academic Press, 1997), chaps 2–5.

3 The leading case recognizing self-representation as a fundamental right is *Feratta* v. *California,* 422 U.S. 806, 835n46 (1975). But the US court in *Feratta* added a caveat – which the Trial Chamber overlooked – stating that "a right of self-representation is not a license to abuse the dignity of the courtroom." US appellate courts have subsequently held that the right of self-representation is subject to exceptions – such as when the defendant acts in a disruptive manner or when self-representation interferes with the dignity or integrity of the proceedings: see *Tuitt* v. *Fair*, 822 F.2d 166, 177 (1ST Cir. 1987), cert. denied, 484 U.S. 945 (1987); *United States* v. *Mack*, 362 F.3d 597, 601 (9TH Cir. 2004); *United States* v. *Cauley*, 697 F.2d 486, 491 (2d Cir. 1983), cert. denied, 459 U.S. 1222 (1983); *United States* v. *West*, 877 F.2d 281 (4TH Cir. 1989), cert. denied, 493 U.S. 959 (1989); *United States* v. *Harris*, 2004 U.S. Dist. LEXIS 8849 (DNJ, 2004).

4 See *Prosecutor* v. *Slobodan Milosevic*, Case No. IT-02-54, Oral Ruling by the Trial Chamber, 18 December 2002, transcript page 14574. The Trial Chamber, however, agreed to keep the position under review, but later confirmed its ruling that Milosevic could continue to defend himself: see *Prosecutor* v. *Slobodan Milosevic*, Case No. IT-02–54, Reasons for Decision on the Prosecution Motion Concerning Assignment of Counsel, ICTY Trial Chamber, 4 April 2003, available on-line via links at <http://www.un.org/icty/ind-e.htm>. At the Trial Chamber's invitation, however, the registrar had appointed several amici curiae to ensure that legal issues favouring the defence would be brought to the tribunal's attention, although the amicus attorneys are not permitted to play any role in the actual trial proceedings.

5 Michael P. Scharf, "Making a Spectacle of Himself, Milosevic Wants a Stage, Not the Right to Provide His Own Defense," *The Washington Post*, 29 August 2004, B2; Marlise Simons, "Richard May, Milosevic Judge, Dies at 65," *The New York Times*, 2 July 2004, 17.

6 Marc Champion, "Court of Opinion: With Hague Case, Defiant Milosevic Wins at Home; As Daily Coverage Keeps Serbs Riveted to TV, Many Feel as If They're on Trial," *The Wall Street Journal*, 10 January 2003, A1, final edition.

7 Paul R. Williams and Michael P. Scharf, *Peace with Justice: War Crimes and Accountability in the Former Yugoslavia* (Oxford: Rowman and Littlefield, 2002), 122–3.

8 Mirko Klarin, "War Crimes Manipulation; Slobodan Milosevic's Refusal to Accept Help in His War Crimes Trial is Making it Difficult to Provide Him a Fair Hearing," *London Free Press*, 24 August 2002, F4, final edition.

9 Champion, *supra* n6.

10 Ibid.

11 Ibid.

12 Joseph Lelyveld, "The Defendant; Slobodan Milosevic's Trial, and the Debate Surrounding International Courts," *The New Yorker*, 27 May 2002, 82.
13 Champion, *supra* n6.
14 Ibid.
15 Ibid.
16 *Prosecutor* v. *Milosevic*, Case No. IT-02-54-T, Reasons for Decision on Assignment of Defence Counsel, 22 September 2004, para. 33.
17 *Prosecutor* v. *Milosevic*, Case No. IT-02-54-AR73.7, Decision on Interlocutory Appeal of the Trial Chamber's Decision on the Assignment of Defence Counsel, 1 November 2004.
18 Ibid., para. 13.
19 Ibid., para. 15.
20 Ibid., paras 17–18.
21 Ibid., para. 19.
22 Ibid., para. 20.
23 *Prosecutor* v. *Slobodan Milosevic*, Case No. IT-99-37-I, Initial Appearance, 3 July 2001, transcript pages 1–2. This appearance related to the first indictment, now known as the Kosovo indictment: *supra* n1.
24 *Prosecutor* v. *Dusko Tadic aka "Dule"*, Case No. IT-94-1-AR72, Decision on the Defence Motion for Interlocutory Appeal on Jurisdiction, ICTY Appeals Chamber, 2 October 1995, reproduced in *International Legal Materials* 35, no. 1 (1996): 32.
25 Ibid., paras 32–6.
26 See article IX of the General Framework Agreement for Peace in Bosnia and Herzegovina (Dayton Accords), signed in Paris on 14 December 1995, reproduced in *International Legal Materials* 35, no. 1 (1996): 75.
27 *Milosevic* v. *The Netherlands*, Case No. KG 01/975, ELRO No. AD3266, Hague District Court, 31 August 2001, reproduced in *International Legal Materials* 41, no. 1 (2002): 86.
28 *Milosevic* v. *The Netherlands*, Application No. 77631/01, European Court of Human Rights, 19 March 2002, reproduced in *International Legal Materials* 41, no. 4 (2002): 801.
29 See article 16(4) of the Statute of the International Tribunal for the Prosecution of Persons Responsible for Serious Violations of International Humanitarian Law Committed in the Territory of the Former Yugoslavia since 1991, UN Doc. S/RES/827 (1993).
30 Ibid., art. 13.
31 Champion, *supra* n6.
32 Konstantinos D. Magliveras, "The Interplay between the Transfer of Slobodan Milosevic to the ICTY and Yugoslav Constitutional Law," *European Journal of International Law* 13, no. 3 (2002): 661–78, 676.

33 *Stocké* v. *Germany*, Ser. A No. 199, 13 EHRR 839.

34 *Bozano* v. *France*, Ser. A No. 111, 9 EHRR 297.

35 *Prosecutor* v. *Dragan Nikolic*, Decision on Interlocutory Appeal Concerning Legality of Arrest, Case No. IT-94-2-AR73, 5 June 2003, paras 28 and 32.

36 Scharf, *supra* n2, 11–12.

37 *Final Report to the Prosecutor by the Committee Established to Review the nato Bombing Campaign against the Federal Republic of Yugoslavia*, 8 June 2000, reprinted in *International Legal Materials* 39, no. 5 (2000): 1257. The original report is at <http://www.un.org/icty/pressreal/nato061300.htm>.

38 Ibid., 1282.

39 While there is no US judge on the Milosevic trial bench, one of the trial attorneys is a former US Department of Justice prosecutor, and much of the evidence used by the prosecution has been provided by US authorities.

40 Quoted in Michael P. Scharf and William A. Schabas, *Slobodan Milosevic on Trial: A Companion* (New York: Continuum Publishing, 2002), 109.

41 Marlise Simons, "Milosevic Requests Subpoena of Western Leaders in Crimes Trial," *The New York Times*, 18 June 2004, A11.

42 Ibid.

43 Williams and Scharf, *supra* n7, 176–7.

44 "Yugoslavia: Hague Tribunal Fires 'Amicus Curiae' in Milosevic Case," *BBC Monitoring Europe*, 10 October 2002.

45 *Prosecutor* v. *Slobodan Milosevic*, Case No. IT-02–54, Decision concerning an Amicus Curiae, ICTY Trial Chamber, 10 October 2002, reproduced in *International Legal Materials* 41, no. 6 (2002): 1342.

46 *Prosecutor* v. *Slobodan Milosevic*, Order Replacing a Judge in a Case Before a Trial Chamber, Case No. IT-02–54-T, 10 June 2004.

47 *Rules of Procedure and Evidence,* adopted on 11 February 1994, Rule 15(E), reproduced in Virgina Morris and Michael P. Scharf, *An Insider's Guide to the International Criminal Tribunal for the Former Yugoslavia*, vol. 2 (Irvington-on-Hudson, NY: Transnational Publishers, 1995), 51.

48 Bruce Zagaris, "International Tribunals on War Crimes Continue," *International Enforcement Law Reporter* 20, no. 5 (2004): 204–5.

49 Heikelina Verrijn-Stuart, "What Remains of the Case against Milosevic," *International Justice Tribune*, 30 September 2004; *Prosecutor* v. *Slobodan Milosevic*, Decision on Motion for Judgment of Acquittal, Case No. IT-02–54-T, 16 June 2004, para. 289.

50 Champion, *supra* n6.

51 Lelyveld, *supra* n12.

52 Dusko Doder, "Book Review of Slobodan Milosevic and the Destruction of Yugoslavia by Louis Sell," *The Nation*, 27 May 2002, 25, final edition.

53 Andre Purvis, “Star Power in Serbia; Slobodan Milosevic’s Performance at his War Crimes Trial has Won Him Increased Popularity at Home,” *Time*, 30 September 2002, 46.

54 Lelyveld, *supra* n12; “Q&A with Zain Verjee,” Transcript, CNN International: Q&A Early Afternoon, 12 February 2002, on-line: <http://edition.cnn.com/TRANSCRIPTS/0202/12/i_qaa.01.html>.

55 Telford Taylor, *The Anatomy of the Nuremberg Trials* (London: Bloomsbury, 1993), 334–7.

56 Peter Maguire, *Law and War: An American Story* (New York: Columbia UP, 2000), 241.

57 Ibid., 246.

58 See, for example, The American Jewish Committee, *German Attitudes toward Jews, The Holocaust and the United States*, on-line: <http://www.ajc.org/InTheMedia/PublicationsPrint.asp?did=708>. The German popular view of the Nuremberg trials must be viewed in light of the aggressive “reorientation” program which the US imposed on Germany in the decade after the end of the Second World War, as well as Germany’s own domestic war crimes trials that began in the 1960s. See Donna E. Arzt, “Nuremberg, Denazification and Democracy,” *New York Law School Journal of Human Rights* 12, no. 3 (1995): 689–758.

3

The Application of International Law Immunities in Prosecutions for International Crimes

DAPO AKANDE*

The debate about whether state officials who commit international crimes should be held responsible in external fora is informed by the basic tension that exists between the desire to protect human rights and calls to respect state sovereignty. This debate involves the interplay between two branches of international law. On one side, there is the well-established law of state and diplomatic immunities which protect a state and its agents from the jurisdiction of other states. This law proceeds from notions of sovereign equality and is aimed at ensuring that a state does not unduly interfere with other states and their agents.[1] On the other side is the development of a newer branch of international law which is based on humanitarian values and which defines certain types of conduct as crimes under international law (international criminal law).[2]

Since states often fail to institute domestic prosecution of their own officials and agents who are alleged to have committed international crimes, renewed attention has been paid to the possibility of subjecting state agents to prosecution in foreign domestic courts or in international courts. For such prosecution in foreign domestic courts to take place, it usually has to be shown, first, that those courts have jurisdiction over crimes committed abroad by foreigners against foreigners (i.e., that they have universal or quasi universal jurisdiction) and, second, that such jurisdiction extends to state agents (i.e., that international law immunities are unavailable).

Although there has been a significant increase in recent years in attempts to institute prosecutions for alleged international crimes in the national courts of states other than the state where the acts occurred,[3] it has not proved easy to establish the two propositions cited above. Indeed, it has become apparent that the views that states possess universal jurisdiction over international crimes committed abroad and that incumbent and former state officials are subject to foreign domestic prosecution for such crimes are by no means universally held.[4]

International law immunities may be relied on in order to prevent prosecution of state officials by the International Criminal Court (ICC). This chapter first considers, however, whether state officials accused of committing international crimes in their home state are immune from the domestic criminal jurisdiction of other states. The question of immunity from foreign national jurisdictions must be considered for two reasons. Firstly, despite the creation of the ICC, it is expected that the majority of prosecutions for international crimes will take place in domestic courts. This is not only because the ICC has not, as yet, achieved universal acceptance,[5] but also because of the complementarity provisions of the Rome Statute of the International Criminal Court (ICC Statute).[6] Under those provisions, the ICC may not exercise jurisdiction in cases in which a state is willing to investigate or prosecute, or has genuinely done so. Thus, the jurisdiction of the ICC supplements national jurisdictions. Secondly, because the ICC has no independent powers of arrest, it must depend on states to arrest and surrender suspects. When those suspects are either serving or former state officials present in the territory of another state, they might be entitled under international law to immunity from the jurisdiction of the "host" state. In such circumstances, the host state must examine whether that immunity prevents it from arresting and surrendering the suspect to the ICC.

As this chapter is devoted to examining the application of international immunities in criminal proceedings, it does not specifically address those questions of immunity which arise in civil proceedings that are instituted abroad against foreign states and foreign officials accused of human rights violations. Since the famous *Filártiga* case,[7] there has been a significant amount of such civil litigation in the courts of the US under the Alien Tort Claims Act 1789[8] and the Torture Victim Protection Act 1991,[9] as well as in the courts of other states.[10] Because the theories that have been proposed by some writers and judges in order to remove the immunity of states and state officials in civil proceedings also apply to criminal proceedings, some of what is said in this chapter will be relevant to these civil cases.

Part one of this chapter introduces the different types of immunity that are available to state officials when abroad and sets out the distinction between immunity *ratione personae* and immunity *ratione materiae*. Brief consideration is given to how state and diplomatic immunities apply in foreign domestic prosecutions for international crimes. It is argued that while immunity *ratione personae* continues to apply in cases of international crimes, developments in international law mean that the reasons for applying immunity *ratione materiae* do not extend to prosecutions for international crimes.

Part two examines whether international law immunities may be pleaded before international tribunals. It is argued that despite the fact that immunities are primarily designed for horizontal inter-state relationships, there are important reasons of principle and policy for recognizing that international immunities may also be pleaded before international tribunals. However, whether or not those immunities are available in practice depends on the text of the instrument creating the tribunal and on whether the state of the official is bound by that instrument.

Finally, part three examines the application of immunities in proceedings initiated by the ICC. This part analyses the tension between the two provisions of the ICC Statute that deal with immunities: articles 27 and 98. It considers whether article 98(1) – which directs the Court not to proceed with a request for arrest or surrender of a person where such a request would require the requested state to violate the immunities that international law accords to that person – may be relied on both by parties to the ICC Statute (states parties) and by non-parties. Similar consideration is given to article 98(2) of the ICC Statute, which requires the Court not to request an arrest or surrender where this would compel the requested state to violate an agreement precluding surrender to the Court. Although it may be argued that even states parties may rely on the provisions of article 98, it is argued that the better view is that only non-parties may benefit from them because this view alone gives meaningful effect to article 27 and to the objects and purposes of the statute.

I. STATE AND DIPLOMATIC IMMUNITIES IN NATIONAL PROCEEDINGS CONCERNING INTERNATIONAL CRIMES

It is commonly accepted that state officials are immune in certain circumstances from the jurisdiction of foreign states.[11] These immunities are derived, firstly, from the customary international law of state immunity, which is concerned with preventing states from exercising control over the public acts of other states. Secondly, under customary international law and applicable treaties, diplomatic agents of states are entitled to immunity from the criminal and civil jurisdiction of the foreign state to which they are accredited.[12] While some officials enjoy a broad immunity because of their status or office (immunity *ratione personae*), the immunity of others relates only to acts performed in their official capacity (immunity *ratione materiae*). This part now briefly examines the scope of these immunities and the rationale underpinning them. In particular, it will be considered whether these immunities remain applicable in criminal proceedings in which an official or diplomat is accused of committing a crime under international law.[13]

A. Immunity Ratione Personae *(Immunity Attaching to an Office or Status)*

The first type of immunity applicable to certain state officials consists of those immunities which attach to a particular office and are possessed only as long as the official is in that office ("personal immunity" or "immunity *ratione personae*"). These immunities are limited to a small group of senior state officials, especially heads of state, heads of government, and foreign ministers.[14] They also apply to diplomats and other officials on special mission in foreign states.[15] These immunities are conferred on officials with primary responsibility for the conduct of the international relations of the state and stem from the recognition that the smooth conduct of international relations and international cooperation between states requires an effective process of communication between them.[16] The effectiveness of this process of communication and cooperation in turn requires that the state agents charged with the conduct of international relations be able to travel freely, as this enables them to perform their functions without the fear or possibility of harassment by other states.[17] In short, these immunities are necessary for the maintenance of a system of peaceful cooperation and coexistence amongst states.[18] As the International Court of Justice (ICJ) has pointed out, there is "no more fundamental prerequisite for the conduct of relations between states than the inviolability of diplomatic envoys and embassies."[19]

Since heads of states, diplomats, and other officials accorded immunity *ratione personae* will be hindered in the exercise of their functions if they are arrested and detained when in a foreign state, these officials are absolutely immune from the criminal jurisdiction of the foreign state. In the *Arrest Warrant Case*, the ICJ held that this type of immunity applies not only in relation to the official acts of this limited group of senior officials but also in relation to private acts.[20] For the same reason, the immunity applies whether or not the act in question was done at a time when the official was in office or before entry to office.[21] Consequently, the arrest and prosecution of these senior officials, as well as the mere issuance and circulation of a warrant for their arrest, would constitute a violation of international law.[22] However, because immunity *ratione personae* is conferred in order to permit free exercise of diplomatic functions, it attaches only for as long as the person is in office.

The ICJ has confirmed that the absolute nature of the immunity from criminal process accorded to a serving foreign minister is maintained even when it is alleged that he or she has committed an international crime and even when the foreign minister is abroad on a private visit.[23] The Court stated that "it has been unable to deduce ... that there exists under customary international law any form of exception to the rule according immunity from criminal jurisdiction and inviolability to incumbent Ministers for Foreign Affairs, where they are suspected of having committed war crimes or crimes against humanity."[24]

This principle – which must be taken as applying to all those serving senior state officials and diplomats possessing immunity *ratione personae*[25] – has been justified on the ground that an absence of immunity in relation to human rights violations committed abroad is likely to hinder international cooperation without significantly increasing the protection of human rights.[26] According to this reasoning, the effect of any rule that removes immunity will simply be to prevent foreign leaders from travelling abroad.

The principle that immunity *ratione personae* is maintained even when it is alleged that the senior serving official has committed an international crime has been applied in recent years by several national courts.[27] Judicial opinion and state practice[28] on this point are unanimous. No case can be found in which it was held that a state official possessing immunity *ratione personae* is subject to the criminal jurisdiction of a foreign state when it is alleged that he or she has committed an international crime.[29]

While the existence and scope of immunity *ratione personae* appears to be reasonably settled, questions remain as to which government officials are entitled to benefit from this absolute immunity from foreign criminal prosecution. In the *Arrest Warrant Case*, the ICJ stated that these immunities are available to "diplomatic and consular agents [and] certain holders of high-ranking office in a state, *such as* the Head of State, Head of Government and Minister for Foreign Affairs."[30] While it has long been clear that serving heads of states, heads of governments,[31] and diplomats[32] possess absolute immunity *ratione personae* in criminal cases, the position of foreign ministers has sometimes been controversial.[33] However, in the *Arrest Warrant Case*, the ICJ held – without reference to any supporting state practice – that absolute immunity *ratione personae* also applies to foreign ministers because they are responsible for the international relations of the state and "in the performance of these functions, he or she is frequently required to travel internationally, and thus must be in a position freely to do so whenever the need should arise."[34]

Although basing this type of immunity on the fact that the official concerned is charged with international functions would be consistent with the rationale for such immunity, it would considerably extend the range of officials entitled to immunity *ratione personae*. The current state of international affairs requires a very wide range of officials (senior and junior) to travel in the exercise of their functions. Ministers other than those specifically designated with responsibility for foreign affairs often represent their state internationally. They may have to conduct bilateral negotiations with other governments or represent their governments at international summits. Indeed it is difficult to think of any ministerial position that does not require at least some level of international involvement.[35]

In the past, it has not been recognized that the mere fact that an official acts in the exercise of international relations is sufficient grounds for conferring immunity *ratione personae*. However, where officials represent their states at international organizations, they will usually be accorded immunity by treaty.[36] Furthermore, it may well be that, under customary international law as well as treaty law, the person of any official sent abroad on a special mission by a state is inviolable, with the result that he or she may not be arrested or detained.[37] This rule would be entirely consistent with the policy underlying immunity *ratione personae*.

B. *Immunity* Ratione Materiae *(Immunity Attaching to Official Acts)*

State officials who are not entitled to immunity *ratione personae* are nevertheless immune from the jurisdiction of other states when they perform acts in their official capacity. This is called "functional immunity" or "immunity *ratione materiae*."[38] Since this type of immunity attaches to the official act, it may be relied on not only by serving state officials but also by former officials with respect to official acts performed while they were in office.[39] It may also be relied on by persons or bodies that are not state officials or organs but have acted on behalf of the state.[40] The application of immunity *ratione materiae* to state officials has occurred more often in civil than criminal cases.[41] The reason for this is not difficult to decipher. The criminal jurisdiction of states is primarily territorial and state officials do not usually exercise their official functions in the territory of other states. Thus, the circumstances in which state officials will be criminally prosecuted in a foreign state for an act done in the exercise of their official capacity are limited. Nevertheless, the assertion of immunity *ratione materiae* in criminal cases is not unknown and the reasons for which it is conferred apply a fortiori in criminal cases.[42]

Two related policies underlie the conferral of immunity *ratione materiae*. Firstly, this type of immunity constitutes a substantive defence in that it indicates that the individual official is not to be held legally responsible for acts that are in effect those of the state.[43] Secondly, the immunity of state officials in foreign courts prevents circumvention of the immunity of the state, which could otherwise be achieved by bringing proceedings against those acting on behalf of the state.[44] In this sense, this immunity operates as a jurisdictional or procedural bar as it prevents courts from indirectly exercising control over acts of the foreign state through proceedings against the official who carried out the act.

Even though serving or former state officials are generally entitled to immunity *ratione materiae* in relation to their official acts, such immunity from foreign domestic criminal jurisdiction does not exist when the person is charged with an international crime. There have been a significant number of domestic prosecutions of officials of foreign states for international crimes.[45] All of these decisions proceed – at least implicitly, and sometimes explicitly[46] – on the basis of a lack of immunity *ratione materiae* in respect of such crimes.

Two principal reasons have been advanced in support of this argument. Firstly, it has been argued that although officials possess immunity *ratione materiae* in respect of official acts, acts amounting to international crimes are not to be considered as official acts.[47] Secondly, it has been argued that there is no immunity with respect to international crimes, because these crimes constitute violations of *jus cogens* norms (i.e., peremptory norms of international law from which no derogation is permitted) and those peremptory norms have a higher status than, and ought to prevail over, the rules according immunity.[48] For reasons explored more fully elsewhere,[49] both of these arguments are unpersuasive. They misunderstand the basis upon which state immunity is accorded and suggest a false conflict between the rule according state immunity and the relevant *jus cogens* norms. In any event, the argument that immunity may not be accorded for acts in violation of *jus cogens* has been rejected by the ICJ,[50] the European Court of Human Rights,[51] and most national courts to have considered the issue.[52]

Whilst international crimes, when committed by state officials, will often constitute official acts, there is a separate rule which removes immunity *ratione materiae* in proceedings relating to these crimes. This immunity is not available in such proceedings, because the reasons for conferring such immunity[53] do not apply to prosecutions for international crimes. Firstly, the general principle that only the state, and not its officials, may be held responsible for acts done by officials in their official capacity does not apply to acts that amount to international crimes.[54] On the contrary, it is well established that the official position of individuals does not exempt them from individual responsibility for acts that are crimes under international law, and thus does not constitute a substantive defence.[55]

Secondly, to the extent that international law has subsequently developed rules which permit domestic courts to exercise universal jurisdiction over certain international crimes and to the extent that those rules contemplate prosecution of crimes committed in an official capacity, the second reason for immunity *ratione materiae* disappears. In those circumstances, immunity *ratione materiae* cannot logically coexist with such a grant of jurisdiction. To apply the prior rule according immunity in such cases would deprive the subsequent jurisdictional rule of practically all meaning. This constitutes the best explanation for the decision of the English House of Lords in the *Pinochet Case [No. 3]*. Most of the judges in that case held that since the Torture Convention limited the offence of torture to acts committed in the exercise of official capacity, the granting of immunity *ratione materiae* would necessarily have been inconsistent with the provisions of the convention that accord universal jurisdiction over the offence.[56] Accordingly, immunity *ratione materiae* must be regarded as having been displaced by the rule according universal jurisdiction for acts of torture.

Similarly, since grave breaches of the 1949 Geneva Conventions and other war crimes committed in an international armed conflict are almost by definition acts committed by military and other officials of states, the treaty rules according universal jurisdiction over such crimes cannot logically coexist with the grant of immunity *ratione materiae* to state officials.[57] However, because genocide, crimes against humanity, and war crimes committed in an internal armed conflict may be committed by non-state actors, the rules permitting universal jurisdiction with respect to these crimes do not cover exactly the same persons as are accorded immunity *ratione materiae* (as is the case with torture and war crimes committed in an international armed conflict). Nevertheless, these jurisdictional rules contemplate the domestic prosecution of state officials and, for that reason, prevail over the prior rule according immunity *ratione materiae*.[58] Therefore, immunity *ratione materiae* does not exist with respect to domestic criminal proceedings for any of the international crimes set out in the ICC Statute.

II. ARE INTERNATIONAL LAW IMMUNITIES AVAILABLE BEFORE INTERNATIONAL TRIBUNALS?

Since state and diplomatic immunities are derived from notions of state equality and are designed for horizontal inter-state relationships, it may be thought that these immunities cannot be pleaded before international tribunals.[59] In the *Arrest Warrant Case*, the ICJ stated that "the immunities enjoyed under international law ... do not represent a bar to criminal prosecution in certain circumstances. ... an incumbent or former Minister for Foreign Affairs may be subject to criminal proceedings before certain international criminal courts, where they have jurisdiction."[60]

A similar view has also been taken by the Special Court for Sierra Leone[61] in proceedings against the former head of state of Liberia, Charles Taylor.[62] Taylor challenged the validity of his indictment on the basis that it was issued when he was still in office and it was therefore contrary to the immunity of a head of state under international law.[63] However, the Appeals Chamber of the Special Court (agreeing with the Office of the Prosecutor and the amici curiae appointed by the Court) rejected the challenge.[64] Relying on the statutes of the Nuremberg and Tokyo International Military Tribunals, the International Criminal Tribunal for the Former Yugoslavia (ICTY), the International Criminal Tribunal for Rwanda (ICTR), and the ICC,[65] as well as the *Arrest Warrant* and *Pinochet* cases, the Special Court held that "the principle seems now established that the sovereign equality of states does not prevent a Head of State from being prosecuted before an international criminal tribunal or court."[66]

However, the view that international law immunities may never be pleaded in proceedings instituted before international courts and tribunals oversimplifies the matter.[67] Whether or not those wanted for prosecution by an international criminal tribunal may rely on international law immunities to exempt themselves from its jurisdiction depends, firstly, on the provisions of the statute establishing that tribunal. While these texts tend to include a general rule to the effect that the official position of a defendant may not be relied on as a bar to prosecution,[68] it is important to pay attention to the manner in which immunity is provided.[69]

Secondly, and more importantly, the possibility of relying on international law immunities (particularly immunity *ratione personae*) to avoid prosecutions by international tribunals depends on the nature of the tribunal: how it was established and whether the state of the official sought to be tried is bound by the instrument establishing the tribunal. In this regard, there is a distinction between those tribunals established by UN Security Council resolution (i.e., ICTY and ICTR) and those established by treaty. Because of the universal membership of the UN and because decisions of the Council are binding on all UN member-states,[70] the provisions of the ICTY and ICTR statutes are capable of removing the immunity of practically all states. But this is only because those states are bound by and have indirectly consented (via the UN Charter) to the decision to remove immunity.[71] On the other hand, since only parties to a treaty are bound by its provisions,[72] a treaty establishing an international tribunal cannot remove immunities that international law grants to officials of states that are not party to the treaty. Those immunities are rights belonging to the non-party states and those states may not be deprived of their rights by a treaty to which they are not party.[73]

It is not an adequate response to assert that immunities are conferred by international law only with respect to inter-state relations and in proceedings before national courts. These immunities are conferred in order to prevent foreign states from unduly interfering with the affairs of other states and from exercising judicial jurisdiction over another state in circumstances where the state concerned has not consented. It makes little difference whether the foreign states seek to exercise this judicial jurisdiction unilaterally or through some collective body to which the state concerned has not consented. To suggest that immunity is non-existent before an international tribunal that has not been consented to by the relevant state is to allow subversion of the policy underpinning international law immunities. Indeed, the amici curiae to the Special Court recognized this point in stating that "if the Special Court had not been established pursuant to Security Council resolution the situation may be materially different: for example, two states may not establish an international criminal court for the purpose, or with the effect, of circumventing the jurisdictional limitations incumbent on national courts."[74] It is difficult to understand how the amici curiae, having admitted this much, could have reached the conclusion that a serving head of state cannot claim immunity before an international tribunal[75] – a conclusion expressly stated to apply whether or not the tribunal was established under chapter VII of the UN Charter.

The ICTY has recognised, in *Prosecutor* v. *Blaškić*,[76] that there are circumstances in which international immunities may be pleaded before an international tribunal. In that case, the Appeals Chamber held that because state officials are entitled to functional immunity (immunity *ratione materiae*) with respect to official acts, the tribunal was not entitled to issue an order that would require state officials to produce documents they held in their official capacity. While the Appeals Chamber acknowledged that the rule according immunity *ratione materiae* was based on sovereign equality and "undoubtedly applies to relations between States *inter se*," it held that the rule "must also be taken into account, and indeed it has always been respected, by international organizations as well as international courts."[77] In *Prosecutor* v. *Krstic*, the Appeals Chamber appeared to contradict its earlier decision in *Blaškić* when it stated that "it may be the case (it is unnecessary to decide here) that, between states, such a functional immunity exists against prosecution for those acts (attributable to the State), but it would be incorrect to suggest that such an immunity exists in international criminal courts."[78] However, the statement in *Krstic* relates to immunity *ratione materiae* and probably amounts to nothing more than a decision that such immunity does not extend to prosecutions for international crimes. Indeed the *Krstic* Appeals Chamber did not question the general principle that functional immunities available to state officials restrict the power of the international tribunal to issue orders to state officials. It only questioned the scope of that immunity.[79]

In sum, the statement by the ICJ that international immunities may not be pleaded before certain international tribunals must be read subject to the condition, first, that the instruments creating those tribunals expressly or implicitly remove the relevant immunity[80] and, second, that the state of the official concerned is bound by the instrument removing the immunity. Therefore, a senior serving state official who is entitled to immunity *ratione personae* (for example a head of state) is entitled to such immunity before an international tribunal to which the state concerned has not consented.

III. THE ICC STATUTE AND IMMUNITY

This part of the chapter considers the application of immunities in proceedings initiated by the ICC. Section A below highlights the tension between the two provisions in the ICC Statute that deal with immunities – articles 27 and 98. In section B, detailed attention is given to whether states parties, non-parties, and international organizations may benefit from the provisions of article 98. Those provisions direct the Court not to request the arrest or surrender of a person where such a request would require the requested state to violate the immunities that international law accords to that person or to violate an international agreement precluding surrender to the Court. Finally, Section C considers whether it is the ICC or national authorities that are competent to decide on whether a person wanted by the Court is entitled to immunity from arrest and surrender.

A. *The Tension between Articles 27 and 98 of the ICC Statute*

As indicated in part two above, the determination of whether state, diplomatic, or other immunities are available in relation to the ICC must begin with an examination of the text of the ICC Statute. Two provisions of the statute bear on questions of immunity: articles 27 and 98. Article 27 primarily addresses the position of state officials in relation to the ICC itself. Article 27(1) provides that "this Statute shall apply equally to all persons without any distinction based on official capacity. In particular, official capacity as a Head of State or Government, a member of a Government or Parliament, an elected representative or a government official shall in no case exempt a person from criminal responsibility under this Statute, nor shall it, in and of itself, constitute a ground for reduction of sentence." This provision has now become standard in the founding instruments of international criminal tribunals. Similar provisions were inserted into the relevant agreements for the Nuremberg and Tokyo tribunals after World War II as well as the statutes of the ICTY and the ICTR.[81] Article 27(1) primarily addresses the substantive responsibility of state officials for international crimes rather than questions of immunity. Its main effect is to establish that the official capacity of a person does not relieve him or her of individual criminal responsibility, and it thus eliminates a substantive defence that may be put forward by state officials.[82]

It may be argued that article 27(1) and similar provisions do not deal with immunity at all since a statement that a person may be legally responsible does not address whether that person is subject to the jurisdiction of a particular forum, that is, whether that forum may determine that responsibility. Those jurisdictional issues are addressed, in part, by the law on international immunities and the possession of immunity does not mean that the person concerned may not be legally responsible for the act in question.

However, deeper analysis shows that article 27(1) does have the effect of removing at least some of the immunities to which state officials would otherwise be entitled.[83] First of all, questions of legal responsibility are not wholly separate from questions of immunity. As has already been argued, one of the reasons for conferring immunity with respect to official acts is that they are generally regarded as acts of the state, and therefore acts for which the state and not the official ought to be held responsible.[84] To the extent that an international rule establishes that the official himself or herself ought to be held responsible for the act, that reason for immunity disappears. Secondly, by providing that the ICC Statute applies to state officials, article 27(1) establishes that those officials are subject to prosecution by the ICC even when they acted in their official capacity. Therefore, article 27(1) is also jurisdictional in nature. Not only does the second sentence implicitly exclude immunities based on the official nature of the act, the first sentence also implicitly establishes that the official status of defendants does not exclude them from the jurisdiction of the ICC.

Perhaps as a result of doubts as to whether article 27(1) completely removes the possibility of reliance on immunities in proceedings before the ICC, article 27(2) contains an explicit denial of international and national law immunities. It provides that "immunities or special procedural rules which may attach to the official capacity of a person, whether under national or international law, shall not bar the Court from exercising its jurisdiction over such a person." This provision is new. It has no counterpart in the Nuremberg or Tokyo tribunal agreements or in the ICTY and ICTR statutes. Article 27(2) conclusively establishes that state officials are subject to prosecution by the ICC and that provision constitutes a waiver by states parties of any immunity that their officials would otherwise possess vis-à-vis the ICC.

However, the removal of immunity vis-à-vis the ICC by article 27 is not the end of the matter. Because the ICC does not have independent powers of arrest and must rely on states to arrest and surrender wanted persons,[85] the immunities of state officials in national jurisdictions become important. To the extent that the ICC is seeking arrest and surrender from the state of the official concerned, article 27 constitutes a waiver of national law immunities by parties to the ICC Statute. States parties are therefore obliged to arrest and surrender their own officials even if those officials would otherwise be entitled to immunity under national law.[86] However, where an official is in a state other than his or her state and is entitled under international law to immunity from arrest and criminal process in the other state, the matter is more complicated. To deal with this issue, article 98(1) of the ICC Statute provides that "the Court may not proceed with a request for surrender or assistance which would require the requested State to act inconsistently with its obligations under international law with respect to the State or diplomatic immunity of a person or property of a third State, unless the Court can first obtain the cooperation of that third State for the waiver of the immunity."[87] Thus, although article 27 provides that a state official's possession of international immunity shall not bar *the* ICC from exercising jurisdiction, article 98 directs the Court not to take action that would result in the violation by *states* of their international obligations to accord immunity to foreign officials.[88]

It is likely that the Court will gain custody of indicted state officials mostly through the cooperation of *other* states parties on whose territory the officials happen to be. This is because non-parties to the ICC Statute have no obligation to surrender their nationals or officials to the ICC and because parties may, in breach of their obligations, refuse to handover their own officials.[89] However, the Court's ability to gain custody of state officials and the denial of immunity provided for in article 27 may be undermined by the fact that officials may be entitled to rely on international immunities in order to prevent *other* states from arresting them. Whether or not this proves to be a significant barrier to the exercise of the ICC's jurisdiction will depend on the interpretation given to article 98(1).

B. Who May Benefit from Article 98?

1 THE POSITION OF OFFICIALS AND DIPLOMATS OF STATES NOT PARTY TO THE ICC STATUTE

Although the ICC is entitled to exercise jurisdiction over nationals of states that are not party to its statute,[90] nothing in the ICC Statute can operate to remove the immunities that officials of non-parties would ordinarily possess under international law.[91] Part 9 of the ICC Statute imposes an obligation on parties to cooperate with requests from the ICC for the arrest and surrender of persons on their territory. However, states parties would be in breach of their international obligations to non-parties if they arrested and surrendered to the ICC an official of a non-party who is entitled to immunity from arrest and prosecution.[92] In these circumstances, article 98(1), by directing the Court not to proceed with a request for arrest, ensures that ICC parties will not be placed in the position of facing competing legal obligations to the ICC and to other states. Indeed, since the ICC operates in effect by "delegation" from (or in the place of) its states parties,[93] the immunity of officials of non-parties applies not only in relation to states parties but also in relation to the ICC itself. Thus, the Court itself is prevented by international law from taking steps that would amount to a violation of those immunities.[94] In particular, the ICC would be prevented from even issuing an arrest warrant under article 58 of the ICC Statute.[95] This follows from the decision of the ICJ in the *Arrest Warrant Case*,[96] where it was held that the issuance and circulation of an arrest warrant for a person entitled to immunity violates that immunity even where no subsequent steps are taken.[97]

2 THE POSITION OF OFFICIALS AND DIPLOMATS OF PARTIES TO THE ICC STATUTE UNDER ARTICLE 98(1)

Although it is clear that article 98(1) applies to immunities enjoyed by officials of non-parties, it is less clear whether that provision also refers to immunities ordinarily enjoyed by officials of ICC parties. The question is whether article 98(1) prevents the Court from requesting that one state party surrender the official of another state party present on the territory of the first, where the official would normally have immunity under international law. The answer depends on the relationship between articles 27 and 98. In particular, the answer depends on whether the waiver of immunity in article 27 is a waiver not only in relation to the ICC, but also in relation to the exercise of authority by other parties where those other parties are acting in support of the exercise of ICC jurisdiction.

The view that article 98(1) applies only to officials of non-parties has been taken by scholars[98] and by some ICC parties.[99] This view is reflected in the legislation of a number of ICC parties implementing their obligations under the ICC Statute. For example, under section 23(1) of the British International Criminal Court Act 2001[100] "any State or diplomatic immunity attaching to a person by reason of a connection with a state party to the ICC Statute" does not prevent his or her arrest in Britain or surrender to the Court. However, where the state or diplomatic immunity attaches by reason of a connection to a non-state party, section 23(2) in effect provides that proceedings for arrest or surrender may continue only where the non-state party has waived the immunity. Virtually identical provisions and language can be found in the relevant legislation of Malta and the proposed legislation of Ireland.[101] The relevant legislation of Canada and New Zealand goes even further and appears to provide that no person may rely on international law immunities in proceedings instituted pursuant to an ICC request for arrest and surrender.[102] Nevertheless, in light of the discussion in the previous section, the Canadian and New Zealand provisions should not be interpreted as applying to officials of states not party to the ICC Statute.[103]

The effect of the provisions just referred to is that a serving head of state of an ICC party who is on an official visit to the state concerned, or a serving diplomat of an ICC party accredited to that state, may be arrested and surrendered to the Court if the ICC so requests.[104] The immunities *ratione personae* that ordinarily apply to such persons[105] would therefore not apply. Because this is a far-reaching conclusion that constitutes a significant change from the legal position which existed before creation of the ICC, it is imperative that cogent and convincing reasoning support it.

The cases in which the ICC will wish to direct a request for surrender of the official of one state party to another state party are likely to be those in which the official's own state, probably in breach of its obligations, has refused to surrender the accused.[106] Absent voluntary appearance by the official or surrender of him or her by a non-state entity, surrender of the official by another state offers the only realistic possibility of securing custody. It has therefore been argued that the effectiveness of the ICC Statute is best served by an interpretation that permits the Court to direct its requests for the surrender of officials of states parties to other states.[107] However, because any interference with the immunity that international law accords to serving senior state officials and diplomats constitutes an extremely serious interference with the state concerned and with its international relations, the fact that a denial of immunity would increase the effectiveness of the ICC is not sufficient ground for implying that there exists a waiver of immunity. On the contrary, it must be shown that such a removal of an otherwise applicable immunity is either stated expressly in the ICC Statute or must necessarily be implied from its provisions.

On one view, the text of article 98(1) itself resolves the question of whether it extends to officials of states parties since that provision refers to the "immunity of a person ... of a *third State*" (emphasis added). According to this view, the expression "third State", when used in the law of treaties usually refers to states not party to the relevant treaty,[108] and therefore refers in article 98(1) to states that are not party to the ICC Statute. However, this argument is neither compelling nor decisive. The fact that article 98(1) speaks of "third States" does not necessarily mean that it excludes states parties. It is more likely that "third State" in that provision is not used to refer to non-parties but rather to a state other than the one with custody of the suspect. As Paola Gaeta has noted, in other parts of the ICC Statute where reference is made to states not party to the Statute, it is not the term "third State" that is used but terms such as "non-contracting States" and "States not parties."[109] Significantly, the other uses of the term "third State" in the ICC Statute probably do not refer only to non-parties. It is unlikely that, for example, the prohibition under article 108 of extradition to a third state by states that have custody of persons sentenced by the ICC was meant to cover only non-parties. Likewise, when the ICC Statute uses the term "third party" in connection with requests by the ICC to states parties to provide documents or information disclosed in confidence by a third party, that term explicitly includes states parties as well as non-parties.[110]

A more compelling argument in support of the view that article 98(1) benefits only non-parties is that an interpretation that allows officials of states parties to rely on international law immunities when they are in other states would deprive the ICC Statute of its stated purpose of preventing impunity and ensuring that the most serious crimes of international concern do not go unpunished.[111]

Furthermore, the removal through article 27 of immunity from the Court's jurisdiction would be nullified in practice if article 98(1) were interpreted as allowing parties to rely on the same immunities in order to prevent the surrender of their officials to the Court by other states.[112] This argument is supported by the principle that "an interpreter is not free to adopt a reading that would result in reducing whole clauses or paragraphs of a treaty to redundancy or inutility."[113] Thus, the removal of immunity in article 27 must be interpreted as applying not only in relation to the ICC itself but also in relation to states acting at the request of the ICC.

This argument is supported by the fact that, as discussed above, the removal is not only contained in article 27(2), which stipulates that immunities are not to bar the ICC from exercising jurisdiction, but also in article 27(1). Steffen Wirth has pointed out that when the parties agreed in the first sentence of article 27(1) that the ICC Statute applies to their officials, they thereby agreed that all parts of the ICC Statute, including the cooperation regime in part 9, apply to those officials.[114] Since the international law immunities of officials of states parties are removed by the ICC Statute, another state on whose territory such an official is present would therefore not be acting "inconsistently with its obligations under international law"[115] by arresting and surrendering such officials to the ICC.

In response to the arguments just set out, it may be maintained that an interpretation of article 98(1) that extends its application to officials of ICC parties does not deprive article 27 of all meaning. Even under such an interpretation of article 98, article 27 would allow the ICC to conduct an investigation and even issue an arrest warrant under article 58, for persons who would otherwise be immune.[116] Furthermore, article 27 would bar any reliance on immunity once the ICC has taken an accused person connected with a state party into custody.[117] On this view, article 27 is directed solely at the position of state officials vis-à-vis the Court and does not affect the immunity of those officials from the jurisdiction of other states. Rather than having been waived by article 27, those immunities, according to this view, are expressly preserved by article 98(1). Thus, article 98(1) would prevent the Court from requesting that a host state arrest and surrender an official of another state who is entitled to international law immunities. However, the Court would remain free to request the surrender of the official from his or her home state, which has an obligation under part 9 of the ICC Statute to cooperate with the Court in executing the request.

While interpreting article 98(1) as also applying to officials of parties to the ICC Statute does not totally negate the effect of article 27, this interpretation leaves only a very small scope of application for article 27(2). Firstly, it is incorrect to assert that the waiver of international law immunities in article 27(2) at least allows the

Court to conduct an investigation and issue arrest warrants for officials of ICC parties in circumstances where it would otherwise have been unable to do so. If article 98(1) were interpreted as preventing the Court from requesting that host states arrest those officials of other ICC parties that possess immunity under international law, then the warrants issued under article 58 could be directed only at the official's home state. Such an interpretation would render that part of article 27(2) that removes the immunity of officials under *international law* redundant. Since officials do not possess immunities under international law with respect to their home state, the removal in article 27(2) of "immunities or special procedural rules which may attach ... under ... international law" could not have been for the purpose of allowing the ICC to issue arrest warrants that operate only in relation to the official's home state.

Secondly, the view that article 27 operates solely in relation to the *ICC* and removes immunity only when the *Court* has custody of accused persons (but not when they are still within the territory of a state other than their own) will mean in practice that the provision will rarely apply. In the vast majority of cases, the Court is expected to obtain custody of accused officials through surrender either by their own state or another state. Where an official in the Court's custody has been surrendered by his own state, reliance on article 27 to remove immunity from the exercise of ICC jurisdiction is hardly necessary, as the surrender itself constitutes a waiver. If article 98(1) is interpreted as allowing states parties to rely on immunities to prevent the surrender of their officials to the ICC by other states, it would mean that the removal of immunity contained in article 27 is effectively applicable only in the minority of cases in which custody is secured through the acts of non-state entities[118] or through voluntary appearance.[119] To confine what on its face appears to be an important provision to these limited and exceptional circumstances would defeat the objects and purposes of the ICC Statute.

To give meaningful effect to article 27, article 98(1) must be interpreted as applying only to officials of non-parties. Thus, article 98(1) does not prevent the Court from requesting the surrender of officials of parties even where those officials would otherwise be protected by international law immunities from arrest by national authorities of other states. Correspondingly, parties to the ICC Statute have an obligation under part 9 to comply with the Court's requests for arrest and surrender where an official of another state party is on their territory. The ICC Statute therefore gives parties the power (or more accurately the *obligation*) to arrest and surrender senior officials, including a serving head of state or a serving head of diplomatic mission, when – and only when – such persons have been indicted by the ICC and it has issued a warrant for their arrest.

The practice of several parties subsequent to their ratification of the ICC Statute supports the view that article 27 operates to remove the immunity of officials of states parties in the territory of other states that are acting at the Court's request. Reference has already been made to the implementing legislation of Canada, the UK, Malta, Ireland, and New Zealand, which all incorporate article 27 into their law and explicitly deny immunity to officials of states parties in domestic proceedings concerning a request for arrest and surrender by the ICC.[120] Moreover, the provisions in the South African and Swiss legislation appear to take the same view of article 27.[121] Although this subsequent practice in the application of the ICC Statute involves only a minority of parties and does not "*establish the agreement of the parties* regarding its interpretation,"[122] it certainly supports the view that article 98(1) does not prevent the Court from requesting the arrest of officials (even senior serving officials) of states parties.

Conferral of the power to arrest a visiting head of state or serving ambassador is practically unprecedented (though not unknown)[123] in international relations and may lead to significant tensions and disruptions in those relations if that power is not exercised judiciously. It is not certain that the drafters of the relevant parts of the ICC Statute consciously contemplated (at the time of drafting) the possibility that states would be empowered to arrest a serving head of state or ambassador.[124] Nevertheless, as demonstrated above, this power follows from the text of the ICC Statute. In addition, the objects and purposes of the ICC Statute as expressed in the preamble and article 27 make clear that the drafters did intend that even the most senior state officials of ICC parties should not be excluded from the exercise of ICC jurisdiction. Likewise, the drafters took the view that international law immunities ought not to stand in the way of the exercise of such jurisdiction by the Court. Whilst tensions will doubtless arise from the arrest by one state of the head of state or diplomats of another state, the fact that such arrests cannot be unilaterally initiated by the host state but must follow an investigation and a request from the ICC and the fact that the state of the head of state or diplomat must be an ICC party ought to reduce these tensions to some degree.

3 THE POSITION OF PARTIES AND NON-PARTIES UNDER ARTICLE 98(2)

If article 98(1) applies only to officials of non-parties, the question arises as to whether the same holds true for article 98(2). Under that provision, "the Court may not proceed with a request for surrender which would require the requested state to act inconsistently with its obligations under international agreements pursuant to which the consent of a sending state is required to surrender a person of that state to the Court, unless the Court can first obtain the cooperation of the sending state for the giving of consent for the surrender."

Like the first paragraph of article 98, the second paragraph is designed to avoid a situation in which a state – to which a request for surrender or arrest has been directed by the Court – is subjected to conflicting obligations. Article 98(2) allows states to honour treaty obligations prohibiting the surrender of persons sent to their territory by other states.[125] In particular, this paragraph allows states to respect the provisions of Status of Forces Agreements (SOFAs), which prohibit states, on whose territory armed forces of another state are located, from arresting troops and related personnel of the sending state.[126] That provision would also cover extradition agreements providing that a person who has been extradited from one state to another may not be re-extradited to a third state without the consent of the first state.[127]

But can an ICC party rely on the agreements covered by article 98(2) to prevent other states from surrendering the party's personnel to the ICC? This question is of practical importance because a fair number of ICC parties have concluded agreements with other states (mainly the US) which specifically state that neither party may transfer persons of one party, present in the territory of the other, to the ICC without the consent of the first party. It is worth noting that, as currently worded, these agreements with the US are not limited to persons sent by one party to the agreement to the other party.[128] Since article 98(2) only covers agreements that require the consent of the "sending state" for surrender to the ICC, the US agreements (to the extent that they apply to persons who have not been "sent") are not covered by that provision.[129] Therefore, the Court is not obliged to refrain from requesting the arrest of persons who have not been sent, even though the ICC party is bound by the agreement with the US not to surrender the person.

In considering whether ICC parties may rely on agreements covered by article 98(2) to bar a request for surrender by the Court, it is significant that not only have some ICC parties been willing to conclude these agreements with the US,[130] but the provisions of the agreements are reciprocal so that they also benefit persons of the ICC party. In addition, at least one such agreement was concluded for the benefit of a number of ICC parties with a state other than the US. Under the Military Technical Agreement between the International Security Assistance Force (ISAF) and the Interim Administration of Afghanistan ("Interim Administration"),[131] Afghanistan agreed not to surrender ISAF personnel to any international tribunal without the express consent of the contributing nation. At the time the agreement was signed, most of the ISAF troop contributing states were ICC parties and this remained the case thereafter.[132] The only conclusion that can be drawn from these agreements is that at least some ICC parties take the view that ICC parties may rely on agreements covered by article 98(2).[133] Some observers have even argued that *only* agreements benefiting ICC parties are protected by that provision.[134] For reasons discussed earlier,[135] the view that agreements for the benefit of non-parties are not covered by article 98(2) cannot be accepted. The ICC Statute cannot be taken as overriding the rights of non-parties.

At least three reasons demonstrate the importance of construing article 98(2), like article 98(1), as benefiting only non-parties. Firstly, the reasons described above for interpreting article 98(1) in this way also apply to those agreements covered by article 98(2),[136] which confer immunity based on official capacity (e.g., SOFAS).[137] Secondly, there is a significant degree of overlap in the two provisions that suggests that they must be given similar interpretations. The overlap arises because treaties conferring state or diplomatic immunities clearly fall within the language of article 98(2). Whatever the intent of the drafters of the ICC Statute, it cannot be doubted that the Vienna Convention on Diplomatic Relations of 1961 and the UN Convention on Special Missions of 1969 are "international agreements pursuant to which the consent of a sending state is required to surrender a person of that state to the Court."[138]

Thus, if article 98(2) is not limited to non-parties, the limitation of article 98(1) to non-parties would easily be avoided by relying on article 98(2) instead. Thirdly, interpreting article 98(2) as extending to ICC parties while article 98(1) does not would lead to the manifestly absurd result that troops of parties and extradited persons may not be surrendered to the ICC – because of the SOFAS and extradition agreements covered by article 98(2) – but that a serving head of state, head of government, or foreign minister who goes to visit those troops in the same country (or the head of the diplomatic mission) has no immunity and may be surrendered to the ICC. Thus, an interpretation of article 98(2) in context – that is, in light of the interpretation given to article 98(1) – must lead to the conclusion that only agreements for the benefit of non-parties to the ICC Statute come within the scope of article 98(2).

In concluding this examination of article 98(2), it is important to note that agreements which require the consent of a state for the surrender of a person to the ICC and which do not come within the scope of that provision (for example, the US agreements or other agreements intended to benefit ICC parties) may nevertheless be legally effective in preventing such transfers to the ICC. This effect may ensue where the agreement was concluded after the entry into force of the ICC Statute. As an ordinary treaty with no "constitutional" status, the ICC Statute does not prevail over subsequent treaties. Clearly, the obligation to confer immunity under pre-existing agreements between ICC parties is superseded by the provisions of the ICC Statute.[139] However, obligations under agreements between ICC parties entered into after the ICC Statute came into force will, *as between the parties to that later agreement*, prevail over their obligations under the ICC Statute.[140] Likewise, obligations under agreements with a non-party that are not covered by article 98(2) (such as the US agreements) are valid and binding under international law;[141] but these obligations do not detract from the obligations which ICC parties continue to have, under the ICC Statute, to the other ICC parties not party to the later agreement, and to the ICC. Thus, an ICC party that has entered into a relevant agreement not covered by article 98(2) and that has received a request by the ICC to surrender a person covered by that subsequent agreement will have to contend with inconsistent obligations. If the ICC party chooses to surrender a person covered by such an agreement, it will breach valid treaty obligations and be legally responsible to the other party for that breach.

4 THE POSITION OF OFFICIALS OF INTERNATIONAL ORGANIZATIONS

A further question that may arise in connection with requests by the Court to states for the surrender of persons is whether such requests may be issued when the person wanted is an official of (or an expert on mission for) an international organization. While most international officials possess immunity only with respect to acts performed in their official capacity,[142] an official could conceivably be accused of committing an international crime in the exercise of his official duties.[143] For example, it might be alleged that such a crime was committed during the planning or implementation of a peacekeeping or other military operation conducted or authorised by the international organization.[144] Furthermore, the immunity of the most senior officials of international organizations, such as the UN secretary general and assistant secretaries general is analogous to that of diplomats since those senior officials are generally immune from the jurisdiction of states for as long as they hold office.[145] Therefore, while in office, they may not be arrested in relation to any acts they committed before or during office. Similarly, under the UN Immunities Convention, experts on mission are immune from arrest or detention.[146] In all these cases, states are bound to refrain from arresting and surrendering officials or experts of international organizations, even if they are accused of having committed international crimes.

Whether or not the ICC may require the arrest and surrender of an official or expert of an international organization in circumstances where that person is immune from arrest in the host state is not addressed in article 98. The text of that provision makes no mention of immunities accruing to international organizations but is limited to "immunity of a person or property of a third *state*"[147] and "international agreements pursuant to which the consent of a sending *State* is required to surrender a person of that *state* to the Court."[148] While the declaration in article 27(1) that the statute applies equally, irrespective of official capacity, may be taken as including officials of international organizations,[149] this declaration cannot bind the organization as a non-party to the ICC Statute and may not be regarded as a waiver of the immunity of the official.[150] The position remains the same even if all members of the organization are parties to the ICC Statute. Since the organization is a separate legal person, the immunity of its officials and experts are rights belonging to the organization and not to the member states.[151] Only the international organization itself can waive the immunities of its officials and experts,[152] and nothing in the statute can be regarded as having this effect.

Thus, while article 98 does not preclude the ICC from requesting the surrender of officials and experts of international organizations who ordinarily possess immunity, an ICC party that is party to a treaty conferring such immunity would be acting in violation of that treaty if it arrested and surrendered the official or expert. To prevent inconsistent obligations from arising, it would be prudent for the ICC to not request the surrender of officials or experts of international organizations until the organization has waived the immunity of that person.[153] In the case of UN officials, article 19 of the Relationship Agreement between the UN and the ICC provides that the UN undertakes to waive any immunities that may otherwise apply where such persons are wanted for prosecution by the ICC.[154] Importantly, the wording of this provision makes clear that it does not in itself constitute a waiver of immunity but rather an undertaking to waive the immunity. Therefore, if an actual case were to arise, a further act of waiver by the UN secretary general would still be required.

C. Who Decides Whether a Person Is Entitled to Immunity in Another State?

A final question that must be addressed in the application of article 98 is this: Who decides whether a person sought by the ICC is entitled to state or diplomatic immunity or is covered by an agreement precluding surrender? Is that decision to be made by the ICC or by the state on whose territory the person is located? Furthermore, if the ICC is to make the decision, by what procedure is it to do so and will the decision bind the state to which the request for surrender is directed?

Under article 97, a state party that has received a request from the Court "in relation to which it identifies problems which may impede or prevent the execution of the request ... shall consult with the Court without delay in order to resolve the matter." Since article 98 states that "the Court may not proceed with a request for surrender" unless the conditions stipulated therein are met, the Court must first decide whether those conditions apply.[155] This reading is confirmed by rule 195 of the ICC's Rules of Procedure and Evidence,[156] which provides that a requested state that believes that a request for surrender raises a problem under article 98 "shall provide any information relevant to assist the Court in the application of Article 98." Moreover, "[a]ny concerned third state or sending state may provide additional information to assist the Court."[157]

Unfortunately, neither the ICC Statute nor the Rules stipulate the procedure by which the Court is to make a decision in respect of article 98. Although this issue is not specifically included in the list of functions of the Pre-Trial Chamber contained in article 57, on a matter of such importance it can only be assumed that the state concerned is entitled to a decision of the chamber. Arguably, rule 195 grants procedural rights to concerned third states or sending states in any hearings before the Pre-Trial Chamber.

Despite the fact that the Court must first make a decision under article 98, there remains the issue of whether that decision is binding on the state it is addressed to. Once a request for surrender is made, article 89 of the ICC Statute imposes an obligation on parties to comply. But since a request governed by article 98 deals with a situation involving an ICC party's obligations to non-parties, leaving the final decision to the ICC is very far-reaching,[158] as any errors by the Court would render the concerned ICC party legally responsible to the non-party. It may be argued that article 59(2)(c) of the ICC Statute, which provides that a person arrested at the request of the Court shall be brought before the competent judicial authorities of the custodial state for the purpose, amongst other things, of determining whether his or her rights have been respected, allows those judicial authorities to make a decision on immunity. However, disagreements relating to whether or not a requested state is obliged to surrender a person to the Court are disputes "concerning the judicial function of the Court," which under article 119 "shall be settled by the decision of the Court."[159]

The national statutes that deal with the immunity of foreign officials when a request for arrest has been made by the ICC reveal that states have taken differing views on which body is entitled to decide the issue. Both the Canadian Crimes Against Humanity and War Crimes Act 2000[160] and the New Zealand International Crimes and International Criminal Court Act 2000[161] leave the final decision on immunity to the ICC. On the other hand, the Australian and Swiss legislation provide for consultation by the state's executive branch with the ICC but leave the final decision to the relevant national authorities, whose decision appears to be binding on the courts.[162] Similarly, under the UK and Maltese implementing legislation, the relevant minister may certify, with conclusive effect, whether or not a state is a party to the ICC Statute and whether a non-party has waived its immunity.[163] More importantly, the relevant minister may also direct, after consultation with the ICC and the state concerned, that proceedings in the UK or Malta that would ordinarily be barred by state or diplomatic immunities attaching to a person shall not be taken against the person.[164] Thus, a decision by the executive that immunities are available would appear to bind the courts of those countries. However, in the case of an official or diplomat of a non-party, if the executive takes no view or finds that international immunities are not available, the UK or Maltese courts may decide for themselves whether arrest or surrender would be inconsistent with any immunity attaching to that person.

CONCLUSION

The basic aims of those states that drafted the ICC Statute were to ensure "that the most serious crimes of concern to the international community as a whole must not go unpunished" and "to put an end to impunity for the perpetrators of these crimes."[165] These goals can be realized only to the extent that there is an attempt to bring to justice those who initiate and plan these crimes, as opposed to those who merely carry them out. Since history suggests that international crimes are often the work of state agents, a strategy of prosecuting right to the top of the planning chain will entail attempts to prosecute senior state officials. In all probability, the ICC will depend on cooperation from states to secure the custody of persons wanted for trial, and the question of the immunity of state officials from arrest and surrender is therefore likely to prove important in the work of the Court.

When applied to criminal cases alleging the commission of international crimes, the rules of international law concerning immunity must and do strike a fair balance between the need to ensure that undue interference with the functioning of foreign states is avoided and the need to ensure that those who perpetrate international crimes are punished. Thus, very senior state officials, as well as serving diplomats and officials abroad on special mission, are entitled to immunity and may not be arrested or subjected to prosecution whilst in office or working as part of the mission. However, the position is different for other state officials as well as former officials (irrespective of the rank they held). The development of the rule of universal jurisdiction means that all states are entitled to prosecute those persons on their territory who are accused of committing certain international crimes, irrespective of the nationality of the perpetrator or the place where the crime was committed. Where this rule contemplates prosecutions of state officials, those officials that are not entitled to immunity as a result of their current status (immunity *ratione personae*) may not rely on immunity *ratione materiae* in cases in which universal jurisdiction is exercised.

The parties to the ICC Statute have gone beyond the developments in customary international law. In subjecting all state officials to possible prosecution by the ICC and in explicitly removing the international law immunities of senior officials, including heads of state, the ICC parties agreed not only to prosecution by the ICC but also to the possibility that senior officials may be arrested and surrendered to the ICC by other states. This conclusion has been reached despite article 98 of the ICC Statute. Although it is not easy to dismiss the argument that article 98 preserves the international law immunities of officials of ICC parties when they are in a third state, this interpretation must ultimately be rejected because it would render certain parts of article 27 ineffective. The conferral of a power on states to arrest a visiting serving head of state or a serving ambassador is very far-reaching but is probably the only way in practice that such persons will be subjected to the jurisdiction of the Court. In view of the parties' determination under the ICC Statute to ensure that all perpetrators of international crimes are brought to justice, the ICC Statute must be construed in a way that permits this possibility.

Since state immunity is derived from the independence and sovereign equality of states,[166] it is appropriate to set this principle aside where a state is acting in support of an international tribunal. In such a case, the maxim *par in parem non habet imperium* ("an equal has no power over an equal") is hardly applicable because it is the ICC, and not the arresting state, that is ultimately seeking to exercise authority. However, it must be emphasized that this waiver of immunity vis-à-vis other states applies only when the ICC requests an arrest and surrender. It does not apply to domestic prosecutions.

It is equally important to emphasize that it is only parties to the ICC Statute that have waived the international law immunities (*ratione personae*) of their senior officials. Although the ICC may exercise jurisdiction over nationals and officials of non-parties, nothing in the statute can affect the immunities that the officials of non-parties would otherwise enjoy. Accordingly, article 98 of the ICC Statute represents an instruction to the Court and to ICC parties to not interfere with those officials of non-parties who ordinarily possess immunity in international law.

NOTES

♣ A version of this paper was first published in the *American Journal of International Law* 98, no. 3 (2004): 407–33. I am grateful to Sir Franklin Berman, Dr Robert Cryer, Joanna Harrington, Sangeeta Shah, Professor Colin Warbrick, and Elizabeth Wilmshurst.

1 For surveys of this body of law, see Hazel Fox, *The Law of State Immunity* (Oxford: Oxford UP, 2002); James Crawford, "International Law and Foreign Sovereigns: Distinguishing Immune Transactions," *British Yearbook of International Law* 54 (1983): 75–118; and Eileen Denza, *Diplomatic Law: A Commentary on the Vienna Convention on Diplomatic Relations*, 2d ed. (Oxford: Clarendon Press, 1998).

2 For surveys of this body of law, see Antonio Cassese, *International Criminal Law* (Oxford: Oxford UP, 2003) and ibid., "International Criminal Law," in *International Law*, ed. Malcolm D. Evans, 720–56 (Oxford: Oxford UP, 2003).

3 For surveys of domestic prosecutions relying on universal jurisdiction, see Luc Reydams, *Universal Jurisdiction: International and Municipal Legal Perspectives* (Oxford: Oxford UP, 2003) and Committee on International Human Rights Law and Practice, "Final Report on the Exercise of Universal Jurisdiction in Respect of Gross Human Rights Offences," in *Report of the Sixty-Ninth Conference of the International Law Association* (International Law Association: London, 2000), 403, 424 et seq. The association's Web site is at <http://www.ila-hq.org/html/layout_committee.htm>.

4 In three recent ICJ proceedings, states have challenged both of these principles: *Arrest Warrant* Case (*Democratic Republic of the Congo* v. *Belgium*), *International Legal Materials* 41, no. 3 (2002): 536–644; *Certain Criminal Proceedings in France* (*Republic of Congo* v. *France*), (Provisional Measures Request), *International Legal Materials* 42, no. 4 (2003): 852–76; and Liberia's application instituting proceedings against Sierra Leone in respect of the indictment by the Special Court for Sierra Leone of the Liberian head

of state (ICJ press release 2003/26 [5 August 2003], on-line: <http://www.icj-cij.org/icjwww/ipresscom/ipress2003/ipresscom2003–26_xx_20030805.htm>).

5 By the fall of 2005, ninety-nine states were parties to the ICC Statute. On-line: International Criminal Court <http://www.icc-cpi.int/php/statesparties.html>.

6 17 July 1998, UN Doc. A/CONF. 183/9, 2187 UNTS 907, reprinted in *International Legal Materials* 37, no. 5 (1998): 1002, arts. 17–20 [hereinafter ICC Statute]. For an analysis of these provisions, see John T. Holmes, "Complementarity: National Courts versus the ICC" in *The Rome Statute of the International Criminal Court: A Commentary*, vol. 1, eds. Antonio Cassese, Paola Gaeta, and John R.W.D. Jones, (Oxford: Oxford UP, 2002), chap. 18.1; Jann K. Kleffner, "The Impact of Complementarity on National Implementation of Substantive International Criminal Law," *Journal of International Criminal Justice* 1, no. 1 (2003): 86–113.

7 *Filártiga* v. *Peña-Irala*, 630 F.2d 876 (2d Cir., 1980).

8 28 USC §1350.

9 Pub. L. No. 102-256, 106 Stat. 73. See Beth Stephens and Michael Ratner, *International Human Rights Litigation in United States Courts* (New York: Transnational Publishers, 1996); Roger O'Keefe, "Civil Actions in US Courts in Respect of Human Rights Abuses Committed Abroad: Would the World's Oppressors be Wise to Stay at Home?" *African Journal of International and Comparative Law* 9, no. 1 (1997): 15–41; Anne-Marie Burley, "The Alien Tort Claims Statute and the Judiciary Act of 1789: A Badge of Honour," *American Journal of International Law* 83, no. 2 (1997): 461–93.

10 See, for example, *Al-Adsani* v. *Kuwait,* 107 ILR 536 (England: CA, 1996); *Jones* v. *Saudi Arabia* (2004) EWCA Civ. 1394 (England: CA).

11 See generally, C.A. Whomersley, "Some Reflections on the Immunity of Individuals for Official Acts," *International & Comparative Law Quarterly* 41 (1992): 848–58; Mizushima Tomonori, "The Individual as Beneficiary of State Immunity: Problems of the Attribution of Ultra Vires Conduct," *Denver Journal of International Law and Policy* 29, no. 4 (2001): 261–87; Fox, *supra* n1, 352–60, 421–73; Sir Arthur Watts, "The Legal Position in International Law of Heads of States, Heads of Governments and Foreign Ministers," *Recueil des Cours* 247 (1994-III): 13–130; and Chanaka Wickremasinghe, "Immunities Enjoyed by Officials of States and International Organizations," in Evans, *supra* n2, 387.

12 See *Vienna Convention on Diplomatic Relations,* 18 April 1961, 500 UNTS 95, arts 29 and 31 [hereinafter VCDR].

13 The issues considered in this next section are more extensively explored by the author elsewhere: see Dapo Akande, "International Immunities, Human Rights Violations and International Crimes" (forthcoming).

14 See Watts, *supra* n11.

15 VCDR, *supra* n12, arts 29 and 31; *Convention on Special Missions,* 16 December 1969, 1400 UNTS 231, arts 21, 39 and 31.

16 See Wickremasinghe, *supra* n11, 389.

17 See Michael A. Tunks, "Diplomats or Defendants? Defining the Future of Head-of-State Immunity," *Duke Law Journal* 52, no. 3 (2002): 651–82, and at 656: "Head-of-state immunity allows a nation's leader to engage in his official duties, including travel to foreign countries, without fearing arrest, detention, or other treatment inconsistent with his role as the head of a sovereign state. Without the guarantee that they will not be subjected to trial in foreign courts, heads of state may simply choose to stay at home rather than assume the risks of engaging in international diplomacy." The same may be said of others entitled to immunity *ratione personae.*

18 See *Arrest Warrant Case, supra* n4, and specifically the Joint Separate Opinion of Judges Higgins, Kooijmans, and Buergenthal at para. 75: "immunities are granted to high state officials to guarantee the proper functioning of the network of mutual inter-state relations, which is of paramount importance for a well-ordered and harmonious international system." See also Fox, *supra* n1, 427.

19 *United States Diplomatic and Consular Staff in Tehran Case* (*US* v. *Iran*), Judgment of 24 May 1980, ICJ Reports 1980, para. 91.

20 *Arrest Warrant Case, supra* n4, para. 54; Fox, *supra* n1, 441. See also the treaty provisions cited above in note 15.

21 *Arrest Warrant Case, supra* n4, para. 54–5.

22 Ibid., para. 55.

23 Ibid., para. 55.

24 Ibid., para. 58.

25 See generally, Cassese, *International Criminal Law, supra* n2, 271–3; Paola Gaeta, "Official Capacities and Immunities," in Cassese, Gaeta,and Jones, *supra* n6, 975–1002, 983–9; Salvatore Zappalà, "Do Heads of State in Office Enjoy Immunity from Jurisdiction for International Crimes? The *Ghaddafi* Case before the French *Cour de Cassation,*" *European Journal of International Law* 12, no. 3 (2001): 595–611; Hazel Fox, "The Resolution of the Institute of International Law on the Immunities of Heads of state and Government," *International & Comparative Law Quarterly* 51, no. 1 (2002): 119–25.

26 See Tunks, *supra* n17, 678–9.

27 See the *Ghaddafi* case, Arrêt no. 1414, 125 ILR 456 (France: Cour de Cassation, 2001) (criminal proceedings against Colonel Ghadaffi, the Libyan head of state, relating to the bombing of a French airliner dismissed on grounds

of immunity); the *Castro* case (Spain: Audiencia Nacional, 1999), cited by Cassese, *International Criminal Law, supra* n2, 272n20 (criminal proceedings against Fidel Castro, the Cuban head of state, dismissed on grounds of immunity); *Re Sharon & Yaron, International Legal Materials* 42, no. 3 (2003): 596–604 (Belgium: Cour de Cassation, 2003) (criminal proceedings against Israeli prime minister Ariel Sharon alleging crimes against humanity and war crimes dismissed on grounds of immunity); *R.* v. *Bow Street Stipendiary Magistrate and others, Ex parte Pinochet [No.3]*, [1999] 2 All ER 97, 126–7, 149, 179, 189 (England: House of Lords, 1999) (stating that serving heads of state are immune from the criminal jurisdiction of foreign states); *Wei Ye* v. *Jiang Zemin*, 383 F.3d 620 (US: 7TH Cir., 2004) (civil proceedings against Chinese president Jiang Zemin alleging torture, genocide, and other human rights violations dismissed on grounds of immunity); and *Tachiona* v. *United States*, 386 F.3d 205 (US: 2ND Cir., 2004) (civil proceedings against Zimbabwean president Robert Mugabe alleging torture dismissed on grounds of immunity). In early 2004, British district judges rejected, on grounds of immunity, applications for warrants for the arrest of Mugabe and General Shaul Mofaz (the Israeli minister of defence) in relation to allegations of torture and war crimes: see respectively *Application for Arrest Warrant against Robert Mugabe* (England: Bow St. Mag. Ct., 2004), reprinted in *International & Comparative Law Quarterly* 53, no. 3 (2004): 770–1 and *Application for Arrest Warrant against General Shaul Mofaz*, (England: Bow St. Mag. Ct, 2004), reprinted in *International and Comparative Law Quarterly* 53, no. 3 (2004): 771–3.

28 In 2002, the US government issued a suggestion of immunity in a case brought against the then president of China alleging torture, genocide, and other human rights violations: see Sean D. Murphy, "Head-of-State Immunity for Former Chinese President Jiang Zemin" in "Contemporary Practice of the United States Relating to International Law," *American Journal of International Law* 97, no. 4 (2003): 962–91, 974–7, referring to the lower court proceedings in *Wei Ye* v. *Jiang Zemin, supra* n27. In August 2003, Saied Baghban, an Iranian diplomat accused of having been involved in the bombing of a Jewish centre in Argentina was briefly detained in Belgium but then released on grounds of diplomatic immunity: see Richard Beeston, "Iran Threatens to Hit Back over Diplomat's Arrest," *The Times*, 28 August 2003, 17. Similarly, despite accusations that the Israeli ambassador to Denmark was complicit in torture while he was head of Shin Bet, the Israeli Intelligence Service, Denmark has maintained that he is entitled to diplomatic immunity from Danish criminal jurisdiction. See Jacques Hartmann, "The Gillon Affair," *International and Comparative Law Quarterly* 54, no. 3 (2005: 745–55); Andrew Osborn,

"Danish Protests Greet Israeli Envoy," *The Guardian*, 16 August 2001, 13. Likewise, the UK authorities took the view that a serving Israeli defence minister was entitled to immunity from arrest despite the allegation that he had been responsible for war crimes in the West Bank: see Chris McGreal, "Sharon's Ally Safe from Arrest in Britain," *The Guardian*, 11 February 2004, 19.

29 See Tunks, *supra* n17, 663: "no nation has yet gone so far as to actually pass judgment against a sitting head of state." *United States* v. *Noriega*, 117 F.3d 1206 (11TH Cir., 1997) is the only case that can be construed as denying immunity to a head of state. However, it was on the ground that the US government had never recognized General Noriega as head of state that immunity was not accorded in this case. He was viewed simply as the de facto ruler of Panama.

30 *Supra* n4, para. 51 (emphasis added). The use of the words "such as" suggests that the list of senior officials entitled to this immunity is not closed.

31 See Watts, *supra* n11, 54, 106–7; Fox, *supra* n1, 437, 441. See also articles 1, 2, and 15 of *Immunities from Jurisdiction and Execution of Heads of state and of Government in International Law*, a Resolution of the *Institut de Droit International*, adopted on 26 August 2001 (on-line: Institut de Droit International <http://www.idi-iil.org/idiE/resolutionsE/2001_van_02_en.PDF>); and Andrew Dickinson, Rae Lindsay, and James P. Loonam, eds., *State Immunity: Selected Materials and Commentary*, (Oxford: Oxford UP, 2004), 212.

32 VCDR, *supra* n12, arts 29 and 31.

33 Watts, *supra* n11, 106–8.

34 *Arrest Warrant Case*, *supra* n4, para. 53.

35 In *Mofaz*, *supra* n27, District Judge Pratt stated (at 773): "The function of various Ministers will vary enormously depending upon their sphere of responsibility. I would think it very unlikely that ministerial appointments such as Home Secretary, Employment Minister, Environment Minister, Culture Media and Sports Minister would automatically acquire a label of state immunity. However, I do believe that the Defence Minister may be a different matter." Notwithstanding the judge's statement, in modern international affairs it is difficult to see that the ministers listed above would not be involved in travel on behalf of the state.

36 See *Convention on the Privileges and Immunities of the United Nations*, 13 February 1946, 1 UNTS 15 and 90 UNTS 327 (corrigendum), art. IV, s. 11 [heareafter UN Immunities Convention]; *General Convention on the Privileges and Immunities of the Organization of African Unity*, 25 October 1965, art. V (on-line: South Africa, Department of Foreign Affairs <http://www.dfa.gov.za/foreign/Multilateral/africa/treaties/oaupriv.htm>).

37 See *Convention on Special Missions*, *supra* n15, arts. 29 and 31. Some have doubted whether these provisions represent customary international law: see *USA* v. *Sissoko* (1997), 121 ILR 599 (US: SD Fla.); Wickremasinge, *supra* n11, 402.

38 See, for example, *Chuidian* v. *Philippine National Bank*, 912 F.2d 1095 (US: 9TH Cir., 1990) and *Propend Finance Pty Ltd* v. *Sing*, 111 ILR 611 (England: CA, 1997). For other cases, see Tomonori, *supra* n11, 269–73. For a consideration of US and UK law on the matter, see Whomersley, *supra* n11; and Fox, *supra* n1, 352–60.

39 Wickremasinghe, *supra* n11, 403. See also VCDR, *supra* n12, art. 39(2) in relation to former diplomats; and *Vienna Convention on Consular Relations*, 24 April 1963, 596 UNTS 262, art. 43(1) [hereinafter VCCR] in relation to consular officials. Some have doubted whether the immunity *ratione materiae* applicable to former diplomats is of the same nature as the general immunity applicable to other official acts of other state officials. For example, Yoram Dinstein, "Diplomatic Immunity from Jurisdiction *Ratione Materiae*," *International and Comparative Law Quarterly* 15 (1966): 76–89, 86–9, argues that diplomatic immunity *ratione materiae* is broader than the immunity accorded to other state officials. Tomonori, *supra* n11, 281, questions whether other state officials possess immunity *ratione materiae* in criminal proceedings and in relation to ultra vires acts.

40 See H.F. Van Panhuys, "In the Borderland between the Act of State Doctrine and Questions of Jurisdictional Immunities," *International and Comparative Law Quarterly* 13 (1964): 1193–213, 1201. See also *Twycross* v. *Dreyfus*, (1877) 5 Ch.D. 605 (England: CA); *Kuwait Airways Corp.* v. *Iraq Airways Co.* (1995) 3 All ER 694 (England: House of Lords); *Walker* v. *Bank of New York* (1994) 16 OR 3d 504 (Canada: Ontario CA); *State Immunity Act 1978* (UK), c. 33, s. 14(2).

41 For the suggestion that the paucity of domestic criminal cases recognizing the immunity *ratione materiae* of state makes it difficult to prove that this type of immunity applies in criminal proceedings, see Tomonori, *s upra* n11, 262.

42 The most well known case in which this type of immunity was asserted in respect of criminal proceedings is *MacLeod's Case,* for which see R.Y. Jennings, "The *Caroline* and *MacLeod* Cases," *American Journal of International Law* 32 (1938): 82–99, 92. While both the British and American governments accepted that there was immunity under international law from both civil and criminal processes, Macleod was actually subject to trial owing to the inability of the US federal government to interfere with the prosecution. However, in the *Rainbow Warrior Case* (1986), 74 ILR 241, the French

government's assertion that military officers should not be tried in New Zealand once France had accepted international responsibility was rejected by New Zealand. See also the few cases cited by Tomonori, *supra* n11, 262.

43 See Cassese, *International Criminal Law, supra* n2, 266; and Fox, *supra* n1, 510–13. In *Attorney General of Israel* v. *Eichmann* (1962), 36 ILR 5, 308–9, the Israeli Supreme Court stated: "The theory of 'Act of State' means that the act performed by a person as an organ of the state – whether he was Head of the state or a responsible official acting on the Government's order – must be regarded as an act of the state alone. It follows that only the latter bears responsibility therefore, and it also follows that another state has no right to punish the person who committed the act, save with the consent of the state whose mission he performed. Were it not so, the first state would be interfering in the internal affairs of the second, which is contrary to the conception of the equality of states based on their sovereignty." However, the court was not prepared to accept that this theory applied in all cases. In *Prosecutor* v. *Blaškić* (Objection to the Issue of *Subpoena duces Tecume*) IT-95-14-AR108, (1997), 110 ILR 607, 707, para. 38, the Appeals Chamber of the ICTY stated: "[state] officials are mere instruments of a state and their official action can only be attributed to the state. They cannot be the subject of sanctions or penalties for conduct that is not private but undertaken on behalf of the state. In other words, state officials cannot suffer the consequences of wrongful acts that are not attributable to them personally but to the state on whose behalf they act: they enjoy so-called 'functional immunity'. This is a well established rule of customary international law going back to the eighteenth and nineteenth centuries, restated many times since." See also the correspondence in the *MacLeod Case, supra* n42.

44 See Wickremasinghe, *supra* n11, 403; Fox, *supra* n1, 353–4. See also *Zoernsch* v. *Waldock*, [1964] 1 WLR 675, 692 (England: CA, per Diplock LJ); *Chuidian* v. *Philippine National Bank*, *supra* n38 and *Propend Finance Pty Ltd* v. *Sing*, *supra* n38.

45 See Antonio Cassese, "When May Senior State Officials Be Tried for International Crimes? Some Comments on the *Congo* v. *Belgium* Case," *European Journal of International Law* 13, no. 4 (2002): 853–75, 870–1 (referring to cases in which Israeli, French, Italian, Dutch, British, American, Polish, Spanish, and Mexican courts have entertained proceedings against foreign state officials, particularly foreign military officers, in respect of war crimes, crimes against humanity, and genocide.)

46 See, for example, *Eichmann*, *supra* n43, 44–8 (District Court of Jerusalem), 308–11 (Israeli Supreme Court), and *Pinochet [No. 3]*, *supra* n27.

47 See *Pinochet [No.3]*, *supra* n27, 113 and 166 (England, House of Lords, per Lords Browne Wilkinson and Hutton); *R.* v. *Bow Street Stipendiary Magistrate and others, ex parte Pinochet [No.1]*, [1998] 4 All ER 897, 939–40, 945–6 (England: House of Lords, per Lords Nicholls and Steyn). It is amazing these judges could have reached this conclusion in respect of torture, which under article 1 of the *Convention against Torture and Other Cruel, Inhuman or Degrading Treatment or Punishment*, 10 December 1984, 1465 UNTS 85 [hereinafter Torture Convention] is limited to acts "of a public official or other person acting in *an official capacity*" (emphasis added). See also the Joint Separate Opinion of Judges Higgins, Kooijmans, and Buergenthal, *Arrest Warrant Case*, *supra* n4, para. 85 and their citation to the *Bouterse* case at para. 42. See also *Jones* v. *Saudi Arabia* (2004) EWCA Civ. 1394 (England: CA). A similar position has been taken in a number of US civil cases under the *Alien Tort Claims Act*, Act 28 USC §1350: see, for example, *In re Estate of Ferdinand Marcos*, 25 F.3d 1467, 1469–72 (9TH Cir., 1994); *Xuncax* v. *Gramajo*, 886 F. Supp. 162, 175 (D. Mass., 1995); and *Cabiri* v. *Assasie-Gyimah*, 921 F. Supp. 1189, 1197–8 (SDNY, 1996). See further, Tunks, *supra* n17, 659–60; Tomonori, *supra* n11, 283 *et seq.*; Alexander Orakhelashvili, "state Immunity and International Public Order," *German Yearbook of International Law* 43, (2002): 227–67, 238–9.

48 See Andrea Bianchi, "Immunity Versus Human Rights," *European Journal of International Law* 10, no. 2 (1999): 237–78, 265: "As a matter of international law, there is no doubt that *jus cogens* norms, because of their higher status, must prevail over other international rules, including jurisdictional immunities." See also Mathias Reimann, "A Human Rights Exception to Sovereign Immunity: Some Thoughts on *Prinz v. Federal Republic of Germany*," *Michigan Journal of International Law* 16, no. 2 (1995): 403–32, 421–3; Michael Byers, "Comment on *Al-Adsani* v. *Kuwait*," *British Yearbook of International Law* 67 (1996): 537–42, 539–40; Alexander Orakhelashvili, "State Immunity in National and International Law: Three Recent Cases before the European Court of Human Rights," *Leiden Journal of International Law* 15, no. 3 (2002): 703–14, 712–3; ibid., "International Decisions: *Arrest Warrant Case*," *American Journal of International Law* 96, no. 3 (2002): 677–84; ibid., "State Immunity and International Public Order," *supra* n47, 255 *et seq.*

49 See Akande, *supra* n13.

50 See *Arrest Warrant Case*, *supra* n4, para. 58 and the text associated with note 24.

51 *Al-Adsani* v. *United Kingdom*, (2001) 123 ILR 24, para. 61, where the judges held by nine to eight that "notwithstanding the special character of the

prohibition of torture in international law, the Court is unable to discern in the international instruments, judicial authorities or other materials before it any firm basis for concluding that, as a matter of international law, a state no longer enjoys immunity from civil suit in the courts of another state where acts of torture are alleged.")

52 See *Al-Adsani* v. *Kuwait*, 107 ILR 536 (England: CA, 1996); *Prinz* v. *Federal Republic of Germany*, 103 ILR 594 (US: DC Cir., 1992); *Smith* v. *Libya* reprinted in *International Legal Materials* 36, no. 1 (1997): 100–10 (US: 2ND Cir., 1996); *Persinger* v. *Islamic Republic of Iran*, 90 ILR 486 (US: DC Cir., 1996); *Sampson* v. *Federal Republic of Germany*, 975 F. Supp. 1108 (US: ND Ill., 1997); *Bouzari* v. *Iran*, [2004] OJ No. 2800 (QL), application for leave to appeal to the Supreme Court of Canada denied 27 January 2005 (Canada: Ontario CA, 2004); *Germany* v. *Margellos*, Case No. 6/17–9–2002 (Greek Special Supreme Court, 2002); *Distomo Massacre Case*, BGH-III2R 245/98 reprinted in *International Legal Materials* 42, no. 5 (2003): 1027–52, 1033–4 (Germany: SC, 2003).

53 See *supra* n44–5.

54 See Cassese, "When May Senior State Officials Be Tried," *supra* n45, 870 *et seq.*; ibid., *International Criminal Law*, *supra* n2, 267 *et seq.*; Gaeta, *supra* n25, 981–3; Zappalà, *supra* n25, 601–5; Steffen Wirth, "Immunity for Core Crimes? The ICJ's Judgment in the *Congo* v. *Belgium* Case," *European Journal of International Law* 13, no. 4 (2002): 877–93, 891.

55 See *In re Goering and Others* 13 ILR 203, 221 (Int. Mil. Tribunal, Nuremberg, 1946). The fact that official capacity does not amount to a substantive defence has been included in the statutes of a number of international criminal tribunals: *London Agreement for the International Military Tribunal at Nuremberg*, 8 August 1945, 82 UNTS 279, art. 7 [hereinafter London Agreement]; *Charter of the International Military Tribunal for the Far East*, 19 January 1946, (1946) TIAS 1589, art. 6 [hereinafter Tokyo Tribunal Charter]; *Statute of the International Criminal Tribunal for the Former Yugoslavia*, 25 May 1993, SC Res. 827 (1993), art. 7(2); *Statute of the International Criminal Tribunal for Rwanda*, 8 November 1994, SC Res. 955 (1994), art. 6(20); ICC Statute, *supra* n6, art. 27(1); and *Statute of the Special Court for Sierra Leone*, 16 January 2002, art. 6(2) (on-line: Special Court for Sierra Leone <http://www.specialcourt.org/documents/Statute.html>).

56 See *Pinochet [No. 3]*, *supra* n27, 114, 169–70, 178–9, 190 (per Lords Browne-Wilkinson, Saville, Millett, and Phillips).

57 See *Geneva Convention for the Amelioration of the Condition of the Wounded and Sick in Armed Forces in the Field (Geneva Convention I)*, 12 August 1949, 75 UNTS 31, art. 49; *Geneva Convention for the*

Amelioration of the Condition of Wounded, Sick and Shipwrecked Members of Armed Forces at Sea. Geneva (Geneva Convention II), 12 August 1949, 75 UNTS 85, art. 50; *Geneva Convention relative to the Treatment of Prisoners of War (Geneva Convention III)*, 12 August 1949, 75 UNTS 135, art. 129; *Geneva Convention relative to the Protection of Civilian Persons in Time of War (Geneva Convention IV)*, 12 August 1949, 75 UNTS 287, art. 146; *Protocol Additional to the Geneva Conventions of 12 August 1949, and Relating to the Protection of Victims of International Armed Conflicts (Protocol I)*, 8 June 1977, 125 UNTS 3, art. 85(1).

58 See Akande, *supra* n13, for the fuller development of these arguments.

59 See Gaeta, *supra* n25, 991: "Strictly speaking, under international law individuals are only entitled to enjoy personal immunities *vis-à-vis* the authorities of the state where they are authorized to discharge official functions (the 'receiving or territorial state'). Clearly these immunities cannot be relied upon before the ICC; hence they cannot preclude the exercise of the Court's jurisdiction."

60 *Arrest Warrant Case*, *supra* n4, para. 61.

61 The Special Court for Sierra Leone is an international tribunal created under a treaty between the UN and Sierra Leone to prosecute persons that have committed serious international crimes during the country's civil war. See further, Special Court for Sierra Leone, on-line: <http://www.sc-sl.org>. Unlike the ICTY and ICTR, the Special Court is not established by a UN Security Council resolution and is not able to bind all UN members. While SC Res. 1315 (2000) encouraged the establishment of the Special Court, it is not the legal basis for its creation. See Report of the Secretary General on the Establishment of a Special Court for Sierra Leone, UN Doc. S/2000/915, para. 9. See further, Robert Cryer, "A 'Special Court' for Sierra Leone?" *International and Comparative Law Quarterly* 50, no. 2 (2001): 435–46; John R.W.D. Jones, Claire Carlton-Hanciles, et al., "The Special Court for Sierra Leone," *Journal of International Criminal Justice* 2, no. 1 (2004): 211–30.

62 *Prosecutor* v. *Charles Taylor*, Immunity from Jurisdiction, Case No. SCSL-03-I, 31 May 2004. On 7 March 2003, the court's prosecutor issued an indictment charging Charles Taylor (then the head of state of Liberia) with responsibility for crimes against humanity and war crimes committed on the territory of neighbouring Sierra Leone during the civil war in that state. In June 2003 while Taylor was in Ghana for peace talks with Liberian rebels, the prosecutor sought his arrest based on the indictment. The Ghanaian government declined to do so. See, Paul Welsh, "Liberian Leader's Strange Day in Ghana," *BBC News*, on-line: <http://news.bbc.co.uk/1/hi/world/africa/

2965110.stm>. After Charles Taylor stepped down from power in Liberia, he was allowed to live in exile in Nigeria. See "Nigeria Defends Taylor Exile," *BBC News*, on-line: <http://news.bbc.co.uk/1/hi/world/africa/3142659.stm>.

63 Oral hearings relating to the defence motion to quash the indictment against Taylor were held on 31 October and 1 November 2003. For a summary of these proceedings, see Reports on Appeal Hearings, on-line: <http://www.specialcourt.org/documents/WhatHappening/ReportsOnAppealHearings.html>.

64 *Prosecutor* v. *Charles Taylor*, supra n62.

65 See the provisions referred to in note 55 above.

66 *Prosecutor* v. *Charles Taylor*, supra n62. The court's judgment drew from and approved the submissions of amici curiae Philippe Sands and Alison McDonald, and Diane Orentlicher. The former argued that "international practice and a majority of academic commentary supports the view that ... an international criminal court or tribunal (whether or not it has been established under Chapter VII of the UN Charter) may exercise jurisdiction over a serving head of state and that such person is not entitled to claim immunity under customary international law in respect of international crimes." See *Prosecutor* v. *Charles Taylor*, Case No. SCSL-03-I, *Submissions of the Amicus Curiae on Head of State Immunity (Sands & McDonald)*, paras 56(3) and 118(3), on-line: International Criminal Court <http://www.icc-cpi.int/library/organs/otp/Sands.pdf>. This submission (at para. 51) cites an earlier draft of this chapter as one of the works taking the opposite view, specifically that international immunities might be available before international tribunals.

67 See Fox, *supra* n1, 431; Gaeta, *supra* n25, 991 *et seq.*

68 See the provisions referred to in note 55 above.

69 Because the decision was taken not to prosecute the Japanese emperor after World War II, article 6 of the Tokyo Tribunal Charter, *supra* n55 (unlike article 7 of the London Agreement, *supra* n55) does not explicitly provide that a person's position as head of state may not be relied on as exempting individual responsibility. Also, while article 27 of the ICC Statute denies immunity, article 98 preserves it for certain persons.

70 *Charter of the United Nations*, 26 June 1945, 59 Stat. 1031, art. 25.

71 It may be questioned whether the UN Security Council is able to override the immunities normally accruing to representatives of states that are not UN members. This is a question that may have been raised in 1999 when the ICTY indicted the then head of state of the Federal Republic of Yugoslavia (FRY), Slobodan Milosevic, and other senior members of the FRY government. At the time of the indictment there was some doubt as to whether the FRY

was a UN member. To the extent that the FRY was not a UN member, it is arguable that an attempt by other states to execute the indictment and arrest warrant would have engaged the legal responsibility of the arresting state or even that of the UN. By the time Milosevic was handed over to the ICTY in June 2001, the FRY had been admitted to the UN, with this having occurred in 2000. In any event, surrender by the FRY would have constituted a waiver of any available immunities. For an analysis of the status of the FRY in the UN prior to 2000, see Yehuda Z. Blum, "UN Membership of the 'New' Yugoslavia: Continuity or Break?" *American Journal of International Law* 86, no. 4 (1992): 830–3; Michael Scharf, "Musical Chairs: The Dissolution of States and Membership in the United Nations," *Cornell International Law Journal* 28, no. 1, (1995): 29–69; Michael Wood, "Participation of Former Yugoslav States in the United Nations and in Multilateral Treaties," *Max Planck Yearbook of United Nations Law* 1 (1997): 231–57, 241–51; Matthew Craven, "The *Genocide* Case, The Law of Treaties and State Succession," *British Yearbook of International Law* 68 (1997): 127–63, 131–5; Dapo Akande, "The Jurisdiction of the International Criminal Court over Nationals of Non Parties: Legal Basis and Limits," *Journal of International Criminal Justice* 1, no. 3 (2003): 618–50, 628–31.

72 *Vienna Convention on the Law of Treaties*, 23 May 1969, 1155 UNTS 331, art. 34 [hereinafter VCLT].

73 See Liberia's challenge at the ICJ: ICJ Press Release 2003/26, *supra* n4. See also Cesare P.R. Romano and André Nollkaemper, "The Arrest Warrant against the Liberian President, Charles Taylor," *ASIL Insights*, June 2003, on-line: American Society of International Law <http://www.asil.org/insights/insigh110.htm>.

74 *Submissions of the Amicus Curiae on Head of State Immunity*, supra n66, para. 78. See also, Tunks, *supra* n17, 665n75, noting that the ICJ's statement in the *Arrest Warrant Case* that immunity does not exist before international tribunals only holds true with respect to officials whose home country has assented to the jurisdiction of that tribunal: "No other country has jurisdiction over a third party's head of state, and, consequently, no two states (or groups of states) may agree by treaty to waive the immunity of a third party's head of state without that other nation's consent."

75 See note 66 above and associated text.

76 See *Prosecutor* v. *Blaškić*, *supra* n43, 707 *et. seq.*, paras. 38–43.

77 Ibid., 710, para. 41.

78 *Prosecutor* v. *Krstić*, Case IT-98-33-A, *Decision on Application for Subpoenas*, 1 July 2003, para. 26, on-line: <http://www.un.org/icty/krstic/Appeal/decision-e/030701.htm>.

79 The Appeals Chamber held in *Krstić* (ibid. at para. 27) that while state officials could not be compelled to produce a document in their possession in their official capacity, they could be compelled to give evidence of what they saw or heard in the course of exercising their official functions.

80 Judge Shahabuddeen in his dissenting opinion in *Krstic* (*supra* n78, at paras. 11–12) states: "In my view ... there is no substance in the suggested automaticity of disappearance of the immunity just because of the establishment of international criminal courts. ... International criminal courts are established by states acting together, whether directly or indirectly as in the case of the Tribunal, which was established by the Security Council on behalf of states members of the UN. There is no basis for suggesting that by merely acting together to establish such a court states signify an intention to waive their individual functional immunities. A presumption of continuance of their immunities as these exist under international law is only offset where some element in the decision to establish such a court shows that they agreed otherwise."

81 *Supra* n55.

82 Fox, *supra* n1, 429–30.

83 See Cassese, *International Criminal* Law, *supra* n2, 267 *et seq.*; *Arrest Warrant Case*, *supra* n4, para. 58; Gaeta, *supra* n25, 981–2.

84 See the text *supra* n43.

85 States parties have an obligation to cooperate with the ICC with regard to arrest and surrender of wanted persons (ICC Statute, *supra* n6, arts. 86 and 89).

86 See Gaeta, *supra* n25, 996–1000; Bruce Broomhall, *International Justice and the International Criminal Court: Between Sovereignty and the Rule of Law* (Oxford: Oxford UP, 2003), 139–41. As a result of the waiver of national law immunities in article 27(2), some states parties (such as France) have been obliged to amend the provisions of their constitutions granting immunity to the head of state or government: *Re Treaty Establishing the International Criminal Court*, 125 ILR 442, Decision No. 98–402 DC (France: Constitutional Council, 1999).

87 In addition, article 98(2) provides that "the Court may not proceed with a request for surrender which would require the requested state to act inconsistently with its obligations under international agreements pursuant to which the consent of a sending state is required to surrender a person of that state to the Court, unless the Court can first obtain the cooperation of the sending state for the giving of consent for the surrender."

88 Broomhall, *supra* n86, 141.

89 The risk of this happening is quite high, since the principle of complementarity adopted in the ICC Statute means that the ICC will only exercise its

jurisdiction in cases in which the national state has failed to genuinely exercise its own jurisdiction (ibid., 143–4).

90 See ICC Statute, *supra* n6, art. 12(2)(a) (providing for ICC jurisdiction with respect to crimes committed on the territory of an ICC party.) The author, and others, have argued that states are legally entitled to create, by treaty, an international tribunal with criminal jurisdiction over nationals of non-parties: Akande, *supra* n71; Michael Scharf, "The ICC's Jurisdiction over the Nationals of Non-Party States: A Critique of the US Position," *Law and Contemporary Problems* 64, no. 1 (2001): 67–117; Gennady M. Danilenko, "ICC Statute and Third States," in Cassese, Gaeta, and Jones, *supra* n6, 1871; Jordan J. Paust, "The Reach of ICC Jurisdiction over Non-Signatory Nationals," *Vanderbilt Journal of Transnational Law* 33, no. 1 (2000): 1–15. The US, and others, has taken the contrary view and argued that the exercise of ICC jurisdiction over nationals of non-parties is illegitimate and even unlawful: Madeleine Morris, "High Crimes and Misconceptions: The ICC and Non-Party States," *Law and Contemporary Problems* 64, no. 1 (2001): 13–66; Ruth Wedgwood, "The Irresolution of Rome," *Law and Contemporary Problems* 64, no. 1 (2001): 193–214, 199–200; David Scheffer, "The United States and the International Criminal Court," *American Journal of International Law* 93, no. 1 (1999): 12–21, 18.

91 See the texts at notes 72 to 74 above. While the provisions of the ICC Statute may eventually influence the development of customary law so that international law immunities are never available in cases of international crimes, it is clear that this is some way from the present position.

92 Part two above contains a discussion of the circumstances in which international law immunities are available where a person is accused of committing an international crime.

93 See Akande, *supra* n71.

94 See the discussion in the text at notes 69–79.

95 It appears that the arrest warrant issued under article 58(1) by the ICC's Pre-Trial Chamber after the conclusion of investigations by the prosecutor is preliminary to and different from the request for arrest to which article 98(1) relates. The latter is provided for in part 9 of the ICC Statute (specifically, articles 89–92). The fact that there is a difference is implicit in the requirement that a request for arrest under article 91 must be supported by a copy of the arrest warrant.

96 *Supra* n4, paras 70–1. Some of the dissenting judges in this case (Judge Oda and Judge ad hoc Van den Wyngaert at paras 13 and 78–80 of their respective opinions) have argued that the mere issuance or international circulation

of an arrest warrant is not a violation of applicable immunities because there is no obligation on the receiving state to carry it out. See also *Submissions of the Amicus Curiae on Head of State Immunity (Sands & McDonald)*, *supra* n66. This argument is unconvincing because the mere issuance and circulation of the warrant is sufficient and likely to restrict the ability of the relevant serving senior state officials (such as heads of state, heads of government, and foreign ministers) to travel and carry out their international functions. The very purpose of immunity *ratione personae* is to permit the senior serving state officials to carry out their international functions.

97 Arguably, the position of diplomatic and consular officials is different, since international law only accords immunities to these officials in the state to which they are accredited or through which they transit (VCDR, *supra* n12, arts 39 and 40; VCCR, *supra* n39, arts 53 and 54). Other states have no obligation to refrain from arrest and the issuance and circulation of an arrest warrant to those other states will not be a violation of immunities accorded by international law.

98 Broomhall, *supra* n86, 145; Gaeta, *supra* n25, 993–6; Steffen Wirth "Immunities, Related Problems, and Article 98 of the Rome Statute," *Criminal Law Forum* 12, no. 4 (2001): 429–58, 452–4; William Schabas, *An Introduction to the International Criminal Court*, 2d ed. (Cambridge: Cambridge UP, 2004), 114–15.

99 In the margins of the July-August 1999 session of the ICC Preparatory Commission, delegates from Canada and the UK circulated a paper in which they stated: "The interpretation which should be given to article 98 is as follows. Having regard to the terms of the Statute, the Court shall not be required to obtain a waiver of immunity with respect to the surrender by one state Party of a head of state or government, or diplomat, of another state Party." The text of the paper is reproduced in Broomhall, *supra* n86, 144. The informal paper was circulated after discussions among the "Like Minded" group of countries on the relationship between articles 27 and 98.

100 (UK), 2001, c. 17.

101 See *International Criminal Court Act* (Malta), 2002, c. 453, art. 14, inserting a new art. 26S into the *Extradition Act* (Malta), c. 276. Articles 26S(1) and (2) are identical to sections 23(1) and (2) of the British Act. See also section 60(1) of Ireland's *International Criminal Court Bill 2003* which reads: "In accordance with Article 27, any diplomatic immunity or state immunity attaching to a person by reason of a connection with a state party to the Statute is not a bar to proceedings under this Act in relation to the person."

102 *International Crimes and International Criminal Court Act 2000* (New Zealand), 2000 No. 26 (Amendment 2000 No. 67), s. 31(1): "The existence of any immunity or special procedural rule attaching to the official capacity of any person is not a ground for: (a) refusing or postponing the execution of a request for surrender or other assistance by the ICC; or (b) holding that a person is ineligible for surrender, transfer or removal to the ICC or another state under this Act; ..." This provision is, however, subject to sections 66 and 100, which permit proceedings to be stayed while the ICC makes a determination under ICC Statute, art. 98. See also *Crimes Against Humanity and War Crimes Act* (Canada), SC 2000, c. 24, s. 48, inserting a new section 6.1 into the *Extradition Act* (Canada), SC 1999, c. 18, which reads as follows: "Despite any other Act or law, no person who is the subject of a request for surrender by the International Criminal Court ... may claim immunity under common law or by statute from arrest or extradition under this Act." See also *Crimes Against Humanity and War Crimes Act* (Canada), SC 2000, c. 24, s. 70, amending section 16 of the *state Immunity Act*, SC 1991, c. 41, s. 13.

103 It is likely that the courts in these countries will apply the common law rule that ambiguous legislation ought to be construed in a manner consistent with the state's international obligations rather than in a manner contrary to them. See *Salomon* v. *Customs and Excise Commissioners*, [1967] 2 QB 116 [England, CA]; *Murray* v. *Schooner Charming Betsy*, (1804) 2 Cranch 64, 118 [US SC].

104 Under article 26S(4) of the Maltese act, *supra* n101 and section 23(4) of the UK act, *supra* n100 (but not under the Irish bill), the minister or secretary of state may, after consultations with the ICC and the other state, direct that proceedings which, but for subsections (1) and (2), would be prohibited by state or diplomatic immunity, shall not be taken.

105 See part two for a discussion of these immunities.

106 Broomhall, *supra* n86, 143–4.

107 Ibid., 145.

108 See VCLT, *supra* n72, arts 34–8.

109 Gaeta, *supra* n25, 993. See, for example, ICC Statute, *supra* n6, art. 90(4).

110 ICC Statute, *supra* n6, art. 73. See also article 93(9)(b) which provides that where a request for assistance from the Court "concerns information, property or persons which are subject to the control of a third state or an international organization by virtue of an international agreement, the requested states shall so inform the Court and the Court shall direct its request to the third state or international organization."

111 See the fourth and fifth paragraphs of the preamble to the ICC Statute, which read: "*Affirming* that the most serious crimes of concern to the international community as a whole must not go unpunished and that their effective prosecution must be ensured by taking measures at the national level and by enhancing international cooperation,

Determined to put an end to impunity for the perpetrators of these crimes and thus to contribute to the prevention of such crimes."

112 Gaeta, *supra* n25, 993–4; Broomhall, *supra* n86, 145; Wirth, *supra* n98, 452.

113 *United States – Standards for Reformulated and Conventional Gasoline*, WT/DS2/9, 1996, 23 [WTO Appellate Body].

114 Wirth, *supra* n98, 452.

115 ICC Statute, *supra* n6, art. 98(1).

116 See note 95 above.

117 See Otto Triffterer, "Article 27," in *Commentary on the Rome Statute of the International Criminal Court: Observers' Notes, Article by Article*, (Baden-Baden: Nomos, 1999), 513, margin note 24.

118 It cannot be excluded that private parties, and peacekeeping or peace enforcement forces operating under a mandate from an international organization will be involved in surrendering persons to the ICC. A number of persons were transferred to the ICTY by NATO forces operating in Bosnia and Croatia. In one case, there appeared to be collusion between private parties and the NATO force: *Prosecutor* v. *Nikolic, Interlocutory Decision of Appeals Chamber*, IT-94-2-AR73 (June 2003). Since peacekeeping or peace enforcement forces are composed of state forces, it is arguable that any limitations that apply to states (e.g., the immunities retained in article 98) would also apply to such forces.

119 Gaeta, *supra* n25, 994; Triffterer, *supra* n117.

120 See notes 101–2 in the UK/Canada paper referred to in note 99. For a collection of national legislation implementing the ICC Statute, see on-line: Coalition for the International Criminal Court <http://www.iccnow.org/resourcestools/ratimptoolkit/nationalregionaltools/legislationdebates.html>; Amnesty International <http://web.amnesty.org/web/web.nsf/pages/implementation>; Council of Europe <http://www.coe.int/T/E/Legal_Affairs/Legal_co-operation/Transnational_criminal_justice/International_Criminal_Court/>; and University of Nottingham School of Law <http://www.nottingham.ac.uk/law/hrlc/hrlc_enacted%20legislation.htm>.

121 *Federal Law on Cooperation with the International Criminal Court* (Switzerland), 22 June 2001, art. 6, providing that the Swiss Federal Council "shall decide on questions of immunity relating to Article 98 in connection with Article 27 of the Statute which arise in the course of the execution of

requests." See also article 4, which provides for consultations with the ICC where it appears that a request from the ICC could violate state or diplomatic immunity. See also *Implementation of the Rome Statute of the International Criminal Court Act, 2002* (South Africa), s. 10(9), which provides that the fact that a person is or was a head of state or government, a member of government or parliament, an elected representative, or a government official does not constitute a ground for refusing to issue an order for surrender to the ICC. It is arguable that this provision only refers to domestic and not foreign officials. However, the fact that section 4(2) states that the official position of these persons shall not constitute a defence despite any other law to the contrary, "including customary and conventional international law," suggests that it contemplates foreign officials as well.

122 See VCLT, *supra* n72, art. 31(3)(b). Emphasis added.

123 In 1999, Slobodan Milosevic, at that time head of state of the Federal Republic of Yugoslavia, was indicted by the ICTY (see *supra* n71 and the text associated with notes 69–75 above).

124 Articles 27 and 98 were drafted by different committees: Triffterer, *supra* n117. It is not clear whether any thought was given to the consistency of the two provisions in regard to one another or to the question of whether article 98 applied to ICC parties.

125 For an analysis of article 98(2), see Akande, *supra* n71, 642–6; Salvatore Zappalà, "The Reaction of the US to the Entry into Force of the ICC Statute: Comments on UN SC Resolution 1422 (2002) and Article 98 Agreements," *Journal of International Criminal Justice* 1, no. 1 (2003): 114–34.

126 See, for example, *Agreement Between the Parties to the North Atlantic Treaty Regarding the Status of their Forces*, 19 June 1951, 199 UNTS 67 [hereinafter NATO SOFA]. Some have doubted whether the NATO SOFA and others come within the scope of article 98(2): see Dieter Fleck, "Are Foreign Military Personnel Exempt from International Criminal Jurisdiction under Status of Forces Agreements?" *Journal of International Criminal Justice* 1, no. 3 (2003): 651–70; Paust, *supra* n90, 10; Amnesty International, "International Criminal Court: US Efforts to Obtain Impunity for Genocide, Crimes against Humanity and War Crimes," AI Index: IOR 40/025/2002, Section III, on-line: Amnesty International <http://web.amnesty.org/library/index/engior400252002>; Wirth, *supra* n98, 455. The author has argued elsewhere (Akande, *supra* n71, 644) that NATO SOFA, arts VII(3)c and VII(5) fall within the language of article 98(2). Moreover, it is generally admitted that article 98(2) was drafted with the intention of applying to SOFAS: see Kimberly Prost and Angelika Schlunck, "Article 98," in Triffterer, *supra* n117, 1133 margin note 6.

127 For example, *European Convention on Extradition*, 13 December 1957, ETS No. 24, art. 15. See Akande, *supra* n71; Wirth, *supra* n98, 455; Prost and Schlunck, *supra* n126, 1133 margin note 6.

128 Under these agreements, "'Persons' of one Party present in the territory of the other shall not, absent the expressed consent of the first Party, (a) be surrendered or transferred by any means to the International Criminal Court for any purpose, or (b) be surrendered or transferred by any means to any other entity or third country, or expelled to a third country, for the purpose of surrender to or transfer to the International Criminal Court." For the purposes of the agreement "'persons' are current or former Government officials, employees (including contractors), or military personnel or nationals of one Party." For the text of the agreement, see Sean D. Murphy, "U.S. Bilateral Agreements Relating to the ICC," in "Contemporary Practice of the United States," *American Journal of International Law* 97, no. 1 (2003): 179–208, 201–2.

129 See Akande, *supra* n71, 643–4; Zappalà, *supra* n125, 129. See also James Crawford, Philippe Sands, and Ralph Wilde, *Joint Opinion regarding Bilateral Agreements Sought by the United States under Article 98(2) of the Statute of the International Criminal Court*, 5 June 2003, on-line: Human Rights First (formerly Lawyers Committee for Human Rights) <http://www.humanrightsfirst.org/international_justice/Art98_061403.pdf>, arguing that these agreements are inconsistent because (1) they deal with persons who cannot objectively be treated as having been "sent" by a state and (2) the object and purpose of the ICC Statute precludes a state party from entering into an agreement the purpose or effect of which may lead to impunity. For similar views, see Council of the European Union, "EU Guiding Principles concerning Arrangements between a State Party to the Rome Statute of the International Criminal Court and the United States Regarding the Conditions to Surrender of Persons to the Court," annexed to the *Council Conclusions on the International Criminal Court*, 30 September 2002, on-line: <http://ue.eu.int/cms3_fo/showPage.asp?id=404&lang=en&mode=g> [hereinafter EU Guiding Principles].

130 By May 2005, 100 states had reportedly signed such agreements with the US (though only a third of that number had ratified those agreements or signed executive agreements). Forty-one of the signatories are parties to the ICC Statute. For a list, see on-line: Coalition for the International Criminal Court <http://www.iccnow.org/documents/USandICC/BIAsByRegion_current.pdf>. There has been debate about whether article 98(2) covers agreements entered into after the entry into force of the ICC Statute or only pre-existing agreements. The better view is that it covers

both. See Akande, *supra* n71, 645; Zappalà, *supra* n125, 122–3; Crawford, Sands, and Wilde, *supra* n129, para. 38.

131 January 2002, s. 1(4), Annex A, on-line: UK Ministry of Defence <http://www.operations.mod.uk/isafmta.pdf>.

132 For the composition of ISAF at its inception, see Centre for Defense Information, "Fact Sheet: International Security Assistance Force (ISAF) in Afghanistan," 14 February 2002, on-line: <http://www.cdi.org/friendlyversion/printversion.cfm?documentID=1161>. For a more recent list, see International Assistance Security Force <http://www.afnorth.nato.int/ISAF/index.htm>.

133 This is evidently not the view of the EU, which has stated that the "nationality of persons [is] not to be surrendered: any solution should only cover persons who are not nationals of an ICC state Party." EU Guiding Principles, *supra* n129.

134 See EC Commission Legal Services, "Effective Functioning of the International Criminal Court Undermined by Bilateral Agreements as Proposed by the US" reprinted in *Human Rights Law Journal* 23, no. 1–4 (2002): 158–9; Human Rights Watch, "United States Efforts to Undermine the International Criminal Court: Impunity Agreements," 4 September 2002, on-line: Coalition for the International Criminal Court <http://www.iccnow.org/documents/otherissuesimpunityagreem.html>. Those taking this view argue that to interpret article 98(2) as extending to agreements with non-parties would result in impunity in cases where the non-party decides not to prosecute. It is then argued that such an interpretation must be rejected since one of the purposes of the ICC Statute is the prevention of impunity. According to this view, article 98(2) is only a "routing device," allowing the ICC party on whose territory a national of another ICC party is found to comply with its treaty obligations to the latter ICC party but leaving the court free to request surrender from the latter state.

135 See section two, part A *supra*. See further Akande, *supra* n71, 643.

136 It must be admitted that it is more difficult to interpret the wording of article 98(2) as applying only to agreements concluded by non-parties. That provision prevents requests for surrender that would "require the requested state to act inconsistently with its obligations under international agreements pursuant to which the consent of a sending state is required." Firstly, this language does not explicitly exclude agreements concluded by parties. Secondly, while obligations under the ICC Statute (such as those in article 27) are part of the "obligations under international law" of states parties and can therefore be taken into account under article 98(1), it may be argued that article 98(2) only requires consideration of the obligations under the other international agreement and not the obligations under the statute.

While, between the same parties, the obligations under the ICC Statute would normally prevail over those in prior agreements (VCLT, *supra* n72, art. 30(3)), it might be argued that article 98(2) effectively specifies that the ICC Statute is subject to the agreements referred to in that provision. In such circumstances, the provision of that other agreement will prevail: VCLT, *supra* n72, art. 30(2).

137 While extradition agreements within the scope of article 98(2) (see *supra* n127) will not be covered by the waiver in article 27, it has been argued that the right of ICC parties, under those extradition treaties, to demand that persons they extradite are not transferred to the Court has been waived by article 89 of the ICC Statute. See Wirth, *supra* n98, 455.

138 See Akande, *supra* n71.

139 VCLT, *supra* n72, art. 30(3).

140 Ibid.

141 Ibid., art. 30(4)(b).

142 See, for example, UN Immunities Convention, *supra* n36, art. V, s. 18(a). There are several treaties dealing with the immunities of international organizations. However, the provisions in those treaties dealing with immunity from arrest and criminal process tend to be uniform.

143 See part two above for the argument that acts which amount to international crimes are nevertheless to be regarded as official acts where they are done under "colour of law."

144 See Henry G. Schermers and Niels M. Blokkers, *International Institutional Law*, 3d rev. ed. (Cambridge, MA: Kluwer Law International, 1995) 358, §534; Paul C. Szasz and Thordis Ingadottir, "The UN and the ICC: The Immunity of the UN and its Officials," *Leiden Journal of International Law* 14, no. 4 (2001): 867–85, 880.

145 See, for example, UN Immunities Convention, *supra* n36, art. V, s. 19. Since many heads of international organizations have previously been senior state officials or government members, it is not inconceivable that they may be accused of having committed or been involved in the commission of an international crime prior to their appointment by the organization. For example, it was alleged that Kurt Waldheim, a former Austrian UN secretary general from 1972 to 1981, was involved in the commission of war crimes during World War II.

146 See, for example, UN Immunities Convention, *supra* n36, art. VI, s. 22(a).

147 ICC Statute, *supra* n6, art. 98(1).

148 Ibid., art. 98(2). This provision is wide enough to cover treaty provisions conferring immunity on the representatives of states to international organizations since it is the member state and not the organization that is usually

empowered to waive the immunity. See, for example, UN Immunities Convention, *supra* n36, art. IV, s. 14.

149 See Triffterer, *supra* n117, 509.

150 Szasz and Ingadottir, *supra* n144, 881–2.

151 This follows from the principle that an official or expert of an international organization is entitled to immunity even from the jurisdiction of his own state. See *Difference Relating to Immunity from Legal Process of a Special Rapporteur of the Commission on Human Rights*, Advisory Opinion of 29 April 1999, *ICJ Reports* 1999, 62, para. 46; and *Applicability of Article VI, Section 22 of the Convention on the Privileges and Immunities of the United Nations*, Advisory Opinion of 15 December 1989, *ICJ Reports* 1989, 177, paras 51–2. See also C.F. Amerasinghe, *Principles of the Institutional Law of International Organizations* (Cambridge: Cambridge UP, 1996), 370.

152 See, for example, UN Immunities Convention, *supra* n36, art. V, s. 20 and art. VI, s. 23.

153 The Court is empowered to request cooperation and assistance from international organizations: ICC Statute, *supra* n6, art. 87(6).

154 "If the Court seeks to exercise its jurisdiction over a person who is alleged to be criminally responsible for a crime within the jurisdiction of the Court and if, in the circumstances, such person enjoys, according to the Convention on the Privileges and Immunities of the United Nations and the relevant rules of international law, any privileges and immunities as are necessary for the independent exercise of his or her work for the United Nations, the United Nations undertakes to cooperate fully with the Court and to take all necessary measures to allow the Court to exercise its jurisdiction, in particular by waiving any such privileges and immunities in accordance with the Convention on the Privileges and Immunities of the United Nations and the relevant rules of international law." *Relationship Agreement between the United Nations and the International Criminal Court*, 4 October 2004, ICC-ASP/3/RES.1, on-line: International Criminal Court <http://www.icc-cpi.int/library/asp/ICC-ASP-3-Res1_English.pdf>.

155 See Crawford, Sands, and Wilde, *supra* n129, paras 58–9, which argue that where the ICC has requested or intends to request the surrender of a person, it is for the Court to decide whether a bilateral non-surrender agreement covering the person is consistent with article 98(2).

156 Rules of Procedure and Evidence, 3–10 September 2002, ICC-ASP/1/3, on-line: International Criminal Court <http://www.icc-cpi.int/library/officialjournal/Rules_of_Proc_and_Evid_070704-EN.pdf>.

157 Ibid.

158 Broomhall, *supra* n86, 145 and Wirth, *supra* n98, 458 argue that the final decision should be left to the ICC.

159 See Crawford, Sands, and Wilde, *supra* n129, para. 58(6).

160 SC 2000, c. 24, s. 48, amending section 6 of the *Extradition Act*, SC 1999, c. 18. See also *Crimes Against Humanity and War Crimes Act* (Canada), SC 2000, c. 24, s. 70, amending section 16 of the *State Immunity Act*, SC 1991, c. 41, s. 13.

161 2000 No. 26 (Amendment 2000 No. 67), s. 31. Under sections 66 and 120, the New Zealand executive may request the ICC to make a final determination on whether or not article 98 applies to a request for surrender. However, if the ICC advises that it intends to proceed with the request, the New Zealand authorities must comply.

162 *International Criminal Court Act 2002* (Australia), No. 41 2002, s. 12; *Federal Law on Co-operation with the International Criminal Court* (Switzerland), 22 June 2001, arts 4(d) and 6.

163 *International Criminal Court Act 2001* (UK), 2001, c. 17, s. 23(3); *International Criminal Court Act 2002* (Malta), c. 453, art. 14, inserting a new article 26S(3) into the *Extradition Act* (Malta), c. 276.

164 *International Criminal Court Act 2001* (UK), 2001, c. 17, s. 23(4); *International Criminal Court Act 2002* (Malta), c. 453, art. 14, inserting a new article 26S(4) into the *Extradition Act* (Malta), c. 276.

165 ICC Statute, *supra* n6, preamble.

166 Fox, *supra* n1, 30.

4

Exaggerating the ICC

DAVID WIPPMAN♣

The ongoing debate over the legitimacy and utility of the newly formed International Criminal Court has been freighted with overblown rhetoric by its supporters and opponents alike. Proponents describe the Court as the most significant new international institution created in many years. To them, it represents revolutionary progress in the struggle to supplant the rule of the jungle with the rule of law. The Court, they claim, will be a powerful new weapon in the fight to end the prevailing "culture of impunity," deter atrocities, promote national reconciliation in divided societies, and trigger major progress in efforts to promote the rule of law.

Critics view the Court as a drastic intrusion on state sovereignty, a forum for politicized prosecutions, and a deliberate means to restrain national security decision-making (particularly by the US). They see the Court as an undemocratic and unaccountable institution, and fear that the Court's prosecutor might become a "global Ken Starr."[1] Worse, they suggest that the Court will impede political resolution of protracted conflicts and hinder the ouster of rights-abusing dictators by removing amnesty and exile from the diplomatic toolbox.

To some extent, overstatements are inevitable as both sides seek to marshal the political and other resources necessary to support (or impede) the development of a new and costly international institution. Similarly inflated projections have accompanied the creation of other international judicial institutions, most notably the International Court of Justice (ICJ) and its predecessor, the misnamed Permanent Court of International Justice. Proponents characterized those institutions as "essential to the world's progress," and a vital means of securing international peace by substituting judicial resolution of disputes for armed conflict.[2] In retrospect, these international courts can claim to have played a valuable if modest role in international affairs. The courts' decisions have undoubtedly facilitated the resolution of a number of international disputes, but no one now suggests that the ICJ is a "significant instrument for maintaining international peace."[3]

Within the US, ironically, Republicans have historically tended to be more effusive concerning the potential for "world peace through law and courts" than Democrats.[4] Thus, President Dwight D. Eisenhower, for example, called for global acceptance of the ICJ's compulsory jurisdiction, proclaiming that it would be far "better to lose a point now and then in an international tribunal and gain a world in which everyone lives at peace under the rule of law."[5] But others, especially within the US Senate, have often expressed much darker visions of international judicial institutions, "arguing that the United States, protected by two oceans and a powerful military, and endowed with a tradition of fair play and non–self-aggrandizement, has little reason to subordinate its national self-reliance to a compact with less fortunate or more venal nations."[6] Critics lamented what they saw as a loss of US sovereignty and feared an anti-American bias in international fora.

Professors Franck and Lehrman label these alternating currents in American attitudes towards international courts "messianism" and "chauvinism." Despite the fundamental differences between the state-to-state claims heard in courts such as the ICJ and the charges against individuals heard in international criminal tribunals, the same terms – messianism and chauvinism – might readily be applied to describe some of the rhetorical excesses surrounding the ICC.

The intensity of ICC rhetoric has been heightened by anger at US opposition to the Court. Many Court supporters, often in surprisingly undiplomatic language, accuse the US of arrogance, a short-sighted focus on a narrowly defined national interest, and a refusal to play by rules applicable to everyone else. Increasingly, the US is seen as an obstacle to the larger project of international cooperation through international law and institutions. The US position on the

ICC is commonly lumped together with the US rejection of other important treaties and institutions, including the Landmines Convention, the Kyoto Protocol on global warming, and the ABM treaty.

The unfortunate result of the polarization of the debate over the ICC is that it obscures what may realistically be expected of the new institution, and potentially distorts the allocation of political and financial resources in the fight against the crimes the new Court is designed to address. The reality is that claims on both sides are substantially overstated. In practice, the Court will be hampered by legal, financial, and political constraints; there is little empirical evidence to support the deterrence claims; national legal systems in the countries where atrocities are most widespread are usually inadequate and will often be unable to fulfill the role assigned to them by the Court's statute; and the signalling/rule-of-law promotion function of the Court is likely therefore to be relatively modest. But the Court can contribute to the marginalization of extremists in some contexts, and it can, over the long term, reinforce normative constraints against the commission of atrocities, even if only at the margins. Moreover, the Court will probably avoid the gray area cases most feared by the US and other critics, so its impact on state sovereignty and national security decision-making is likely to be modest.

I. PRACTICAL CONSTRAINTS ON THE ICC'S PURSUIT OF ACCOUNTABILITY

The most basic function of any criminal court is to provide a particular form of accountability by ensuring that persons guilty of criminal law violations face penal sanctions. Undoubtedly, the Court will perform this function to some extent; the Court will try and sanction some number of individuals for crimes within its jurisdiction (presently, genocide, crimes against humanity, and war crimes).[7] But Court proponents view it as a vehicle to provide accountability in a much more important and transformative sense. They claim it will help substitute a "culture of accountability" for a "culture of impunity."

Proponents are generally vague about the way in which this expected transformation will occur. The commonly expressed hope is that the ICC will contribute to a developing political culture of accountability by reinforcing norms of acceptable behaviour through its judicial pronouncements, by deterring potential violators through the threat of prosecution, and by defusing potential conflicts and promoting national reconciliation through the individualization of guilt.

Even assuming that prosecutions can contribute significantly to the achievement of these ends, much will depend on whether the Court can overcome important practical limitations. As Reed Brody, the advocacy director for Human Rights Watch, posed the question: "Will the gaping jurisdictional loopholes in the ICC Statute, a total reliance on governmental cooperation, and a US refusal to allow the UN Security Council to submit cases to the Court make the institution an expensive but underemployed bureaucracy? Or will widespread ratification and a political determination to pursue the worst criminals render the court a potent weapon to combat impunity in the 21st century?"[8]

A. Jurisdictional Loopholes

The ICC Statute's jurisdictional provisions, while too robust for the US and other critics, may prove too weak to accomplish the aims of Court supporters. As a result of a hotly contested compromise, the Court may exercise its jurisdiction over covered crimes only if the state on whose territory the crimes are committed or the state whose national is accused has accepted the Court's jurisdiction, either by ratifying the ICC Statute or accepting the Court's jurisdiction over a particular situation ad hoc. Many ICC advocates lament this compromise. In most instances, the territorial state and the state of nationality are likely to be the same. As a result, the Court will often be unable, absent a UN Security Council referral, "to intervene where serious violations of humanitarian law are committed by the political authorities of a State non-party to the Statute in the territory of that State, and against their own nationals. The Pol Pot or Milosevic scenarios would not be covered."[9]

This "critical flaw"[10] in the Court's jurisdictional regime might be overcome through widespread ratification of the Court's statute, or through regular UN Security Council referrals. But there is reason to be skeptical that either will occur, at least in the near term. As of May 2005, ninety-nine states have ratified the ICC Statute, and more are expected to do so. But most states experiencing ongoing military conflicts are not parties to the statute. Notable exceptions include Afghanistan, Colombia, and the Democratic Republic of the Congo. But the trend is what a realist might expect: most countries that are engaged in or anticipate armed conflicts giving rise to war crimes and related charges have not joined the ICC regime. Notably absent are Israel, most of the Arab states, and states experiencing brutal conflicts in Asia and sub-Saharan Africa. Similarly absent are the largest and most powerful states, including the US, China, India, and Russia (the latter has signed but not ratified the Court's statute).[11]

This major gap in the reach of the ICC Statute could be remedied by the UN Security Council, which has the authority to refer situations to the Court. Indeed, Elizabeth Wilmhurst, a member of the United Kingdom delegation in Rome, suggests that "because of the jurisdictional limits of the Court, many or most of the cases before it in the early dates are likely to be those referred by the Council."[12] But that possibility seems largely foreclosed by the vehemence of US opposition to the ICC. The Bush administration, at least, is extremely reluctant to accept UN Security Council referrals for fear of legitimating an institution it vigorously opposes. No doubt there will be situations in which the United States will feel compelled to accept a UN Security Council referral, as it did with Darfur. But in most cases the US will likely push alternative fora: national courts, mixed tribunals similar to those now operating in Kosovo, or even military tribunals. The US has, after all, been prepared to frustrate UN peacekeeping operations in order to obtain immunity for its peacekeeping personnel. It is thus likely in most cases to see the cost of working around the ICC as acceptable, even in situations in which it wants to refer cases to an international tribunal.

B. Procedural Hurdles

The Court's limited jurisdictional reach is exacerbated by the procedural devices open to states (and individual defendants) wishing to obstruct the work of the ICC. As Leila Sadat and Richard Carden observe, the ICC Statute's "extremely complex and potentially burdensome procedural regime governing challenges to jurisdiction and admissibility... may prevent the Court from efficiently fulfilling its primary mission to administer justice."[13] This procedural regime was instituted to implement the principle of complementarity (which gives national court's primary authority to investigate and prosecute cases within the Court's jurisdiction) and to screen out inappropriate invocations of the Court's jurisdiction. But the result is that at almost every stage of the Court's proceedings multiple parties can raise challenges to admissibility and jurisdiction, and most of these are subject to interlocutory appeal. Because "it is all too easy for disputes about jurisdiction to be abused," it seems "likely that the Court will be spending a great deal of time on motions relating to admissibility and jurisdiction."[14] For similar reasons, Hans Peter Kaul, a German delegate to the Rome negotiations who championed a strong Court, concludes that the ICC Statute in effect creates two different Courts: one "very strong" (when acting on the basis of a UN Security Council referral), and one "quite weak" (when acting on the basis of a state complaint or action of the ICC prosecutor).[15] But for the reasons noted above, UN Security Council referrals are likely to be infrequent, leaving only the "quite weak" court operative.

To make matters worse, "the Court's enforcement jurisdiction is so feeble that it has the potential to completely undermine the efficacy of the Court."[16] The Court has no authority to compel states to comply with its orders, and no right in most cases to carry out investigative or other work in the territory of requested states without the consent and cooperation of the authorities in those states. Further, the Court will be completely dependent on the cooperation of states for the execution of its "arrest warrants, judgments, orders to seize assets, or sentences."[17] Sadat and Carden conclude that "given the difficulty that the ICTY, in particular, has had with the arrest of suspects and conduct of investigations, even when backed with the power of the Security Council, the future of the ICC looks gloomy indeed."[18]

In some instances, this assessment may be overly pessimistic. Political changes within states can substantially improve the prospects for cooperation. In Rwanda, military success brought to power a government committed to the prosecution of those responsible for genocide and related crimes. As a result, a number of senior figures involved in the Rwandan genocide have been brought to trial, and various other states in Africa and elsewhere have assisted the International Criminal Tribunal for Rwanda (ICTR) in apprehending suspects and in locating evidence. Moreover, in the last few years, after the publication of Sadat and Carden's article, state cooperation with the ICTY improved significantly. A number of senior indictees, most notably Milosevic, have been apprehended and brought to trial. Nonetheless, inadequate state cooperation remains a significant problem for the effective operation of both the ICTY and the ICTR.

The ICC is likely to experience even greater problems in this regard. It cannot count on internal political change in states of the sort that took place in Rwanda. Moreover, unlike the ICTY and ICTR, it cannot count on the assistance of the UN Security Council in obtaining state cooperation, given the attitude of the present US government. Moreover, it cannot count on pressure from key international development and lending organizations, which have contributed significantly to cooperation in countries such as Croatia and Serbia. This is because, in many cases, there simply may not exist the kind of international consensus that rendered it at least episodically possible to apply significant political and economic pressure to countries obstructing ICTY investigations.

C. Financial Constraints

Both the Yugoslavia and Rwanda tribunals are large and expensive institutions. Although formed in 1993 with the very modest annual budget of $276,000 US, the ICTY has mushroomed into an institution with twenty-five judges (sixteen permanent and nine *ad litem*) and over 1,200 staff. Its budget for 2004–05 was an extraordinary $271,854,600.[19] The ICTR has also grown dramatically. It now has a staff of over 870, and its budget for 2002–03 was $177,739,400.[20] The combined budget of the two tribunals thus exceeds $400 million, an amount equal to approximately one-seventh of the UN's 2004–05 peacekeeping budget (approximately $2.8 billion).[21]

The budgets of the two institutions have grown to keep pace with the escalating number and cost of legal proceedings. At the same time, as detailed below, the number of cases actually tried by the two existing tribunals remains very small. Simply put, trials before the international criminal tribunals have proven to be long and costly.

It is at best an open question whether the ICC will be funded at a level comparable to the existing tribunals. Among other things, the Court will not receive any US financial support; provision of such support is not only contrary to US policy, it is prohibited by US law.[22] The US has been the biggest financial backer of the existing tribunals, and it remains to be seen whether other states will pick up the slack. The Court's proposed budget for 2005 was €69,564,000, to support among other things an anticipated staff of 526.[23] The budget and staff will undoubtedly grow as the Court begins trying cases. Amnesty International suggests that the budget will expand to $100 million annually, but even at that level, the Court will possess only a fraction of the resources currently devoted to the two existing tribunals. Moreover, for reasons noted above, much of the ICC's time, energy, and budget is likely to be devoted to resolving multiple challenges to jurisdiction and admissibility. And unlike each of the existing tribunals, which have the luxury of focusing their efforts on a single country or area, the ICC's focus is global. Under the circumstances, it is hard to imagine states supplying the level of financial support that would be needed in order to make the ICC an effective institution, and doubtful whether it would be a wise use of resources to try.

D. US Opposition to the Court

The Clinton administration signed the ICC Statute, and was prepared to adopt a policy of constructive engagement, working to protect US interests without seeking directly to undermine the Court.[24] But the Bush administration entered office determined to oppose the ICC. In May 2002, the administration formally renounced the US signature of the ICC treaty.[25] In the summer of 2002, the US demanded that UN peacekeepers be exempted from the jurisdiction of the Court by means of a UN Security Council request under article 16 of the Court's statute. The US vetoed the extension of the mandate for the peacekeeping mission in Bosnia and Herzegovina (UNMIBH) when the other members of the UN Security Council unanimously opposed the proposed exemption as inconsistent with the object and purpose of the ICC. Britain eventually formulated a compromise: the UN Security Council agreed to request that the ICC prosecutor defer for one year (with the possibility of renewal) any investigation into crimes by members of UN peacekeeping operations who are nationals of states not party to the ICC Statute.[26] The US also launched a campaign to persuade other states to enter into bilateral "article 98 agreements" that would preclude parties to the agreements from surrendering each other's nationals to the Court.[27] As of May 2005, one hundred states had signed such agreements. These and other US actions undermine the Court in several ways.

First, to the extent that the article 98 agreements prove effective,[28] they further limit the scope of the Court's jurisdictional reach. Almost half of the states that have entered into such agreements with the US are parties to the Court's statute, and they are now barred from surrendering to the ICC US nationals that might be accused of committing covered crimes on their territory. Second, and more important, US opposition, especially combined with opposition from other powerful states, undermines the legitimacy of the institution and its claim to represent the international community. Third, US opposition will render the Court considerably less able to fulfill its mission than it might otherwise have been. The US supplies the two existing ad hoc tribunals not just with money but with vital intelligence information, political and diplomatic support, and, on occasion, military assistance for the apprehension of suspects. None of that will be made available to the ICC. While European and other like-minded states may fill the gap to some extent, it is doubtful that they are able or prepared to commit the necessary resources.

It is, of course, possible (and even probable) that future US presidents will view the ICC with less hostility than President Bush has shown. The Clinton administration, while unwilling to recommend ratification, was prepared to act as a "good neighbor" to the Court.[29] Assuming (as seems very likely) that the Court acts responsibly, US concerns may come to be seen as largely groundless, and the US might begin, at least tacitly, to accept the Court and on occasion to cooperate with it. But any significant cooperation would require a fundamental change in the prevailing mood within both the executive and legislative branches. In this regard, recent trends are not encouraging. The US in the post–Cold War era seems to be moving towards an increasingly unilateralist posture in international affairs, accompanied by a growing willingness to reject or disregard multilateral institutions and treaties that might constrain US freedom of action. The US willingness to go to war with Iraq with or without UN support is only one of a series of unilateralist decisions made by both Democrats and Republicans; it follows US rejection of the ABM treaty, the Kyoto Protocol on global warming, and the Landmines Convention, among others. Thus, Court supporters who predict that the US will eventually come around on the ICC, as it has on some other international human rights treaties, may have a long time to wait.[30] Moreover, should the ICC exercise questionable judgment in its early years, or adopt a definition of aggression that does not include a UN Security Council screen, or investigate a US national, US hostility to the Court will almost certainly sharply intensify, regardless of who is in the White House.

To all the practical limitations noted above, Court enthusiasts may respond that the ICC is designed to be a court of last resort. Under article 17 of the Court's statute, national courts are given primacy; the Court will undertake investigations and prosecutions only when national courts are unable or unwilling genuinely to do so. In theory, then, the Court could fulfill its function without trying any cases at all, simply by serving as an incentive to states to pursue cases themselves. Accordingly, the Court's limited resources might not pose as large an obstacle as might at first appear.

The problem with this line of reasoning is that states have never shown much interest in prosecuting the crimes covered by the Court's statute. Impunity has proven to be the rule rather than the exception. And the existence of a Court hobbled by structural and practical limitations is unlikely to provide much of an incentive for states to undertake serious investigations and prosecutions (as opposed to pro forma actions designed to avoid ICC action) that they would rather not undertake for domestic political reasons. Accordingly, complementarity does not significantly address the jurisdictional and other constraints detailed above.

II. DETERRENCE AND ITS LIMITS

For many, the strongest argument for an international criminal court is that it will help deter the commission of future atrocities.[31] Deterrence may be defined as "the ability of a legal system to discourage or prevent certain conduct through threats of punishment or other expression of disapproval."[32] But deterrence is difficult to achieve, especially in the international context. As Reed Brody observes, "there is growing evidence that the deterrence function of criminal law is, at best, limited on a national level. There is even less empirical evidence to suggest that rulers and their henchmen are dissuaded from atrocities by prosecutions of their counterparts elsewhere in the world – which remain the exception."[33]

The historical experience with efforts at deterrence has not been encouraging. During World War II, the US and UK issued a series of highly publicized warnings that violations of the laws of war would be punished.[34] Similarly, while conflicts in the former Yugoslavia were underway, the UN Security Council and various individual states repeatedly warned combatants that those committing atrocities would eventually be prosecuted. In each case, atrocities persisted at a high level despite the warnings. Thus, as Professor Theodor Meron (now a judge on the ICTY) has observed, "there is no empirical evidence of effective deterrence in either case."[35]

Of course, the fact that atrocities continue despite the threat or actual commencement of criminal prosecutions does not mean such threats or prosecutions have no effect. Some potential perpetrators of atrocities may have been deterred even if others were not. Indeed, there is at least modest anecdotal evidence to suggest that some individual actors in the former Yugoslavia adhered more closely to the requirements of international humanitarian law than they would have otherwise, for fear of prosecution.[36] But overall, the evidence suggests that the uncertain risk of a future international criminal prosecution usually will not prove sufficient to achieve deterrence at a level significant enough to have a visible impact on the course of events in war-torn societies.

In general, theories of deterrence assume that a sufficiently credible threat of prosecution will induce individuals to refrain from committing crimes out of self-interest. But numerous obstacles stand in the way of this seemingly simple outcome. As Paul Robinson and John Darley observe with reference to national legal systems:

> the behavioral sciences increasingly call into question the assumption of criminal law's *ex ante* influence. Potential offenders commonly do not know the legal rules, either directly or indirectly, even those rules that have been explicitly formulated to produce a behavioral effect. Even if they do know those rules, the cost-benefit analysis potential offenders perceive – which is the only analysis that matters – commonly leads to a conclusion suggesting violation rather than compliance, either because the perceived likelihood of punishment is so small, or because it is so distant as to be highly discounted, or for a variety of other reasons. And, even if they know the legal rules and perceive a cost-benefit analysis that urges compliance, potential offenders commonly cannot or will not bring that knowledge to bear to guide their conduct in their own best interests, such failure stemming from a variety of social, situational, or chemical influences. Even if no one of these three hurdles is fatal to law's behavioral influence, their cumulative effect typically is.[37]

Many of the same features inhibiting deterrence at the national level exist with even greater force at the international level.

A. Knowledge of the Law

In the context of national legal systems, "people rarely know exactly what activities the criminal law has criminalized."[38] They tend to rely "on their own moral intuitions to predict the legal rule."[39] To the extent that they misunderstand the law, its deterrence function is obviously limited.

In many instances, knowledge will not be an issue when it comes to genocide, crimes against humanity, and war crimes. No one can reasonably fail to realize that the massacre of civilians or the killing of prisoners of war is unlawful. In other contexts, however, knowledge of the law may well be an issue. Humanitarian law is replete with gray areas. Whether a particular target is legitimate, a particular action proportionate, or a particular order lawful will often prompt considerable debate even among international lawyers. More importantly, in the context of large-scale internal conflicts, where most covered crimes are committed, confusion regarding the applicable legal rules and, perhaps more importantly, a misguided sense of what the rules *should be* can have a significant limiting effect on efforts to achieve deterrence.

As one commentator observes, the deterrence

> calculation depends on an individual's threshold ability to recognize that a particular action may be subject to punishment at all. In the context of violations of international humanitarian law, average citizen-actors may never reach that threshold. For participants in mass violence, "criminal conduct that is normally characterized as 'deviance' is transformed into acceptable, even desirable, behavior. ... [This] indicate[s] that in circumstances conducive to international offences, individuals may not perceive their actions to be wrong and therefore may not adopt the cost-benefit cognitive framework upon which deterrence relies."[40]

This bleak assessment is at least partly borne out by a study conducted several years ago by the International Committee of the Red Cross (ICRC). The ICRC interviewed a cross-section of the population in six war-torn countries in an effort to ascertain, among other things, why combatants violate international humanitarian law.[41]

The case study of Bosnia is particularly revealing. The vast majority of combatants in Bosnia understood in general terms the limits imposed on warfare by international humanitarian law. They accepted the legitimacy of the applicable norms, and believed those norms should generally be followed. But at the same time, most did not view their own actions – even when they involved attacks on civilians – to be wrongful.[42]

The survey suggests that many Bosnians, perhaps most, viewed the conflict in "total war" terms. The conflict "mobilized the whole of society" with remarkably high percentages serving as combatants or civilian support. Losses on all sides were high, and ethnic antagonism was rampant. As a result of the high degree of societal involvement in the conflict and the way in which the conflict was fought, "many people in Bosnia-Herzegovina [were] ready to accept that the line between combatants and civilians was blurred during wartime: they [were] prepared to attack populated villages and towns; wage war on civilian areas to hurt the enemy; plant landmines even at risk to civilians; and, where necessary, torture prisoners."[43] Thus, knowledge of the law in the abstract did not translate into a recognition that particular conduct undertaken in a particular context was wrongful.

B. The Rational Choice Myth

Deterrence arguments take the following form: potential perpetrators can be dissuaded from committing a crime if the likely cost to them (as measured by the probability of prosecution and conviction) exceeds the expected benefit from the crime at issue.[44] This argument assumes two things: a favourable cost-benefit analysis, and an actor motivated wholly or at least primarily by rational self-interest calculations. Both assumptions are deeply problematic.

1 PERCEIVED COSTS

Even if we assume that potential perpetrators compare the risks and costs of prosecution with the political and personal gains to be achieved by participation in ethnic cleansing or similar acts, most would probably attach little weight to the risk of prosecution. Three elements come into play in such calculations: the probability of punishment, its severity, and its timing. On each criterion, the likely deterrent effect of international criminal prosecutions is slight.

Probability. International criminal tribunals are simply not equipped to try more than a tiny fraction of those who commit genocide and related crimes. This is certainly true of the Yugoslavia and Rwanda tribunals. The ICTY tried only six offenders in its first six years of operations. As political changes within the former Yugoslavia and increased international support enabled the tribunal gradually to expand its operations, the numbers have increased significantly, but remain low overall. As of March 2003, ten years into the ICTY's life, thirty-five accused have been tried, sixteen have received final sentences, and forty-seven more are currently in custody.[45] The ICTR has taken sixty suspects into custody, tried ten, and issued final sentences for only seven.[46]

While the work of the tribunals has been impressive in many respects, the number of individuals prosecuted has been minuscule relative to the total number of offenders.[47] And while both tribunals have apprehended some of the most senior figures responsible for atrocities within their respective jurisdictions, other senior figures, such as Ratko Mladic and Radovan Karadzic, remain at large.

These limited numbers are partly a function of the difficulties of obtaining international cooperation and financial support, and (in the case of the ICTY) the reluctance of troop contributors in the former Yugoslavia to anger ethnic supporters of indicted suspects or to put security forces directly at risk by asking them to apprehend armed suspects residing in areas where they might be able to count on significant local support. More fundamentally, the numbers reflect the inherent limits of a single tribunal asked to deal with the aftermath of large-scale inter-group violence.

Because of budgetary constraints, the ICC is likely to have even less capacity than the two existing tribunals to conduct large numbers of prosecutions. Yet its jurisdictional reach, at least on paper, is much broader. This means that the number of cases the ICC can handle with respect to any given conflict is likely to be vanishingly small.

And while the ICC relies on complementarity as a device to encourage trials at the national level, its own inability to hold large numbers of trials undercuts the incentive for states to hold their own trials. Moreover, states emerging from large-scale internal conflicts rarely have justice systems capable of effective (and unbiased) war crimes prosecutions, and in any event will usually be overwhelmed by the sheer numbers of cases. In the former Yugoslavia, for example, despite efforts by the ICTY and Western states to strengthen local judicial capacity, courts there "are simply not equipped to provide fair and impartial trials for all ethnic groups."[48] In Rwanda, the government by 1999 had issued more than 20,000 indictments and held almost 2,000 trials.[49] But the government had some 125,000 accused in custody, and acknowledged it would take 200 years to try them all.[50] In short, low-level perpetrators will in most situations face only a negligible risk of prosecution.[51]

High-level offenders, the Milosevics and Kambandas of the world, presumably face a much greater risk of prosecution than low-level offenders (though many senior officials responsible for atrocities in Rwanda and the former Yugoslavia remain at large). But as discussed below, high-level offenders also have considerably more to gain from the conduct at issue.

Severity. All things considered, most accused would greatly prefer an international court to a domestic one. The ICC cannot impose the death penalty, and if it operates like the Yugoslavia and Rwanda tribunals, it will impose sentences that are substantially lighter than those national courts would impose in either locale. Some European states view long sentences, especially life sentences, as inhumane, and that attitude seems to have influenced ICTY sentencing decisions. Moreover, incarceration when it occurs is likely to take place under relatively comfortable conditions in the prisons of cooperating European states. As a Rwandan government critic acidly observed about the ICTR, "it doesn't fit our definition of justice to think of the authors of the Rwandan genocide sitting in a full-service Swedish prison with a television."[52] Unfortunately, the lesser the perceived penalty, the lower the expected deterrence.

Delay. Most individuals heavily discount future consequences, well beyond what a rational cost-benefit calculus would suggest.[53] As a result, "the effects of punishment in deterring behavior drop off rapidly as the delay increases between the transgressive response and the administration of punishment for that response."[54]

Regrettably, substantial delay is characteristic of international criminal prosecutions. International criminal trials demand high levels of due process, which typically translate into opportunities for procedural delays and multiple appeals. Documentary evidence often does not exist or is unavailable; as a result, the tribunals must rely heavily on extensive and time-consuming witness testimony (and often corroborating witnesses as a check on the possibility of ethnic bias). The net result of these and other constraints is that the handling of each case takes much longer than would be true in most national legal systems. The Milosevic trial, for example, has lasted over three years and still appears far from its conclusion. When long delays in the administration of justice are coupled with a low probability of prosecution and modest penalties, the likelihood of significant deterrence is minimal.

2 PERCEIVED BENEFITS

Against the possible risks and costs of prosecution must be set the perceived potential benefits of the challenged conduct. Participation in atrocities in places such as Bosnia and Rwanda was not limited to a sociopathic criminal fringe. Depressingly, many ordinary civilians joined in the killing.

The ICRC survey in Bosnia suggests some of the reasons why individuals participate in such conduct (and why it is difficult to deter). As noted above, most Bosnians viewed the conflict in "total war" terms. They believed that their own survival, and the survival of their families and ethnic group, was at stake. When asked to explain why civilians were attacked, most of those interviewed focused on "hatred of the other side ... exacerbated by the belief that the other side is doing the same thing."[55] In addition, each side "viewed the conflict as a desperate struggle to defend its own community from attack," which "required suspending the limits" on warfare.[56] For one's own soldiers (the "defenders"), as opposed to the other side's soldiers (the "aggressors"), "the rules [of warfare] would often have to be suspended."[57]

Conversely, because whole communities mobilized to fight this conflict, bringing "civilians and soldiers together in defence of their community," the conflict was viewed in a way that did not "permit a clear distinction" between civilians and soldiers.[58] Instead, it was easy for combatants to assimilate the two and treat both as legitimate targets, particularly when encouraged or ordered to do so by their military and political leaders.

The explanations offered above do not, of course, justify crimes against humanity or war crimes. But when the various motivations for attacks on civilians are combined – the desire to defend one's community, hatred of the other side, a belief that civilians are essentially indistinguishable from combatants and therefore a threat, and encouragement from national leaders – it is not surprising that a slight risk of future prosecution in the apparently distant future will not have a major deterrent effect.

Political leaders in such conflicts have a much greater risk of prosecution, but they also stand to gain much more from the crimes at issue. Most observers believe that Milosevic and the other political leaders most responsible for the wars in Yugoslavia deliberately fostered inter-ethnic violence as a tool to secure political power and personal wealth. For some of them, that strategy has forced them into hiding or landed them in a prison cell in The Hague or elsewhere. For others, however, the strategy has worked fairly well, enabling them to live openly and in comfort.[59] Of these, some hold high-ranking public office; others operate in the shadows as part of the organized criminal networks that permeate the governments and social structures of post-conflict societies in the Balkans and elsewhere.

Whether a greater *ex ante* risk of prosecution might have deterred political leaders in the Balkans to some degree will never be known, but this much is clear: Milosevic and his associates continued to pursue their policies of ethnic cleansing in Kosovo and elsewhere even after they were indicted by the ICTY for similar crimes in Bosnia and Croatia. As Ivana Nizich, a former member of the ICTY's Office of the Prosecutor observes, "the conduct of the Yugoslav Army, the Serbian Interior Ministry, and the leadership of Slobodan Milosevic indicate that they paid little, if any attention, to the Tribunal before or during their military campaign in Kosovo."[60] David Tolbert, a senior legal adviser to the ICTY from 1996 to 2001, concurs, noting that in Kosovo "the tribunal's work did not have a significant deterrent impact on the alleged new crimes."[61] This does not mean the risk of prosecution had no impact; certainly there is evidence that ethnic cleansers in Kosovo took some pains to hide their identities and conceal evidence of their crimes.[62] But the impact was modest, at best.

3 RATIONAL OR IRRATIONAL CHOICES?

The predicate of all rational choice theories is that the decision-makers are rational actors. But as Aram Schvey points out, "according to some critics, the argument that persons commit crimes so long as the expected value of doing so exceeds the cost of punishment is 'totally incorrect, hopelessly naïve, dangerously misleading, and based on complete and utter ignorance of what violent people are actually like.' In other words, criminals do not necessarily act rationally. This is not to say deterrence is impossible because all criminals are irrational; rather, war criminals may not be motivated by a logical decision calculus."[63] Studies of crime at the national level suggest that potential offenders "often are risk-seekers rather than risk avoiders"; they "are people who are less inclined to think at all about the consequences of their conduct or to guide their conduct accordingly."[64] Many may be characterized by impulsive behaviour and minimal self-control.[65]

Propensities to engage in criminal behaviour may be exacerbated by "contextual effects." When crimes are committed by groups (as is often the case in the war crimes context), "an 'arousal effect' leads to sprees and reduced sensitivity to risk," and may also lead to "an increase in esteem in which the group holds the member who boldly breaks the law."[66] Commission of crimes as part of a group leads group members to "badly [underestimate] the risk of being caught."[67] Further, "the individual 'who is lost in a crowd' perceives a loss of accountability for his individual actions... and thus engages in many more anti-social acts."[68] Combined, these factors create a picture that does not fit "the image of a person who is affected by complex rational deterrence considerations."[69]

Moreover, members of groups experience significant social pressure to conform to group norms. As noted earlier, participants on all sides in the conflict in Bosnia felt they were acting to defend their families and their communities. Members of military or paramilitary groups were in addition often operating under orders. While not a defence to war-crimes charges, orders from superiors may have profound effects on an individual's decision-making process. As social psychologist Stanley Milgram has observed, "an act carried out under command is, psychologically, of a profoundly different character than action that is spontaneous. The person who, with inner conviction, loathes stealing, killing, and assault may find himself performing these acts with relative ease when commanded by authority."[70] Milgram explained this unfortunate response to authority as the result of "the fact that a person comes to view himself as the instrument for carrying out another person's wishes, and he therefore no longer regards himself as responsible for his actions."[71]

The natural human tendency to obey authority is compounded by military training, propaganda vilifying members of the opposite community, a belief in the justice of one's cause, and the threat of penalties (including execution) for failure to comply with orders.[72]

Under the circumstances, how much rational cost-benefit considerations dominate the decision-making of low-level offenders is at least an open question. In theory, such considerations should play a much greater role in the decisions of political and military leaders, who are presumably less susceptible to group influence.[73] But as already noted, leaders have more to gain from ethnic cleansing and related acts, and in some prominent cases have not behaved particularly rationally themselves.[74]

C. *The Cumulative-Effect Problem*

As Robinson and Darley point out, "tripping over any" of the hurdles to deterrence noted above "is fatal to a deterrent effect."[75] If actors do not know the applicable law or see the conduct at issue as wrongful, or if they do not see the risks of prosecution as sufficient to outweigh the benefits of the conduct, or if they fail to assess the costs and benefits rationally, deterrence will fail. In light of all of the above, it is hard to see the ICC as having a significant deterrent effect in most cases.

III. MORAL EDUCATION

The overall goal of Court supporters is to reshape attitudes concerning what is and is not tolerable behaviour, to "inculcate the norms of international humanitarian law so thoroughly that the credible threat of external punishment is no longer necessary to prevent offences."[76] Payam Akhavan, a former ICTY legal adviser, suggests the process by which this moral education might occur:

> from the criminal justice system emanates a flow of moral propaganda such that punishment of the individual offender is transformed into a means of expressing social disapproval. In addition to the fear and conscious moral influence of punishment, it is also possible to create "unconscious inhibitions against crime, and perhaps to establish a condition of habitual lawfulness" such that "illegal actions will not present

themselves consciously as real alternatives to conformity, even in situations where the potential criminal would run no risk whatsoever of being caught."[77]

This approach to the prevention of criminal conduct makes considerable sense, at least in theory. As Robinson and Darley observe, "law's most powerful mechanism for gaining compliance lies not with the negative force of the deterrent threat but rather with the positive force of the law as an arbiter of proper conduct. Most people obey the law not because they fear punishment but because they see themselves as persons who want to do the right thing."[78] The criminal law's "moral credibility" may "bring the potential offender to see the prohibited conduct as unattractive because it is inconsistent with the norms of family and friends and, even better, with the person's own internalized sense of what is acceptable."[79] Further, "if the criminal law has such moral credibility that it has the force of social norms, then a violation of the criminal law's rules may trigger moral condemnation by those who know of the offender's violation, even if the law enforcement authorities do not, thus greatly increasing the criminal law's reach in preventing crime."[80]

But "the logical prerequisite to moral education is a threshold level of social consensus that the prosecution process itself is legitimate."[81] To date, that consensus has been sadly lacking within the relevant communities with respect to both the ICTY and the ICTR.[82] Polls in the former Yugoslavia indicate substantial hostility to the ICTY, which many view as biased. The problem was particularly acute during the tribunal's first five years, in part because of its failure to prosecute senior figures and in part because of distorted media portrayals of the tribunal's work. As Sandra Coliver notes, at that point "most Croats and Serbs viewed the Tribunal as utterly biased against their communities, and as more than willing to turn a blind eye to atrocities committed by Bosniaks."[83] Conversely, "large parts of the Bosniak community were disappointed by the Tribunal," viewing it "as a cynical gesture to salve the guilty conscience of the West."[84] As the performance of the tribunal improved, and as independent media began to present tribunal-related information with less of the distortions imposed by ethnic media, attitudes towards the tribunal began to improve.[85] But significant numbers continue to question the ICTY's legitimacy. According to an August 2000 survey, "over 60 percent of Croatian citizens believed the ICTY was 'unfair'";[86] similarly, in March 2003, only 12 per cent of Serbs believed the Federal Republic of Yugoslavia should continue to extradite suspects to The Hague.[87]

The ICTR commands very little respect within Rwanda. Some decry the tribunal's almost exclusive focus on Hutu perpetrators; others criticize the slow pace of justice, instances of tribunal mismanagement, and procedural irregularities.[88] The International Crisis Group summarized attitudes towards the ICTR as follows:

> For the majority of Rwandans, the ICTR is a useless institution, an expedient mechanism for the international community to absolve itself of its responsibilities for the genocide and its tolerance of the crimes of the RPF [Rwandan Patriotic Front]. The Rwandan government complains of the squandering of money and resources while 130,000 prisoners fill its jails and its courts have tried more than 4000 suspects; the survivors of the genocide find the tribunal distant and indifferent to their lot, and the victims of the crimes of the RPF denounce it as an instrument of the Kigali regime, seeing the ICTR as a symbol of victor's justice.[89]

The ICC is likely to encounter similar problems. Overcoming perceptions of victor's justice may prove particularly difficult for the ICC in many instances, since it will have to depend on state cooperation to carry out its mandate. Those in power are far more likely to assist the tribunal with the apprehension and prosecution of their political opponents than of their supporters. But one-sided prosecutions, or an inability to secure prosecution of senior political and military leaders, will simply fuel perceptions of bias and illegitimacy.

Perceptions of the ICTY improved only when the tribunal began to apprehend significant numbers of senior indictees. But even those limited legitimacy gains were made possible only by the concerted political and economic pressure of the US and other Western states on governments in the region. It is doubtful that similar pressure will be brought to bear when Western peacekeepers are not already committed in substantial numbers, as they have been for some years in the Balkans. And bringing too much pressure can backfire. The assassination of Zoran Djindjic highlights the difficulties fragile governments may have in attempting to satisfy Western demands for justice.[90]

It does not follow that international criminal prosecutions do not contribute to the inculcation of important moral and social norms. They may well do so over the long term. And the effects of ICC prosecutions in this respect may be strengthened through parallel prosecutions by national courts. Still, the process of moral-education is not as straightforward as it is often described, and the results to date seem, if not negligible, at least hard to measure. Certainly, whatever moral-education effects the ICTY and ICTR may have had to date, both Rwanda and the Balkans remain societies vulnerable to explosive outbreaks of inter-group violence.

IV. NATIONAL RECONCILIATION AND THE RULE OF LAW

ICC supporters frequently suggest that international criminal prosecutions can promote national reconciliation. In theory, such prosecutions can demonstrate that responsibility for the commission of past atrocities rests with individual perpetrators and not entire ethnic communities. Blame can be "decollectivized," individual guilt assessed, and victims' injuries publicly acknowledged. As a result, the way is opened for opposing communities to reconcile and live together peacefully. At a minimum, international criminal prosecutions may help marginalize or incapacitate extremists, paving the way for moderate political leaders to take power.

Unfortunately, recent experience seems to contradict or at least sharply undermine many of these claims about the conciliatory effects of prosecutions. Members of politically polarized ethnic communities are at least as likely to interpret prosecutions in ways that confirm existing biases as they are to see them as neutral confirmations of individual rather than collective guilt. For many, it is easy to ignore verdicts against one's own ethnic group members, or to dismiss them as biased, while seizing upon verdicts against members of other groups as evidence confirming past prejudice against these groups as a whole. Many people in the Balkans, perhaps most, "see tribunal activities through the polarized lenses of their ethnic groups; rather than promoting reconciliation, the trials may actually confirm preexisting biases."[91] The problem is compounded by the fact that most people get their information from ethnic media, which slant coverage to support ethnic agendas.[92]

In this environment, international trials of ethnic group leaders may simply offer a stage for cagey politicians such as Milosevic to paint for their supporters their own version of history. Thus, Milosevic's trial, far from delegitimizing him, may render him "almost more of a hero in Serbia than he was before."[93] With this evidently in mind, Vojislav Seselj, a former Serb deputy prime minister and ultra-nationalist, voluntarily surrendered to the ICTY. Seselj apparently "relish[es] the prospect of an international audience for his denunciations of Western policy in the Balkans," and intends to play to the Serb audience that gave him one-third of the votes in the Federal Republic of Yugoslavia's December 2002 presidential elections.[94] As evidence mounts against these and other champions of ethnic cleansing, public attitudes may shift. But attention to ICTY trials also declines as the trials wear on.[95]

National court prosecutions, which are intended to play a vital role under the ICC's complementarity framework, have more often that not proven inimical to national reconciliation in the Balkans, and perhaps also in Rwanda. As Neil Kritz has observed, in the Balkans national court trials are not "a method of advancing accountability and reconciliation, but rather ... one more means of continuing the conflict."[96] Too often, national courts pursue the ethnic agenda of the dominant community, rendering trials a means of "brandishing guilt upon rival ethnic groups" and "continu[ing] ethnic hostilities."[97] In theory, the ICTY, under its "Rules of the Road" for local prosecutions, is supposed to intervene when national court trials violate international standards. But constrained by limited resources, the tribunal "has declined to intervene even where violations appeared blatant."[98]

Rwanda's national court trials are even more problematic. As noted earlier, those trials focus almost exclusively on accused Hutu, and are replete with due process problems. Indeed, the Rwandan government has admitted that "judicial institutions in Rwanda have at the best of times been ineffective, run by poorly paid and ill trained personnel. At worst, these institutions have been partisan and corrupt, staffed with many political appointees eager to please the powers that be, the highest bidder, or both."[99] As a result, and despite substantial improvements in recent years, national court trials seem more likely to inflame inter-group hostility than to eliminate it.

The capacity of international tribunals to contribute to national reconciliation is further impaired when the tribunals are remote from the affected populations. Both the ICTY and the ICTR have suffered substantially from their isolation in The Hague and Arusha, respectively. As the International Crisis Group has observed regarding the ICTY:

> Another serious shortcoming of the ICTY is its location in The Netherlands, far from the areas where the crimes took place. The only contact the average Bosnian has with the proceedings of the court are short daily television news stories, which show video footage of the accused wearing headphones, sitting in front of a panel of robed judges in a foreign court setting. As a result, the citizens of Bosnia are almost completely out of touch with the court's day-to-day proceedings. This lack of understanding prevents Bosnians – Serbs, Croats and Bosniaks alike – from hearing the evidence presented in the court.[100]

The same is true for the ICTR, except that "television is extremely rare in Rwanda," and even radio broadcasts are "sparse."[101] As a result, for most Rwandans, the ICTR is "invisible," an "inherently foreign" institution that has "forfeited any impact on Rwandan society" and thus "failed to achieve both its social and educational functions."[102]

The ICTY and ICTR have made efforts in recent years to expand their influence through outreach programs. Among other things, court proceedings have been translated into the local languages. But most people in the Balkans still receive relatively little information about the tribunals, and much of that is filtered through partisan media. The ICC, also based in The Hague, will likely encounter even greater obstacles in this regard, given its lack of geographic focus, limited resources, and absence of US support.

Ultimately, expecting international criminal tribunals to contribute significantly to reconciliation by individualizing responsibility for past atrocities may be asking too much in societies as sharply divided as Rwanda and Bosnia. Reconciliation, if it happens, has to be the product of the much larger and extremely difficult process of post-conflict reconstruction. Criminal trials are part of that process, but they may not play as much of a role as many advocates believe. While Western governments have invested in nation-building efforts in recent years in the Balkans and elsewhere, there is a large gulf between creating the forms and institutions of liberal, Western societies, which Western intervenors know how to do, and actually reshaping the political cultures of those societies in ways that make genuine reconciliation possible. The latter remains a much more elusive goal. Thus, despite some successes, politics in both Bosnia and Rwanda remain polarized along ethnic lines.

But one related area in which the existing tribunals have had a significant positive impact is the marginalization, and in some cases incapacitation,[103] of certain political leaders and political philosophies. In Bosnia, tribunal indictments and related arrests have served to remove or at least sideline some of the extreme nationalist political figures who have contributed to war and ethnic division and would otherwise continue to impede political and legal reform. Even some political leaders involved in ethnic cleansing, but not actually indicted, may have been induced to moderate their policies, "at least in part due to the hope that their 'born again' embrace of a unified Bosnia will spare them from indictment."[104] Similarly, the International Crisis Group contends that the ICTR "has discredited the Hutu leaders who were in power in Rwanda during the 1994 genocide," and has thus "made a decisive contribution to the task of neutralizing Hutu extremism in the political arena and the radical ideology of 'Hutu power' that it propagated."[105] This assessment perhaps overstates the case, given the tribunal's relatively limited reach in most of Rwanda and the power wielded by former genocidaires who have reorganized in the neighbouring Democratic Republic of Congo. In any event, the RPF's military triumph would seem to be the principal factor in the neutralization of Hutu extremism in Rwanda. Still, it seems clear that war crimes prosecutions can at least assist in the political reconstruction of a divided state, even if by themselves they do not have a transformative impact.

V. WHO'S AFRAID OF THE ICC?

Given all the impediments to effective ICC operations, one might well ask why ICC critics worry about this new institution. The answers, of course, vary. Different states have different reasons. But, ironically, on one issue supporters and critics agree: the International Criminal Court can influence national politics. For supporters, that influence will restrain politicians and other actors from adopting policies likely to result in covered crimes. For critics, that influence will unduly interfere with national decision-making, and sometimes impede international peacekeeping and conflict resolution efforts. Both sides may be right, though to a lesser extent than either side is prepared to acknowledge.

Many states have at least some reason to be nervous about the ICC. For states that are engaged in armed conflicts, especially internal armed conflicts (or that anticipate such conflicts in the future), ICC prosecutions might prove embarrassing, even if insufficient to deter atrocities or substantially alter government policies. Governments with generally execrable human rights records, including many Asian and Arab states, fear that the ICC will be used as a vehicle of Western interests, and that their officials might some day be the subject of an ICC investigation or prosecution. China has long been resistant to external supervision of its human rights record, and has reason to resist the dilution of its power as a UN Security Council member. India and Pakistan have reason to fear the Court's exercise of jurisdiction in their mutual conflict.

But the marquee opponent of the ICC is the US. Critics inside and outside the US government have offered a host of reasons for opposing the Court. I do not deal here with US constitutional law concerns, except to say that while these concerns are not frivolous, the US regularly extradites US nationals to stand trial in foreign courts and should be able to do so to a duly constituted international court.[106] Nor do I deal here with international legal objections raised in connection with certain provisions of the Court's statute or the process by which it was drafted. Instead, I focus below on the political arguments made against the ICC: specifically, that it will be an unaccountable and politicized institution and an impediment to US national security decision-making.

A. Accountability and the Risk of Politicized Prosecutions

Accountability concerns are often summarized in the complaint that the Court will engage in politically motivated prosecutions of US nationals. But the issue is larger, and turns on whether the Court's legitimacy requires supervision by a democratically accountable legislative body, and if so, which body that should be. John Bolton, now Under Secretary of State for Arms Control and International Security, puts the argument this way:

> this Statute of Rome creates ... an enormous, potentially enormous, source of executive power: the prosecutor, just kind of out there in the international environment. Beyond control. Certainly beyond control of the US and not part of any ordered structure of accountability ... The argument

that the prosecutor really is "supervised" because he is "supervised" by the Court, which Europeans find very congenial, is something that we have rejected in this country. We've repeatedly rejected the idea that prosecutorial and judicial authority should be combined. Moreover, the idea that the parties signatory to the Statute of Rome, however many it turns out to be, can really supervise the Court is a fantasy. When you are supervised by over 120 or 140 or 160 signatories, whatever it turns out to be, you're not supervised by anybody. The net-net of this is that there really isn't any democratic accountability and no constitutional structures, as we understand those structures. In other words, there's basically no political control. This is something that the proponents of the Court welcome. They say, "This is just great ... the Court will be independent. The prosecutor will be independent." Well, indeed. In this country we have had painful, I mean bitterly painful, experience with the institution of an independent counsel. ... The risk here is that this independent counsel, not subject to any legitimate political accountability in fact, will be politicized and that it will go after, and it will be presented with, cases based principally on political grounds.[107]

Bolton's concerns, which were reflected in US opposition to a *proprio motu* prosecutor (i.e., a prosecutor who can initiate prosecutions on his or her own authority) during the Rome negotiations, should not be dismissed too readily. For Court supporters, an independent prosecutor is essential to overcoming the barriers to prosecution posed by national politics, which have long operated to shield perpetrators of covered crimes. In the US, however, the exercise of prosecutorial authority is seen as legitimate only when it is subject to the overall control of democratically accountable actors in the executive and legislative branches. Bolton's point is that the prosecutor (and to a lesser extent the Court itself) will not be subject to the political checks and balances that keep politicized prosecutions in check in effective national legal systems.

Proponents of the Court point to the numerous safeguards against groundless prosecutions included in the ICC Statute (many at the insistence of the US), and claim that the Court and prosecutor are accountable to the Assembly of States Parties as much or more than courts and prosecutors in national legal systems are accountable to the larger body politic. Whether the Assembly of States Parties will in fact exercise adequate supervision over the Court remains to be seen. Certainly there is reason to doubt that a diverse group of ninety-nine states (with more to come) can actually exercise meaningful supervision in any but the most general sense. Nonetheless, experience with the existing war crimes tribunals suggests that there is very little risk that the Court would permit the prosecutor to turn into a global Ken Starr. The eighteen judges already elected are competent, professional, and unlikely to tolerate overtly politicized prosecutions. And as things stand, states that share US values or can be counted among US allies hold the balance of power in the Assembly of States Parties, with control over the selection, retention, and discipline of the prosecutor. Thus, as a practical matter, the Court and its prosecutor are likely to act reasonably and professionally.

As a general matter, however, it is simply harder for many in the US to place confidence in an independent international institution operating outside of the direct control of an interested body politic than it is for Europeans (who deal with similar institutions within the EU on a daily basis) and others. As Lt Col William Lietzau notes, "Americans, for good reason, are not culturally disposed toward such 'trust' of an institution. Founders of the US established a carefully structured separation of powers that is not as evident in other democratic governments."[108]

More important, the US has greater national interest grounds for fearing politicized prosecutions than other liberal, Western governments. The US military operates abroad in far greater numbers and in more challenging situations than the military of any other country. Resentment at US power is widespread and growing. Thus, as Eric Schwartz observes, US critics of the Court might well ask, "why wouldn't US adversaries seek to use the Court to level the playing field – that is, strike out against the American government through judicial proceedings when other avenues of attack were unavailable?"[109] Not surprisingly, the US attracted the lion's share (over 100) of the 600 complaints filed with the Court as of October 2003,[110] though the Prosecutor's Office had little trouble dismissing those complaints on jurisdictional grounds.

Whether or not any of the complaints lodged against the US have any merit, the US has reason to fear that a prosecutor seeking balance in the work of the Court might choose on occasion to investigate or prosecute a US service member. The ICTY's preliminary investigation of NATO bombing practices during the Kosovo conflict is a case in point. Responding to calls for an investigation from reputable human rights organizations, including the UN's High

Commissioner on Human Rights, Amnesty International, and Human Rights Watch, the ICTY formed a committee to examine NATO's conduct. The Committee eventually concluded that "in all cases, either the law is not sufficiently clear or investigations are unlikely to result in the acquisition of sufficient evidence to substantiate charges against high level accused or against lower accused for particularly heinous offenses."[111] This outcome did not reassure Court critics in the US. To the contrary, the fact that an international tribunal would seriously consider bringing charges against US service personnel carrying out their orders in an intervention aimed at protecting human rights, and in a context in which the tribunal's resources might better be devoted to pursuing the ethnic cleansers whose acts triggered NATO intervention in the first place, suggested that a different prosecutor might well reach a different conclusion in a different case. Critics of the Court in the US note that there are many areas in which the US takes an aggressive interpretation of what international humanitarian law allows, and thus many instances in which US military decisions could be challenged. They fear that a prosecutor might be induced by states hostile to the US to bring such cases.

The chances of this actually happening seem slight. The ICC will have its hands full with instances of gross human rights abuses, and it would be folly to enrage the US by prosecuting a case involving differences in military doctrine on which reasonable people disagree. But such a case is by no means inconceivable, particularly in the context of a military action as internationally unpopular as the recent US war with Iraq.

B. The Court and National Security Decision-Making

For the US, the underlying concern is not that the Court will prosecute the lone service member who shoots up a village or otherwise runs amok, contrary to his or her orders. The US itself would presumably prosecute such a soldier. Rather, the risk is that the Court will pursue cases arising from the implementation of military doctrine. A conviction in such a case would amount to a conclusion by an international tribunal that US policy in that case was not simply illegal but criminal.

Complementarity will not protect the US in such cases. The US will not investigate (much less prosecute) a controversial targeting decision or a particular military action that is later questioned on proportionality grounds, if the decision or action had already been approved at the highest levels. And herein lies the rub: the US fears that the Court will serve as a vehicle to constrain the exercise of US military power. As Bolton puts it, "the real target of the proponents of this court ultimately is the President of the US and his top decision-makers. The proponents are trying to create international structures that inhibit the use, especially, of American force internationally."[112]

This concern (though Bolton overstates it) is reflected in a compromise proposal the US floated during the final weeks of the Rome negotiations. The US proposed that conduct which the state involved is prepared to acknowledge as official action should be excluded from the court's jurisdiction. This proposal was unsuccessful, but it reflects the philosophy that has animated US positions on the ICC since the US first began supporting an international criminal court in 1995. The US views the ICC as an institution that should exercise authority over individuals, but not states. To the extent that the ICC exercises authority over states, even indirectly by means of prosecutions of a state's nationals, the ICC in the US view usurps authority better left to political institutions such as the UN Security Council.

Many Court supporters, of course, wanted very much to break "the Security Council's monopoly" and to shift power from the Council to the ICC.[113] They recognized that relying on the UN Security Council to initiate prosecutions would jeopardize the independence of the Court and permit the permanent members of the council to shelter themselves and their allies from any unwanted exercise of the Court's jurisdiction. The US viewed this effort to shift power away from the UN Security Council as contrary to its interests and resisted; so, too, did other permanent members, though the United Kingdom and France were ultimately swayed by the pull of European unity.

The US points out that the shift may interfere with its national security decision-making. Presumably, the US will still use force when its perceived national interest requires it, even in situations that might trigger the exercise of the Court's jurisdiction. So, in that sense, US concerns seem overblown. But the risk of prosecution may influence US decisions in subtle ways. The US might, for example, prefer to base troops in states that are not parties to the ICC's statute.

More importantly, the US may seize upon the threat of ICC prosecution as an excuse to cut back on peacekeeping and humanitarian missions of the sort that ICC advocates might be expected to support. In fulfillment of its own prophecy on this point, the US has already threatened to veto future UN peacekeeping operations if peacekeepers are not given immunity from the Court. The US has also cut off military aid to a number of countries that have refused to enter into bilateral immunity agreements. While the use of the veto and US foreign aid in this fashion represents an extraordinary triumph of ideology over interest, the US seems prepared to accept the consequences.

In addition, as the US pointed out in Rome, the transfer of coercive authority to the Court and prosecutor may in some instances preclude the use of amnesty and exile as devices to secure the termination of hostilities or the departure of a rights-abusing dictator. Arguments on this issue have a certain chicken-and-egg quality. Court supporters suggest that political leaders can be dissuaded in the first instance from committing atrocities (thus eliminating the need for amnesties and exiles) if they know from the outset they will face prosecution. More realistically, supporters point out that most dictators leave power only when forced out, so that amnesties and exile will rarely prove acceptable solutions in any event. And they contend that it is better to trust in the discretion of a prosecutor than to trust in the discretion of a political body like the UN Security Council. In some cases, the critics may be right that an insistence on prosecutions may impede a negotiated resolution to a civil war or other conflict. After being indicted by the Special Court for Sierra Leone, Charles Taylor, for example, might well have elected to continue the fighting in Liberia if Nigeria had not offered him a safe haven. But such cases are likely to be rare, and must be balanced against the advantages of a Court that is not hamstrung by UN Security Council politics.

In the end, the critical question for the US is whether the relatively modest but potentially real costs to the US of an ICC that can act against US wishes outweigh the benefits to be derived from a standing international criminal court. As overstated as those benefits often are, the Court can in at least some circumstances assist actors (including the US) in efforts to marginalize extremist politicians and propagate minimum international standards of behaviour. That balance seems to favour the ICC, especially when US opposition simply fuels growing international perceptions of US exceptionalism; at a minimum, it favours the Clinton "good neighbour" policy over the Bush administration's open hostility.

CONCLUSION

The tendency of advocates and critics to exaggerate the pros and cons of the ICC may be attributable to a number of factors. Exaggeration may assist each side in efforts to mobilize support for or opposition to the Court. Moreover, vocal Court supporters tend to be international lawyers or human rights activists, who may have a disciplinary bias in favour of such institutions. Conversely, many of the most vocal critics in the US are politicians or government officials such as John Bolton, appealing to a conservative political base.

For both advocates and critics, the debate over the ICC is an exemplar of a larger debate concerning the proper role of international law and institutions in international affairs. As Robert Kagan has suggested, the US, as the sole remaining superpower, tends to view the world in Hobbesian terms, as a place where "international laws and rules are unreliable and where true security and the defence and promotion of a liberal order still depend on the possession and use of military might."[114] As a result, Americans are "less inclined to act through international institutions such as the United Nations, less inclined to work cooperatively with other nations to pursue common goals, more sceptical about international law, and more willing to operate outside its strictures when they deem it necessary, or even merely useful."[115] Conversely, Europeans (the core of the like-minded group supporting a strong ICC), are "turning away from power"; they are therefore "quicker to appeal to international law, international conventions, and international opinion to adjudicate disputes."[116] As Kagan admits, this portrait is a caricature, but it captures an important element of the gulf separating the US from its friends and allies on the ICC, and more broadly, the gulf separating ICC critics and supporters.

But there are costs to exaggerating the ICC. Inflated expectations may lead to rapid (and unfair) disappointment when the Court cannot deliver as advertised. More importantly, overstated rhetoric concerning the benefits of ICC prosecutions may distract us from alternative courses of action that in particular cases may yield far greater benefits.[117] The UN established the ICTY in part in order to alleviate pressure for more forceful action during the breakup of Yugoslavia; the ICTR was set up in part to alleviate guilt for failing to stop the genocide in Rwanda. The ICC may serve a similar purpose in future cases. After all, "if existing means of prosecution can adequately incapacitate offenders, why risk military intervention?"[118]

More broadly, "inflated expectations for prosecution provide an incremental excuse for international actors to cling to a limited range of familiar responses to international offences. Given the difficulty of mobilizing and coordinating political will to achieve international goals beyond narrow national self-interest, even this minor inertial effect may disproportionately deter support for supplemental mechanisms of accountability that better meet the objectives of prosecution."[119] The Rwandan government notes with some bitterness that if it had received the level of financial and political support showered on the ICTR, it could have substantially improved a national judicial system that tries hundreds of genocide suspects for every one tried by the ICTR, but one that does so subject to such serious resource constraints that due process violations are frequent. It is easier for governments to shirk the hard problem of improving national court trials if international attention is focused on a single court in The Hague. Similarly, it will be much harder to pursue promising experiments with mixed tribunals, such as the Special Court in Sierra Leone, if expectations for the ICC are unrealistically high.

The flip side is that overstatements about the threat the ICC poses may not only preclude US support for the ICC but lead to actions that could seriously jeopardize international peace and security, such as the US decision to veto peacekeeping operations absent a grant of immunity to peacekeepers from non-party states. A more realistic appraisal might lead the US to accept the Court, if not to join it.

NOTES

♣ The author would like to thank Jenia Iontcheva, Steven Rickard, Eric Schwartz, Robert Summers, Don Wallace, and the participants in workshops at the University of California at Irvine, the University of Western Ontario, and El Instituto Tecnológico Autónomo de México (ITAM) for helpful comments on an earlier draft of this chapter.

1 Kenneth Starr, the special prosecutor for the Whitewater investigation, uncovered President Clinton's affair with Monica Lewinsky, which ultimately led to the president's impeachment. A Republican, Starr was often criticized as being too partisan. See Howard Fineman and Daniel Klaidman, "The Starr Chamber," *Newsweek*, 30 November 1998.

2 See James B. Scott, *The Status of the International Court of Justice* (New York: Oxford UP, American Branch, 1916), 2.

3 See Hersh Lauterpacht, *The Development of International Law by the International* Court (London: Stevens, 1958), 4.

4 Thomas M. Franck and Jerome M. Lehrman, "Messianism and Chauvinism in America's Commitment to Peace through Law," in *The International Court of Justice at a Crossroads*, ed. Lori F. Damrosch, 3–18 (Dobbs Ferry, NY: Transnational Pub., 1987), 5.

5 Ibid.

6 Ibid., 7.

7 *Rome Statute of the International Criminal Court*, 17 July 1998, UN Doc. A/CONF. 183/9, 2187 UNTS 90, reprinted in *International Legal Materials* 37, no. 5 (1998): 1002, art. 5 [hereinafter ICC Statute]. The ICC Statute contemplates that the Court will also exercise jurisdiction over the crime of aggression once the Assembly of States Parties agrees on a definition. Other crimes may be added to the Court's jurisdiction in the future.

8 Reed Brody, "Book Review," *American Journal of International Law* 96, no. 1 (2002): 268–73.

9 Mauro Politi, "The Rome Statute of the ICC: Rays of Light and Some Shadows," in *The Rome Statute of the International Criminal Court: A Challenge to Impunity*, ed. Mauro Politi and Giuseppe Nesi, 7–16 (Aldershot: Ashgate, 2001), 8.

10 Ibid. Many of the jurisdictional, procedural, and financial weaknesses discussed in this section of the chapter may be attributed in significant part to positions taken by the US in the Rome negotiations. At the same time, some of the strengths of the Court's statute, such as its inclusion of crimes committed in internal conflicts, may also be attributed in significant part to US lobbying. My purpose here is not to assess credit or blame for particular provisions of the Court's statute, but rather to assess how effective the Court is likely to be.

11 As the head of India's delegation to the ICC negotiations observed when explaining India's objections to the ICC Statute, "we are now about to adopt a Statute to which the Governments who represent two-thirds of humanity would not be a party. This is an unusual measure of success": *Explanation of Vote by Mr Dilip Lahiri*, 17 July 1998, on-line: United Nations <http://www.un.org/icc/speeches/717ind.htm>.

12 Elizabeth Wilmhurst, "The International Criminal Court: The Role of the Security Council," in Politi and Nesi, *supra* n9, 39–42, 40.

13 Leila Nadya Sadat and S. Richard Carden, "The New International Criminal Court: An Uneasy Revolution," *Georgetown Law Journal* 88, no. 3 (2000): 381–474, 398.

14 Ibid., 417.
15 Hans Peter Kaul, "The International Criminal Court: Jurisdiction, Trigger Mechanism and Relationship to National Court Jurisdictions," in Politi and Nesi, *supra* n9, 59–64, 62.
16 Sadat and Carden, *supra* n13, 415.
17 Ibid. There are some limited exceptions, most notably in article 57 of the Court's statute, which permits the Pre-Trial Chamber to authorize the prosecutor "to take specific investigative steps within the territory of a State Party without having secured the cooperation of that State," if the judicial system in that state has collapsed. See ICC Statute, *supra* n7, art. 57(3)(d).
18 Ibid., 416–17.
19 *The ICTY at a Glance*, on-line: United Nations <http://www.un.org/icty/glance/index.htm>.
20 *About the Tribunal*, on-line: International Criminal Tribunal for Rwanda <http://www.ictr.org/about.htm>.
21 G.A. Res. 58/298, UN GAOR, 58th Sess., UN Doc. A/RES/58/298 (2004).
22 The American Service Members Protection Act of 2002 (ASPA), Supplemental Appropriations Act for Further Recovery From and Response to Terrorist Attacks on the United States, Pub. L. No. 107-206, §§ 2001–2015, 116 Stat. 820 (2002), prohibits any state or federal agency, including any court, from providing support to the ICC. The statute contains specific prohibitions on the transmittal of letters rogatory, the extradition of persons within the US to the ICC, and the conduct of ICC investigations on territory subject to US jurisdiction. The act contains broad presidential waiver authority, however, and in any event is focused primarily on frustrating ICC efforts to prosecute US nationals. Moreover, section 2015 appears to give back much of what the rest of the act takes away with respect to the US capacity to assist the ICC with the prosecution of foreign nationals. It reads: "Nothing in this title shall prohibit the United States from rendering assistance to international efforts to bring to justice Saddam Hussein, Slobodan Milosevic, Osama bin Laden, other members of Al Qaeda, leaders of Islamic Jihad, and other foreign nationals accused of genocide, war crimes, or crimes against humanity."
23 See Draft Programme Budget for 2005, ICC-ASP/3/2, 26 July 2004. After considerable discussion, the Preparatory Commission settled on a system of funding based on an adaptation from the UN scale of assessments. States parties ordinarily will pay the Court's expenses, although article 115(b) of the Court's statute anticipates that the

General Assembly might approve the use of UN funds to pay for expenses incurred in connection with cases referred by the Security Council.

24 See Eric P. Schwartz, "The United States and the International Criminal Court: The Case for Dexterous Multilateralism," *Chicago Journal of International Law* 4, no. 1 (2003): 223–36.

25 The US sent a letter to the UN stating: "This is to inform you, in connection with the Rome Statute of the International Criminal Court adopted on 17 July 1998, that the United States does not intend to become a party to the treaty. Accordingly, the US has no legal obligations arising from its signature on 31 December 2000. The US requests that its intention not to become a party, as expressed in this letter, be reflected in the depositary's status lists relating to this treaty." (Israel sent a similar letter on 28 August 2002).

26 SC Res. 1422 (2002). On 12 June 2003, the UN Security Council renewed Resolution 1422 by a vote of 12–3, with France, Germany, and Syria abstaining. See SC Res. 1487 (2003). The United States failed to obtain another renewal of the resolution in May 2004 when concerns over abuses at Abu Ghraib prison were growing.

27 The US draft article 98 agreement presented to other governments may be found on-line: <http://www.iccnow.org/documents/otherissues/impunityart98/USArticle98Agreement1Aug02.pdf>.

28 The US argues that the agreements are permitted under article 98(2) of the ICC Statute, which provides: "The Court may not proceed with a request for surrender which would require the requested State to act inconsistently with its obligations under international agreements pursuant to which the consent of a sending State is required to surrender a person of that State to the Court, unless the Court can first obtain the cooperation of the sending State for the giving of consent for the surrender." Critics contend that article 98 was designed to deal with existing Status of Forces Agreements (SOFAS), and that the US bilateral agreements are inconsistent with the object and purpose of the ICC treaty. See, for example, International Federation of Human Rights, *International Criminal Court: No to American Exceptionalism* (December 2002), available at <http://www.iccnow.org/documents/otherissues/impunityart98/FIDHPaperUSandICC.pdf>.

29 See Schwartz, *supra* n24.

30 The US renounced the ICJ's compulsory jurisdiction in 1985, following an adverse decision in *Nicaragua* v. *United States*, [1984] ICJ Reports 392. There has been no serious consideration since then of reversing that renunciation.

31 This section is based in part on David Wippman, "Atrocities, Deterrence, and the Limits of International Justice," *Fordham International Law Journal* 23, no. 2 (1999): 473–88.

32 Payam Akhavan, "Justice in the Hague, Peace in the Former Yugoslavia?" *Human Rights Quarterly* 20, no. 4 (1998): 737–816, 741.

33 Brody, *supra* n8, 272.

34 See Benjamin Ferencz, "International Criminal Courts: The Legacy of Nuremberg," *Pace International Law Review* 10, Summer (1998): 203, 210; Theodor Meron, "From Nuremberg to the Hague," *Military Law Review* 149, (summer 1995): 107–12, 110.

35 Meron, ibid., 110. Payam Akhavan, legal advisor to the Office of the Prosecutor of the ICTY, similarly notes that "the evidence of the tribunal's contribution to the deterrence of ongoing humanitarian law violations remains equivocal." Akhavan, *supra* n32, 744.

36 Akhavan, *supra* n32, 750–1.

37 Paul H. Robinson and John M. Darley, *Criminal Law as an Instrument of Behavioral Control: Should Deterrence Have a Role in the Formulation of Criminal Law Rules?* (draft article on file with author, 2002) 46. Portions of this article have been published in the Georgetown University and Oxford University law journals.

38 Ibid., 5.

39 Ibid., 36.

40 Developments in the Law: International Criminal Law II, "The Promises of International Prosecution," *Harvard Law Review* 114, no. 7 (2001): 1957–82, 1964.

41 ICRC Country Report on Bosnia-Herzegovina, on-line: International Committee of the Red Cross <http://www.icrc.org/web/englsiteengo.nsf/htmlall/onwar_reports/ $file/bosnia.pdf>.

42 Ibid., 13.

43 Ibid., 14.

44 See, for example, Developments in the Law, *supra* n40, 1963–4: "the logic of general deterrence presumes a rational calculation that the likelihood and severity of punishment will outweigh any benefits."

45 The ICTY at a Glance, *supra* n19.

46 About the Tribunal, *supra* n20.

47 In 2000, Jacques Klein, at that time UN coordinator for Bosnia, estimated that 20,000 war criminals remained at large in the former Yugoslavia. See Aram Schvey, "Striving for Accountability in the Former Yugoslavia," in *Accountability for Atrocities: National and International Responses*, ed. Jane Stromseth (Ardsley, NY: Transnational Publishers, 2003), 39, 46n30.

48 David Tolbert, "The International Criminal Tribunal for the Former Yugoslavia: Unforeseen Successes and Foreseeable Shortcomings," *Fletcher Forum World Affairs* 26, no. 2 (2002): 7–19, 12.

49 Statement of Joseph Mutaboba to the UN General Assembly, 9 November 1999. Efforts to try large numbers almost inevitably encounter serious due process concerns. By 2001, the number of completed trials exceeded 5,000, but over 100,000 accused remained in custody, most in appalling conditions. And human rights groups "regularly issue scathing reports condemning Rwanda's treatment of prisoners and the Rwandan trial process." See Jason Strain and Elizabeth Keyes, "Accountability in the Aftermath of Rwanda's Genocide," in Stromseth, *supra* n47, 87, 114. Recognizing that its judicial system could not handle the large numbers of accused, Rwanda recently instituted a system of local courts based on a traditional dispute-resolution model known as *gacaca*, a system replete with its own due process problems (ibid.).

50 See ibid. Even when prosecutions increase significantly in number, they may not foster the desired deterrent effect. In Rwanda, charges of "victor's justice" abound. The governing Rwandan Patriotic Front, while trying thousands of Hutu, has resisted trying its own officials, some of whom have been accused of war crimes during the 1994 civil war or during the ongoing conflict in the neighbouring Democratic Republic of Congo (DRC). In this context, prosecutions may do more to fuel inter-ethnic tensions and spur future atrocities than to deter them. Indeed, deterrence is hard to find in the Rwandan context. Many of those accused of participating in the 1994 genocide continue to engage in atrocities in the DRC, and the Rwandan government is frequently accused of committing its own crimes there.

51 Offenders also "tend to overestimate their own ability to avoid the mistakes that have led to others like them being caught," which further undermines any deterrent effect criminal prosecutions might have. See Robinson and Darley, *supra* n37, 37.

52 Phillip Gourevitch, *We Wish to Inform You That Tomorrow We Will be Killed with Our Families* (New York: Farrar, Straus, and Giroux, 1998), 255, quoted in Strain and Keyes, *supra* n49.

53 Robinson and Darley, *supra* n37, 48–9 (describing experiments showing individuals to be indifferent between receiving $100 immediately or $157 in a year, even though "we know of no banks that are offering 57% interest per year").

54 Ibid., 48.

55 ICRC Report, *supra* n41, 14.

56 Ibid.
57 Ibid., 15.
58 Ibid., 18.
59 Ivana Nizich, "International Tribunals and their Inability to Provide Adequate Justice: Lessons Learned from the Yugoslav Tribunal," *ILSA Journal of International and Comparative Law* 7, no. 2 (2001): 353–68, 357–8.
60 Ibid., 360.
61 Tolbert, *supra* n48, 11.
62 See Wippman, *supra* n31, 480. It's also true that deterrence is hard to measure. A commander ordered to commit a war crime might, for example, simply pretend never to have received the order.
63 Schvey, *supra* n47, 71, quoting James Gilligan, *Violence: Our Deadly Epidemic and its Causes* (New York: G.P. Putnam, 1996), 94–5.
64 Robinson and Darley, *supra* n37, 28.
65 Ibid., 30.
66 Ibid.
67 Ibid., 31.
68 Ibid.
69 Ibid., 32.
70 Stanley Milgram, *Obedience to Authority* (New York: Harper and Row, 1969), xi.
71 Ibid., xii.
72 Ibid., 181–2.
73 See Robinson and Darley, *supra* n37, 64: "we can expect greater deterrent possibilities when dealing with more rational target audiences, such as white collar offenders."
74 Schvey cites the example of Hitler, who "diverted precious resources away from the war effort against the Soviets in order to accelerate the pace of the 'Final Solution,' hastening his defeat." Schvey, *supra* n47, 71n185.
75 Robinson and Darley, *supra* n37, 51.
76 Developments in the Law, *supra* n40, 1966.
77 Akhavan, *supra* n32, 746, quoting Johannes Andenaes, *Punishment and Deterrence* (Ann Arbor: Univ. of Michigan Press, 1974), 34–5.
78 Paul H. Robinson and John M. Darley, *Justice, Liability and Blame: Community Views and the Criminal Law* (Boulder, Colo.: Westview Press, 1995), 5–7.
79 Paul H. Robinson, "Why Does the Criminal Law Care What the Lay Person Thinks Is Just? Coercive vs. Normative Crime Control," *Virginia Law Review* 86, no. 8 (2000): 1839–69, 1840.

80 Robinson and Darley, *supra* n37, 81.

81 Developments in the Law, *supra* n40, 1967.

82 Ibid.: "At present, a large proportion of the populations of the former Yugoslavia and Rwanda may not see the tribunals as sufficiently legitimate to heed the moral lessons the tribunals seek to teach."

83 Sandra Coliver, "The Contribution of the International Criminal Tribunal for the Former Yugoslavia to Reconciliation in Bosnia and Herzegovina," in *International Crimes, Peace, and Human Rights: The Role of the International Criminal Court*, ed. Dinah Shelton, 19–31 (Ardsley, NY: Transnational Publishers 2000), 20.

84 Ibid., 21.

85 Ibid., 24–6.

86 Developments in the Law, *supra* n40, 1967.

87 Steven Erlanger, "Murder in Belgrade: Did Serbia's Leader Do the West's Bidding Too Well?" *The New York Times*, 16 March 2003, p. 4, sec.4, final edition.

88 See Strain and Keyes, *supra* n49, 105–6.

89 International Crisis Group, *International Criminal Tribunal for Rwanda: Justice Delayed* (7 June 2001), iii, on-line: International Crisis Group <http://www.crisisweb.org/projects/africa/rwanda/reports/A400442_02102001.pdf >.

90 See Erlanger, *supra* n87.

91 Developments in the Law, *supra* n40, 1971.

92 See Schvey, *supra* n47, 77: "local media tend to distort the information about the ICTY to fit an ethnic agenda."

93 Catherine Utley, "Where Now for International Justice," *BBC News*, 14 March 2002, quoting Alex Boraine, former co-chair of the South Africa Truth and Reconciliation Commission.

94 Daniel Simpson, "New Defendant in Hague to Aim Defense at Serbs of the Future," *The New York Times*, 20 February 2003, p. A6, final edition.

95 Schvey, *supra* n47, 78, noting a sharp drop in media coverage of the Milosevic trial following opening proceedings.

96 Neil J. Kritz, "Coming to Terms with Atrocities: A Review of Accountability Mechanisms for Mass Violations of Human Rights," *Law and Contemporary Problems* 59, no. 4 (1996): 127–52, 143–4.

97 Schvey, *supra* n47, 67. The same problem characterizes Bosnia's truth commissions, which enable victims to tell their stories in a public forum. Unfortunately, "each of the three ethnic groups has created its own 'truth commission,'" and in each commission, "nationalists from the three ethnic communities ... propagate a history that portrays their group

as the one and only victim of the mass abuses, depicting the other two as evil perpetrators and monsters" (ibid.), quoting Jakob Finci, "Revenge in the Making," UNESCO *Courier*, May 2001, on-line: UNESCO < http://www.unesco.org/courier/2001_05/uk/droits2.htm>).

98 Coliver, *supra* n83, 30.

99 Strain and Keyes, *supra* n49, 115, quoting *The Judicial System in Rwanda: A Report on Justice*, on-line: Rwanda Embassy <http://wwww.rwandaemb.org/justice/justice.htm>.

100 International Crisis Group, *War Criminals in Bosnia's Republika Srpska* (2 November 2000), 75, on-line: International Crisis Group <http://www.icg.org//library/documents/report_archive/A400001_02112000.pdf>.

101 International Crisis Group, *supra* n89, 23.

102 Ibid., 24.

103 Incarcerating war criminals not only limits their political activity, it precludes them from committing further crimes while incarcerated. In national legal systems, a small percentage of the population is often responsible for a high percentage of violent crime; if the same holds true in the international context, incarcerating a significant number of offenders might be expected to have a dramatic impact on the incidence of offences. It is doubtful, however, whether experience at the national level can be readily translated to the international level in this context. Atrocities of the sort likely to attract the attention of the ICC typically occur in armed conflicts in which substantial segments of the population, well beyond the criminal fringe, join in the commission of criminal acts. Rwanda, in which thousands of ordinary people helped kill their neighbours in 1994, is the paradigm case.

104 Coliver, *supra* n83, 27.

105 International Crisis Group, *supra* n89, 8.

106 The US Department of Justice apparently shares this view. See "Is a UN International Criminal Court in the National Interest," Hearing Before the SubCommittee on International Operations of the Committee on Foreign Relations, United States Senate, S. Hrg 105-724, 23 July 1998, 46 (Appendix, Answers to Additional Questions Submitted for the Record by the Committee to Ambassador David J. Scheffer).

107 John Bolton, "Toward an International Criminal Court? A Debate," *Emory International Law Review* 14, no. 1 (2000): 159–97, 164–5.

108 William Lietzau, "International Criminal Law after Rome: Concerns from a US Military Perspective," *Law and Contemporary Problems* 64, no. 1 (2001): 119–140, 136–7.

109 Schwartz, *supra* n24, 3.

110 "All Eyes on International Crime Court," *Edmonton Journal*, 12 October 2003.

111 *Final Report to the Prosecutor by the Committee Established to Review the* NATO *Bombing Campaign against the Federal Republic of Yugoslavia*, 8 June 2000, para. 90, reprinted in *International Legal Materials* 39, no. 5 (2000): 1257.

112 Bolton, *supra* n107, 165–6.

113 Philippe Kirsch, the chair of the Committee of the Whole and now president of the Court, notes that "one of the reasons why an ICC was established was to move away ... [from] the monopoly that the Security Council used to have." *Round Table*, in Politi and Nesi, *supra* n9, 293.

114 Robert Kagan, "Power and Weakness," *Policy Review* 113 (2002): 3–28.

115 Ibid.

116 Ibid.

117 See Developments in the Law, *supra* n40, 1975.

118 Ibid., 1976.

119 Ibid.

5

The US, the ICC, and the Demands of Impartiality

ALEX TUCKNESS

The Bush administration has been very vocal in its opposition to the newly created International Criminal Court (ICC).[1] This stance is significant in its own right, for American support would be of tremendous help as the Court tries to establish itself. The US decision is also of interest because it raises deeper moral issues that transcend the specific case. The attraction of the ICC, I suggest, is that it offers the prospect of a more impartial adjudication of cases involving genocide, crimes against humanity, and war crimes.[2] The "victor's justice" alternative that it is meant to replace predictably leads to powerful nations turning a blind eye to their own human rights abuses and to trials of the defeated before judges whose nations have been harmed by the war. One school of thought holds that the US position is simply foolish because a strong ICC is in the self-interest of the US.[3] This is possible, but in this chapter I explore another possibility: that what is really at stake is the extent to which the US is morally required to set aside the pursuit of its own interests when making such decisions. Suppose, for the sake of argument, that it is *not* in the self-interest, narrowly defined, of the US to join the ICC, but that the ICC regime *is* superior to the US alternative if we assess the two options from the perspective of an impartial observer. The real question then becomes to what extent states are morally obligated to take actions that are not in their self-interest, narrowly defined, but that would be better from an impartial perspective. In this chapter, I examine whether the US has an obligation to join the ICC for this reason, and I suggest a general framework for reflecting on when states have an obligation to limit their claims of sovereignty because of the demands of impartiality.

I. THE CONCEPT OF IMPARTIALITY

The ideal of impartiality is a central one in most conceptions of justice. At its simplest, it refers to someone who makes decisions only on the basis of relevant reasons and who does not allow private considerations to bias the weighting of those reasons.[4] Having insufficient evidence of wrongdoing is grounds for an acquittal; knowing the accused as a citizen of my country, a member of my family, a member of my ethnic group, or a personal friend is not. The concepts "relevant reasons" and "private considerations" are admittedly contested, but not so contested as to be unhelpful in the context of the present discussion.[5]

I limit the term "impartiality" in two ways that make its application more straightforward. First, we are talking only about procedural criminal justice, not a complete theory of substantive justice that would cover questions from freedom of speech to the distribution of global resources. Second, we are talking only about impartiality of *interests*, not impartiality of belief. Partiality of interest exists when a person acts differently than she otherwise would, doing so because she or someone with whom she has some affective tie stands to benefit or be harmed as a result of the decision. Most criminal justice systems have provisions to insure that judges recuse themselves from cases in which one of the parties is a friend or family member. Some systems are obviously stricter about this than others, but the norm is quite widely accepted.

The idea of impartiality of belief is much less clear and much more controversial. John Rawls has suggested that we might define substantive principles of justice based on a norm of impartiality, and his work has inspired a number of related theories.[6] These theories of justice ask persons and peoples to set aside their deepest philosophical or religious commitments because, as others do not recognize such commitments, appeal to these is not impartial. According to these theories, impartiality requires that we appeal only to reasons that other reasonable people could accept without them first having to adopt our larger philosophical or religious commitments as the only true ones. Impartiality of belief requires "bracketing" our deepest religious and philosophical commitments in order to reach agreement with persons who hold different commitments, provided they are willing to do the same. It should be clear that there is no need for this more ambitious theory of impartiality in the present case. My argument does not presuppose a particular theory of criminal justice and there is no claim that persons must be "impartial" between, for example, favouring common law approaches and favouring continental approaches to criminal law.

People from both of these traditions, and indeed from legal traditions around the world, can agree that it is good for criminal procedures to be more just. If we can reform legal processes so that the guilty are more often convicted and the innocent more often acquitted, such an accomplishment is, all else being equal, good. People from these various traditions can also agree on certain practices that have proven effective in this regard. One important practice, often overlooked, is to instruct those who make decisions to be impartial and to enforce these instructions by sanctions in cases where it is evident they have not been so. Another recognized practice is to exclude persons from serving as judges (or jury members) if they have reasons for favouring one side that not all persons would share – familial, ethnic, racial, or national ties are the most obvious. But above all, we do not normally let the person who is accused or the person who is accusing stand as judge in his or her own case, since this would violate what is perhaps the least challenged maxim in jurisprudence, "No one should judge his own case." The human tendency to be biased in one's own favour is too familiar to all. A criminal justice regime that more closely follows the above practices will, all else being equal, better secure justice for the persons under its jurisdiction.

We can apply the concept of impartiality of interests to two different types of objects. The first, as we have been doing above, is actual regimes. We can describe some justice regimes, for example, as more impartial than others. But we can also apply the concept of impartiality to the *criteria* we use for judging between regimes. Again we are using impartiality here in the sense of impartiality of interest rather than impartiality of belief. Some versions of the latter would claim that, when evaluating a criminal justice procedure, a state cannot privilege its own norms of criminal justice since this is showing partiality towards itself. It should instead ask what justice norms would be chosen from a completely impartial perspective. The more limited evaluative criterion that is in use here would simply ask, granted a state's conception of what criminal procedures are most likely to lead to just outcomes, which of the possible regimes would best secure justice for *all* persons under the proposed regime's jurisdiction. What is barred is giving greater weight to justice for one's own citizens than justice for the citizens of other states.

Therefore, when I compare one *justice regime* to another and claim that it is more impartial, I mean only that it does a better job of avoiding certain practices that are widely regarded as tending to biased outcomes. Making a person judge in her own case or in the case of a family member are simple examples. When I say that one *decision procedure* is more impartial, I mean only that it makes a greater demand that the agent set aside personal interests and projects so that the good of the many or justice for the many prevails.

II. THE IMPARTIALITY OF THE ICC

The first question to ask is whether the ICC is more impartial than the best procedure the US might propose as an alternative for adjudicating human rights violations and war crimes. The US position might be formulated in various ways. The US might propose as follows: "No citizen should be subjected to war crimes proceedings without the consent of his or her state."[7] There are some approaches to international law that claim internal human rights abuses, war crimes, and other types of moral infractions are the concern of the state where they take place. This is not, however, an accurate depiction of the US position. The US supported international war crimes tribunals in Yugoslavia and Rwanda despite the fact that these primarily involved intra-state violence. The US also supported and participated in war crimes prosecutions in Germany and Japan after World War II.

Although in all of these cases the US worked in conjunction with other countries, the best characterization of the philosophy behind the US actions is unilateralism. The US wants the freedom to decide whether to initiate war crimes proceedings and the freedom to oppose other nations if they unjustly (according to the US view) attempt to try Americans for war crimes. When other countries are willing to join the effort (as the Allies did after World War II) or when international bodies are willing to authorize it (as in Rwanda), the US is more than happy to cooperate. The US will not, however, commit itself to positions that would hamper its ability to pursue justice unilaterally. The US sometimes uses the UN Security Council (where it has a veto) as an indirect way of accomplishing this goal. Stating that prosecutions must be subject to UN Security Council authorization is mainly a way of insuring that America can veto any prosecution with which it disagrees, preserving the real principle, unilateralism.[8]

Exercising the principle of interpretive charity, the American principle is this: "Each state should be free to pursue justice in war crimes prosecutions and trials according to its own understanding."[9] For the American position to be credible as a justificatory principle, it must be capable of statement in this type of general form. The alternative principle "All states should submit to the jurisdiction of the ICC except the US" fails to meet the moral requirement of generality since there is no plausible reason for claiming that different moral obligations apply to the US than to other states. Indeed, when one person or group claims to be unilaterally exempt from the moral requirements that apply to others, the entire process of moral justification is significantly undermined.

"Free to pursue justice" does not mean that each sovereign must prosecute only its own nationals. It is instead like a Lockean state of nature where there are moral rules that bind all people ("no slaughtering innocent civilians," for example) but their enforcement is left to the various states (and perhaps also non-state actors) that make up the international community. If war crimes are committed in the former Yugoslavia, then *any* state would be justified in intervening to help bring the perpetrators to justice. Likewise, German war crimes could in principle be punished by any state, not just those who happened to defeat it in war (although, practically, such states will be in the best position to do so). In a Lockean moral universe, genocide, crimes against humanity, and war crimes are crimes of universal jurisdiction.[10]

The Lockean analogy is helpful for explaining the reasons why we might expect an impartial observer to prefer the ICC regime to the US alternative. The reasoning is similar to the reasoning that leads people to leave Locke's state of nature.[11] The state of nature does have a certain appeal, because in it each agent has the freedom to act on his own interpretation of natural law. Giving a sovereign the right to judge means persons must accept legal judgments with which they sometimes disagree. But the state of nature has its own inconveniences, most notably that it allows men to be judges of their own cases, something that predictably leads to partial judgments and escalating conflict. Moreover, there is no reason to expect that the side that is in the right will prevail in a contest of strength. Although might does not make right, it decides outcomes in the state of nature. Finally, the law of nature is vague and subject to dispute; a government can issue a more precise code that reduces uncertainty and disagreement. In such a state of nature, Locke claims, people will continually find their lives and property at risk and willingly give up the right to execute the law of nature unilaterally in return for the benefits of the rule of law administered by neutral judges. Locke freely acknowledges that there is a risk that such judges will become tyrants, but believes government is worth the risk. The corresponding benefits and risks in the area of war crimes are obvious. By agreeing to an international criminal court, states (partially) give up the right to pursue justice unilaterally, but they gain both a system in which the judges who decide the case will not be from a state that has a direct interest in the conflict, and one in which the standards used are more clearly articulated beforehand.

Attempts to reason about international politics based on the "domestic analogy" have been criticized for a variety of reasons, but one objection against this approach is particularly important here: the disparity of power between states in international relations is different than the power disparity between individuals. Hobbes and Locke both imagine (at least in the first instance) states of nature populated by individuals who are roughly equal in strength. In international relations, the disparities are much greater. This is perhaps why Hobbes and Locke never drew the same conclusions about the international state of nature that they did for the national state of nature. To see the relevance of this, consider the current position of the US. Because of America's great economic and military strength, it is highly unlikely that another country would invade US territory to apprehend a war criminal. It is similarly unlikely that the US would lose a war and have its soldiers subjected to "victor's justice." At most, the US risks isolated bands of soldiers being captured and tried by enemy forces, forces that would be unlikely to submit to the ICC anyway. On the other hand, it is quite possible that the US might defeat another country in war and want to bring some of that country's soldiers to trial for war crimes. It is quite possible that the US will again intervene in less powerful countries rocked by civil war to prosecute human rights atrocities committed there. In other words, the current international system contains sufficient power discrepancies that the costs associated with the state of nature system are borne almost entirely by weaker states. Powerful states can enjoy the luxury of punishing war crimes at their discretion without seriously worrying that other countries will be able to do the same to them.

What this implies is that the US might very well invoke the principle "Each state should be free to pursue justice in war crimes prosecutions and trials according to its own understanding" fully intending that all states abide by that principle. The US would not, however, support this principle if it were, say, Nicaragua. The US is evaluating the principle from its own perspective as a powerful state. It is precisely to prevent the invocation of principles that are attractive only because of power differences that various theorists have insisted on more impartial *decision procedures* for deciding between competing justice regimes. Rawls famously placed parties behind a veil of ignorance in his original position (both for peoples and for persons).[12] He would have peoples propose principles without knowing their size, wealth, population, or military capacity. The original position and veil of ignorance in this case are a way of expressing our moral intuition that might does not make right and that the powerful should not be able to use their power to extract concessions from the weak. A decision procedure that is even more exacting in its demands of impartiality is utilitarianism. A simple version of utilitarianism would ask which of the competing regimes would create the greatest net happiness for all persons affected, giving equal weight to the interests of all persons regardless of their nationality.

If we take on an impartial perspective that asks "what regime would maximize justice for all," the ICC regime appears to be superior, even accounting for differences in how people define justice. The US position depends on two assumptions. The first is that the US is unlikely to commit war crimes and is fully competent to prosecute and try its own citizens should allegations of war crimes arise. The second assumption is that the ICC will not be impartial, and that it may even have a systemic anti-US bias. America's military power puts it in a position where it is more likely to be the object of criticism.

The first assumption is questionable. If direct attacks on unarmed civilians constitute a war crime, as many commentators believe they do, there are certainly US actions that would fit this characterization. The fire bombing of Tokyo and Dresden and the atomic bombs dropped on Japan killed hundreds of thousands of civilians. To this could be added bombings in Cambodia and the conduct of some American soldiers during the Vietnam War. The My Lai incident, where a large number of unarmed Vietnamese civilians were killed by US troops, is only the most famous example. More recently, the shocking revelations of the treatment of detainees at the Abu Ghraib prison[13] should put to rest any doubts that the perpetration of war crimes by American troops is indeed possible.

Once we acknowledge the real possibility of US troops committing war crimes in the future, we are left with the question of whether the US can be counted on to fairly prosecute war crimes committed by its troops. Since the investigations into the abuses at Abu Ghraib are still ongoing, it is more helpful to look back at the experience of Vietnam. Only one person of the many involved in the My Lai incident was convicted (Lt William Calley), and he was pardoned by President Nixon after serving only a few months of his sentence. Today, even supporters of the Vietnam War acknowledge the barbarity of what took place there; they merely argue that My Lai was the exception.[14] Though it seems hard to believe today, roughly 80 per cent of Americans supported Nixon's decision to pardon Calley in 1974.[15] Although there is likely truth in the claim that he was following orders and being used as a scapegoat to protect those higher up (the main reasons given by the public for supporting a reduction in his sentence),[16] "following superior orders" was not considered a valid excuse when the Allies were trying Germans at Nuremberg, and the actual conduct of Calley more than merited a life sentence. Wars produce a characteristic "rally around the flag" phenomenon that makes it very easy for people to rationalize actions taken by their government and soldiers on their behalf.

The point does not depend on whether the US is a worse offender in the area of war crimes than other countries. There have, in fairness, been instances when the US has gone to great lengths to minimize civilian casualties in the execution of military campaigns. The point is merely that, like every other nation, the US is tempted to breach the rules of war in the pursuit of its ends. Like every other nation, it will also have a natural inclination to rationalize and justify the actions its soldiers take in war, even if these are of questionable character. And again, as with other nations, it is difficult for the US to be an impartial judge when it is judging itself. Whatever imperfections exist in the mechanisms for pursuing justice through the ICC, its overwhelming advantage comes from specifying with a fair amount of precision definitions for the various crimes, procedures for trying persons, and providing for more impartial judges with fewer connections to the states involved in the conflict.

A different US objection would be that important rights of the accused guaranteed by the US Constitution would not be protected by the ICC. Probably the most important example would be with respect to the right of protection from double jeopardy.[17] But if we examine even this problem from an impartial perspective that desires to insure that justice is served in as many cases as possible, the objection is unpersuasive. The idea behind a double jeopardy protection is to prevent the government from repeatedly trying someone until it finds a favourable judge or jury and to spare the accused the very real hardships that go with repeated trials. The danger with granting a blanket protection from double jeopardy is that there may be many instances where there are clear errors at the first trial that result in the acquittal of a guilty person. The US Supreme Court dealt with this issue in the landmark case of *Palko v. Connecticut*[18] where it argued, in essence, that although the Bill of Rights clearly required the federal government to apply the double jeopardy provision strictly, state governments were given more leeway. The court recognized that it was possible to distinguish between those protections that "are not of the very essence of a scheme of ordered liberty" and those that are. A second trial that is motivated by serious legal errors committed during the first trial is very different, as a matter of justice, from repeated politically motivated trials.

The decision to allow the ICC to try persons who have been acquitted in sham trials uses the same logic as *Palko*. If the first trial really was a sham, the interests of justice are served by a new trial before impartial judges. As in the case of *Palko*, a second trial is not unjust if it is held for the right reasons and if it is itself fairly run. The US objection, of course, is that it will not be. "Sham" may be in the eye of the beholder, and in international politics the eyes of every "beholder" will have political bias, some more than others. Once the ICC is granted the power to review cases, it is possible that new, politically motivated trials will be held – exactly the sort of thing a double jeopardy provision is intended to prevent. It must be acknowledged that this is, indeed, a risk.[19] But it was also a risk in *Palko*. The actual judges and prosecutors who will staff the ICC might turn out to be corrupt, but so might US judges and prosecutors. From an impartial perspective, given a choice between (1) a rule that bars the international court from taking action if there have been legal proceedings at the state level and (2) a rule that allows the court to hold new trials in the case of sham acquittals, the second is preferable even with the knowledge that an international court might sometimes abuse this power.

From an impartial perspective, one must weigh the structural factors that would encourage biased judgments in each case. The double jeopardy provision is based on the worry that states will pursue politically motivated convictions, and this is indeed possible at the international level. But war crimes – and the other crimes under the ICC's jurisdiction – are different than many other types of criminal prosecution because at the state level there will be strong political pressure *not* to prosecute or to seek an acquittal. It is the government that must decide to prosecute and it is government judges who will sit at the trial. In most cases, a government that convicts one of its citizens of a human rights atrocity will be implicating itself. The predictable bias towards *not* prosecuting will be very strong.[20] If states that do not want to prosecute realize that they can thwart international action by holding a sham trial, such trials would become sadly frequent. In other words, from the perspective of an impartial legislator considering the political biases of both domestic and international legal actors, the ICC provision seems quite reasonable.

If we evaluate the two regimes from an impartial perspective, the US position comes up wanting. While it is true that an international court will have some amount of bias, it is doubtful that its bias would be on average greater than the bias caused by allowing a state to be judge in its own case. From an impartial perspective, the goal is justice for all peoples of the world, not for one particular state. But this very requirement raises an important objection that must be considered. Is it realistic, or even desirable, to insist that states act with this level of impartiality? There are many reasons for thinking that we would not advocate that states adopt a posture of perfect impartiality, caring no more about whether justice is done to foreigners than to nationals. Below I consider how far the demands of impartiality can be pressed, again using the US and the ICC as a case study.

III. OBJECTIONS TO IMPARTIALITY

Some decision-making criteria require more impartiality than others. Simple versions of utilitarianism, for example, ask the decision-maker to give his own happiness no more weight than the happiness of others. Such a form of utilitarianism requires a high level, some would say an unrealistically high level, of impartiality. Some theories of international justice, though not utilitarian, share with utilitarianism the tendency to use a decision procedure that includes a very demanding conception of impartiality. Just as many people take this as a reason for rejecting utilitarianism, so others reject strongly impartial decision procedures in the realm of international justice. The desire to preserve our own lives, for example, is argued to be so strong that we cannot ask people to be indifferent between saving their own lives and the lives of strangers. Bernard Williams pushes this logic even further in claiming that there are some projects so central to our lives that we cannot be asked to think of morality as more important than them. To use his famous example, if one has a choice between saving one's wife and saving a stranger and one stops to think about whether it is morally permissible to show preference for one's wife in situations like this, the agent has had "one thought too many." His commitment to his wife is not simply a morally permissible preference, it is a commitment that is even more important than his commitment to morality.[21]

In the international context, the argument more often takes the form that we should not ask states to act as perfect altruists in a world where altruism is easily exploited. Michael Walzer, who argues strongly against the view that state interests always trump morality, is willing to grant that in cases of "ultimate necessity," where a people's very way of life is imminently threatened, they may dispense with the moral rules that normally govern warfare.[22] He cites the plight of Britain fighting against the Nazis during the period of the war when Britain's cause looked bleakest. Rawls makes a similar point using the same example.[23] Although the cutoff point varies from author to author, many hold a moral intuition that there are some sacrifices it is simply unreasonable to ask states to make.

One way of understanding this moral intuition is suggested by the Hobbesian idea that "ought" implies "can."[24] The desire to preserve oneself is so strong that persons will often find themselves in positions where they are unable (psychologically, not logically) to act morally. If, given human psychology, it is impossible for humans to act in a given way, then we cannot say that they ought to act in that way. The problem with this argument has always been that such behaviour is not truly impossible, even in a psychological sense. History is filled with examples of persons who endured painful and violent deaths in order to uphold moral principles they thought right. The Hobbesian position is either that such acts are supererogatory – that persons who fail to perform them cannot be blamed[25] – or that such acts are irrational – that persons who act rationally cannot (of course) be blamed. In either case, we have moved from a purely psychological claim to a moral one, since the argument is either passing judgments about what types of actions justly incur moral blame or making moral judgments about the ends a particular agent has chosen to pursue. At this point, we encounter conflicting moral intuitions. There are some who will say "let justice roll though the heavens fall," but many others who will admit that Hobbes is right in at least some cases, who will admit that fear of destruction becomes a legitimate excuse for failing to act morally in some contexts.

There are two related questions that thus must be addressed. First, since impartiality has a strong a priori presumption over partiality in questions of morality, if states should not be required to make decisions on purely impartial grounds, what is the ground for this intuition? Second, assuming states are not required to be completely impartial when deciding whether or not to join international institutions, *how much* impartiality may we demand of them? It does not follow that because considerations of self-interest provide a legitimate excuse in some cases that states must *always* be allowed to act in their self-interest.[26]

IV. THE DEMANDS OF AN IMPARTIAL LEGISLATOR

In this section, I propose a thought experiment that can help in considering both of these questions. I do not claim that it presents the only moral grounds for thinking that the demands of impartiality may be relaxed; more communitarian justifications may also be possible. It does, however, present one ground for relaxing the standards of impartiality and it does so without abandoning the demand of impartiality entirely. The experiment is for each state to ask itself whether an impartial global legislator would require states to limit their sovereignty by joining an international regime of this sort. In this case, they would ask: "What principle would a hypothetical legislator concerned with promoting more just criminal procedures enact for all states to interpret and act upon, realizing that states may be biased in their application of the principle to specific cases?" I first explain the moral intuitions this experiment is intended to capture. I then explain how it finds a helpful middle ground between demands of complete impartiality and allowing states to avoid all moral obligations by invoking self-interest. Finally, I illustrate the application of this framework by considering the US decision to refuse to join the ICC. I should emphasize that this is a thought experiment and not an endorsement that there actually *be* a world state with global legislative powers; it is intended to help international actors discern their moral obligations in the absence of such a system.

The first intuition that this thought experiment is meant to model is that states ought to act on the basis of principles that they would want other states to act on as well. Our earlier discussion showed that this requirement, by itself, is insufficient since a country might adopt a principle that it would want others to act on, but it might still choose it for reasons that are self-serving. The first requirement thus states a formal characteristic the principle must have, but it does not specify the criteria we use for judging between principles.

The second requirement of impartiality is that the interests of all people in being treated justly be given equal weight when selecting the principles. This would mean that the fact that principle A is worse for country X does not determine X's choice if principle A would be better than the alternatives for all affected. It is at this point that the principle of impartiality appears to make an excessive demand.

A third requirement, discussed extensively above, is that we recognize the non-ideal character of the states that will implement the principle: they will often be biased in their own favour and many will refuse to comply with their moral obligations. The legislator would not condone these facts, but would account for them when deciding which principles would best promote the goal: more just criminal procedures for dealing with war crimes.[27]

A state trying to decide whether it should join the ICC would apply the framework as follows. A state will first ask what goal the international legislator would want to promote. When a state considers this question, it will inevitably use its own conception of procedural criminal justice. Again, my position only demands impartiality of interest, not belief. The moral requirement is that the principle of justice be seen as one defining a goal for all people, not just the citizens of the state in question. When specifying the principle, the impartial legislator would consider the divergent ways actors are likely to interpret the principle, the predictable biases of those who will interpret it, and the likelihood of outright non-compliance. Problems associated with the execution of the principle will affect the content of what the legislator chooses. In the present instance, those who disagree about other aspects of justice can agree that those guilty of genocide, crimes against humanity, and war crimes should be punished. The hypothetical impartial legislator's goal is to adopt a set of rules that will most effectively bring the guilty to justice while acquitting the innocent.

If one thinks about the strategy such a legislator would employ, it quickly becomes apparent why the demands of impartiality would not be as onerous as they would initially seem. The principles on which we act are those that would be chosen by an impartial legislator – one cannot simply refuse to obey a principle because it is not in one's interest as a situated actor. The demands of impartiality are, however, mitigated by the fact that a good legislator will be aware of the tendency of persons to fail to follow the rules. From the beginning, we have insisted that the legislator imagine the principle as a hypothetical law addressed to real world agents. A good legislator knows that not all agents will obey the law and tries to identify those situations where self-interest will predictably lead persons to ignore it. The significance of this will vary greatly depending on the nature of the harms involved. In some cases, it will make little difference. If the only harm that non-defectors receive is failure to benefit from the obedience of others (because others, in fact, disobey), then the legislator may conclude that it is better from a moral point of view to have some obey the law than none, even if this situation is unfair. To remedy the unfairness, a good legislator would normally try to sanction those who failed to comply. A state acting on this principle would certainly be justified in working to build up an international regime where those who fail to comply would be punished.

In other cases, a legislator might decide that, given the harms that would follow from large-scale non-compliance, it is better not to impose a legal obligation. Consider the example of military disarmament. Assume for the sake of argument that a world in which no state has the military capacity to project its power into other states would be superior to the status quo. An impartial legislator would realize that the principle "abolish offensive military capability," definitional problems aside, would not be complied with by most states and that any states that actually did comply would be at great risk of attack. A reasonable legislator would not, therefore, require states to disarm, since there would be no way to prevent other states from defecting. Instead, the legislator would direct states to take less drastic intermediate steps that might someday make the desired goal a reality but that would not expose compliant states to undue risk. The legislator will think strategically about what principles will best advance the goal, given foreseen patterns of non-compliance, self-interest, and so on. [28]

This logic is most familiar as a kind of "rule-consequentialism." Many of the objections to rule-consequentialism as the answer to every conceivable moral question are not applicable to the more limited case now under consideration. The "consequence" to be maximized is people being tried justly, not the satisfaction of preferences or a nebulous conception of happiness. In other circumstances, the goal might be something like insuring that each person is treated with dignity and respect. The point of the thought experiment is just to ask which rules one would want a legislator to adopt to further whatever the goal in question is. Additional arguments would be needed where there is disagreement about the proper goal.

A good legislator knows that law-abiding citizens, especially those who will obey the law simply because it is right rather than out of fear of punishment, are a precious resource that must be protected and encouraged. Such a legislator will write laws in such a way that they do not require unreasonable sacrifices on the part of those who obey the principles when the costs they might face from others defecting is high. I should reiterate that we are dealing with a special set of cases where legislators foresee their own inability to force widespread compliance with the law. It is thus different than a situation where the government can effectively enforce a policy (like the draft) that requires great sacrifice on the part of particular individuals but, because it can force individuals to comply with the law, distributes risks in a roughly fair way.

It is thus important to distinguish between two types of cases that will look very different from the legislator's point of view. The first case involves a state that will suffer terribly when it obeys a moral principle in a world where other states are unlikely to reciprocate. A wise legislator is unlikely to ask a state to make such a sacrifice except in the most extraordinary of circumstances. This provides a way to account for those examples where the Hobbesian position is strongest. The second case involves a state acting on a principle without any guarantee that others will also do so, but where the costs of non-compliance by other states are fairly low for the state that obeys. Here the legislator might still direct states to obey the principle (knowing that many others may not) if the net result of such a situation would be better ("better" need not be thought of in utilitarian terms).

The distinction between these two types of cases is particularly important for powerful states. The inequalities of power that exist between states must factor into our assessments of their responsibilities. Powerful states are often in a position to act on a moral principle without fear of significant harm to themselves if they do so. They are also often in a position where they can help establish new norms. The collective action problems that confront international actors can often be solved (even if agents are only self-interested) because real world interactions are repeated over time. A powerful state may be able to establish a norm that it will be in the interest of other states to follow.

V. THE US AND THE ICC

We are now in a position to return to the specific case of the ICC, and to ask whether it would impose an undue burden on the US to participate in such a regime. We have argued above that, on balance, the ICC regime is more likely to promote justice in criminal trials for war crimes, genocide, and crimes against humanity than the unilateralist alternative. In the context of the suggested framework, the goal of an impartial legislator would be to devise principles that would lead to a regime where states are not judges in their own cases. This provides a presumption that the legislator would require states to join the ICC as a way to promote this goal. The previous thought experiment, however, shows that this presumption might be overridden. For it to be overridden based on the model, it would have to be shown that (once the legislator anticipates likely non-compliance and errant compliance) asking states to join the ICC would in the long term undermine the legislator's goal of promoting justice.

In the present case, direct non-compliance by other states is not really the issue since so many states (ninety-four as of 3 May 2004) have already acceded to the ICC Statute. The US is not being asked to take the brave first step to create a new norm, but rather to lend its support to one that is already being supported by many other countries. The real issue then is whether the US would likely be a victim of politically motivated trials by the ICC were it to join. The US worries that its position as a superpower makes it particularly vulnerable to anti-American prejudice in international fora because other nations resent US intervention, even in cases where such intervention is justified.

With respect to the likelihood of this happening, one must acknowledge that it is, in fact, possible. There are many nations with hostile feelings toward the US. From the vantage point of an impartial legislator, one would also acknowledge that some of those feelings may be more justified than many Americans would like to admit. In any case, there are other considerations that mitigate the likelihood of this scenario unfolding. The entire spirit of the negotiation of the ICC Statute was to achieve consensus and bring the US into the fold. Other states realize how important American cooperation is to the success of the ICC and thus have a self-interested reason not to use it as a device to alienate the US. The US is also not the only country jealous of its sovereignty, and if the ICC were to start overturning trials that had been conducted in good faith, rather than trials that were clearly shams, many countries (not just the US) would be extremely concerned about the precedent. The UN Security Council's ability to override the decisions of the

ICC, should the ICC run amok, constitutes yet another safeguard which makes it unlikely that the feared scenarios would take place.[29]

The crucial consideration, however, is that the actual amount of harm a corrupt ICC could do to US interests is fairly small. The US is not at risk of invasion, the collapse of its economy, or the elimination of its cultural ways of life at the hands of the ICC. The actual number of US citizens who might be sentenced to life in prison because of war crimes – the ICC does not hand out death sentences – is quite small compared to the number of people who would be killed in the actual military actions that spawned the cases. The harm is one that would largely be confined to a small number of Americans who might be unjustly sentenced to prison by such a court. Obviously this harm is not trivial, especially to those Americans and their families, but it is not the sort of harm which invokes the kinds of moral considerations that apply when a state's very survival and way of life is threatened.

When we consider this possibility from the perspective of an impartial legislator, we must always compare it to the alternatives. It may sound callous to say that we must simply accept the risk of some Americans being unjustly sentenced by an international court, but *any* legal system will carry the risk of unjust sentences. How many innocent people have been found guilty in American courts?[30] In British courts? We will never know, but the number must be substantial. Any human legal system will be flawed and make errors. Every system is capable of being infected with systemic bias. An impartial legislator would hold that the possible injustices that might result from an international tribunal pale when compared to the wrongs of self-help justice where victors act as judges of the enemies they have defeated or where a state must judge whether it has committed crimes against humanity with respect to its own citizens. The possible harms to the US are not so severe as to dissuade an impartial legislator from imposing an obligation.

Let us now turn to a different scenario. It is honestly difficult to understand the intensity of US opposition to the court simply on the basis of fears that it will prosecute Americans unfairly. The truth is that the intensity of the reaction is also related to a worry shared by many conservatives who have influenced the Bush administration's policy. The views of these conservatives are strongly anti-international. One strain worries that the international community holds values that are at odds with the values that America should hold, and America should therefore be reluctant to limit its national sovereignty.[31] The more extreme strains fear that an international court is the next step toward the end of the state system and the creation of a world government.[32]

Although it is tempting simply to dismiss this latter fear by pointing to the vast distance between the status quo and a world government, I propose to take it seriously and assess it from the prospective of our hypothetical impartial legislator. Some would claim that this view seriously underestimates the harms caused by the "states system" because the US does not bear the brunt of those harms. From an impartial legislator's point of view, the harms of unilateralism are much more apparent than from the perspective of the US. On the other hand, many important commentators, ranging from Kant to Rawls, have seen a world government as something to be avoided and have seen cooperation between states or peoples as a preferable alternative.[33] Since settling this question is far beyond the scope of this chapter, let us assume for the sake of argument that a single world government would be undesirable because it would likely lead to injustice. The question remains, would that fear be a relevant reason for an impartial legislator to oppose the creation of the ICC?

A historical illustration is perhaps appropriate here. If one thinks of the debates over the ratification of the US Constitution in 1789, the fact that the proposed national government would have direct authority over individuals (rather than interacting with them only through the state governments) and that the Supreme Court could review state court decisions represented two tremendously important changes in the structure of the US government. As one reads the ratification debates with the benefit of hindsight, one of the most striking things is how the concerns of the anti-federalists about growing national power – and the large reductions in state sovereignty – proved correct. The ICC is thus important not only for its immediate powers, which are still rather limited, but because of the precedent it sets for other international bodies to act directly without state consent vis-à-vis citizens and to override decisions of national courts. This objection need not be thought of simply as a contrived conspiracy theory. Instead, one might claim that from a legislative point of view a states system is preferable to a world government and that a legislator should be wary of setting precedents that others will exploit at a later time. Just because the current legislator would not go that far does not mean future legislators might not, and this is something that a good legislator should consider.

This is a classic example of a "slippery slope" argument.[34] One way of defeating it is to show other easy identifiable stopping points that can serve as alternatives. One thing that any true world government would need is the power to force even powerful states to abide by its decisions. The permanent member vetoes in the UN Security Council, inequitable as they are in many respects, are recognition of the fact that no such power exists. In other words, we might find a different place to stop the "slide" by insisting that the new international regime not have the power to coerce directly, instead of opposing its power to influence action through the creation of norms. But this line of argument is not persuasive. Few would have imagined that the European Coal and Steel Community would evolve into the European Union. Norms can generate momentum that few would expect.

We do not do the ICC justice if we try to downplay what an enormous step it is in principle, even if its actual powers in the short term will likely be quite limited because of the power of states to interfere with its effective use. It does represent, in principle, a potentially important move away from the states system as we know it. If one assumes, and again the position has not been proven, that the preservation of the states system is a good thing, then this *could* be a reason that a legislator who knows that future legislators and actors will not necessarily stop at the current boundaries might exercise more caution with respect to the ICC.

Although there is thus a *potential* argument that would give a sound moral argument for why the US may not join the ICC, this potential argument is not available to the US based on its present policy. If the US is really operating on the assumption that the states system must be protected against the encroachment of international organizations that would restrict state sovereignty, it should not have supported the international tribunals for Yugoslavia and Rwanda.[35] In each case, it was reading the UN Security Council's powers expansively in order to take actions that were *not* primarily motivated by the preservation of international peace but rather by the desire to punish terrible atrocities that took place within a state. Indeed, these international tribunals provided indispensable momentum for the present ICC. The main difference between the tribunals and the ICC is that the ICC is much more likely to bring charges against the US. The best that can be said for the US is that it is willing to expand the power of international organization at the expense of national sovereignty only if it is done through the UN Security Council (where it has a veto). This reasoning would be rejected in an impartial point of view because it is just a restatement of the unilateralist position described above.

At present, therefore, the US position is not morally tenable. The argument that *might* work, namely that a wise international legislator would take actions to protect national sovereignty and the states system, is not available to the US because it has often ignored that principle when it was the sovereignty of other states that was threatened. The US position must be interpreted as a version of unilateralism in which states can interfere with one another's internal affairs with a fair degree of freedom. An impartial international legislator seeking to promote global justice would reject this regime in favour of one like the ICC, which provides for greater impartiality. Although we cannot demand that states be perfectly impartial when deciding whether to restrict their sovereignty, the current US position cannot show harms substantial enough to indicate that the moral obligation to promote justice from an impartial perspective is overridden.

CONCLUSION

The US decision regarding participation in the ICC serves as an example for a larger class of cases. This is one example of a nation deciding between two courses of action, one of which would likely, from an impartial perspective, provide a more adequate legal framework for securing justice for people around the world, the other of which would, arguably, promote the interests of that country and maintain existing levels of sovereignty. It is possible that it actually would serve US interests, all things considered, to join the ICC. Indeed, that calculation is one that is constantly changing. The ill will towards American unilateralism in the wake of the Iraq war is such that a US administration that decided to cooperate with the ICC might gain important political advantages internationally. In whichever way the calculation of interests works out in this particular case, this question is worth pursuing because we should not assume that the pursuit of justice and self-interest will always coincide. Because they will not, we must wrestle with the question of how much impartiality it is reasonable to ask of states.

The thought experiment used in this chapter asks what a hypothetical legislator would do if that legislator were both committed to justice for all persons impartially and recognized that unrealistically high demands for impartiality often hinder, rather than help, the goal of bringing power to justice. This approach combines a commitment to universal justice with a limited form of pragmatism that asks us to think about the capability of states to pursue justice in an international environment where other states are often unwilling to comply with obligations of justice.[36] This approach can allow for incremental steps in pursuing justice while keeping in view the ultimate goal of creating just institutions for all people.

Between the extremes of complete international anarchy and an all-powerful world government, there are a wide variety of possible arrangements in which international regimes and states share authority. Rather than posing the question in such absolute terms, we should recognize that states will have to make decisions, one international regime at a time, about whether to join. That decision is one that they cannot make on the basis of pre-existing agreements. They will be guided by their interests no doubt, but they should also be guided by considerations of justice. One way to promote justice is to create regimes in which, procedurally, correct verdicts are more likely to emerge. Pursuing impartiality in this procedural sense at the international level, however, may demand very extensive impartiality in a more substantive sense – concern that justice be provided for citizens of other countries as well as for one's own citizens. By asking states to take their own view of justice and consider it as the goal of an impartial global legislator, we inject a needed moral element into these decisions.

NOTES

1 For an excellent analysis of the provisions of the ICC Statute, see William Schabas, *An Introduction to the International Criminal Court*, 2d ed. (Cambridge: Cambridge UP, 2004).

2 It is unclear when, if ever, the court will have effective jurisdiction over the crime of aggression. See *Rome Statute of the International Criminal Court*, 17 July 1998, UN Doc. A/CONF. 183/9, 2187 UNTS 90, reprinted in *International Legal Materials* 37, no. 5 (1998): 1002, art. 5(2) [hereinafter ICC Statute].

3 Joseph Nye, Jr., in his *The Paradox of American Power: Why the World's Only Superpower Can't Go It Alone* (Oxford: Oxford UP, 2002) argues that, in general, unilateralism is not in US interests. For the specific claim

that it is in US interests to support the ICC rather than oppose it, see Michael P. Scharf, "The United States And The International Criminal Court: A Recommendation for The Bush Administration," *ILSA Journal of International and Comparative Law* 7, no. 2 (2001): 385–9.

4 Brian Barry helpfully distinguishes between first order (or common sense) impartiality and second order impartiality. The latter involves viewing each person's conception of the good from an impartial perspective, while common sense impartiality only requires that we abstain from private consideration, favouritism, and so on. It is the common sense notion of impartiality that we use in talking about the way a judge is supposed to make decisions in a courtroom. See Brian Barry, *Justice as Impartiality: A Treatise on Social Justice*, vol. 2 (Oxford: Clarendon Press, 1995), 11–4. Although common sense impartiality is by itself inadequate for developing a full sense of justice, it represents a helpful starting point for this chapter since it represents a point of broad agreement when talking specifically about criminal procedure.

5 "Relevant reason" is the more fundamental of the two concepts since the claim that, for example, a judge should base her decision on public rather than private reasons rests on the prior assumption that public reasons are relevant and private reasons are not.

6 See John Rawls, *A Theory of Justice* (Cambridge, Mass.: Harvard UP, 1971); ibid., *The Law of Peoples* (Cambridge, Mass.: Harvard UP, 1999); and Barry, *supra* n4.

7 I assume here that any principle which purports to justify action must be stated in general terms. It must be a principle to which any state could appeal. Any restrictive terms in the principle must be principles that do not violate the basic principle of impartiality as described above. "Because we are the US" is not a justification. The philosophical presuppositions of this argument are discussed in my book *Locke and the Legislative Point of View* (Princeton: Princeton UP, 2002).

8 An example of the way unilateralist principles inform US attitudes to the ICC is found in article 98(2) of the ICC Statute, *supra* n2, an amendment pressed for by the US. This would authorize the ICC to enter into a "good neighbour" agreement with states that are non-parties (in particular, the US). The US basically wants the option of assisting the court when it prosecutes criminals from "irresponsible nations" (as it did in Rwanda and the former Yugoslavia) without putting itself under the ICC's jurisdiction. See Roseann M. Latore, "Escape out the Back Door or Charge in the Front Door: U.S. Reactions to the International Criminal Court," *Boston College International and Comparative Law Review* 25, no. 1 (2002): 159–76, 166–7.

9 For reasons of brevity, I will focus primarily on war crimes since it is here that the US is most likely to be charged with an offence under the Court's jurisdiction. The arguments apply to disputes over genocide and crimes against humanity as well.

10 For a general discussion of Locke's ideas as they relate to humanitarian intervention and of the challenges these issues pose in a contemporary context, see John Dunn, "The Dilemma of Humanitarian Intervention: The Executive Power of the Law of Nature, after God," *Government and Opposition* 29, no. 2 (1994): 248–61.

11 See John Locke, *Two Treatises of Government*, ed. Peter Laslett (Cambridge: Cambridge UP, 1988), 2.123–31.

12 Rawls, *A Theory of Justice* and *The Law of Peoples*, *supra* n6.

13 Sean D. Murphy, "U.S. Abuse of Iraqi Detainees at Abu Ghraib Prison," *American Journal of International Law* 98 (2004): 591–6.

14 Hadley Arkes, *First Things: An Inquiry into the First Principles of Justice* (Princeton: Princeton UP, 1986), 278.

15 See on-line: University of Missouri-Kansas City School of Law <http://www.law.umkc.edu/faculty/projects/ftrials/mylai/SurveyResults.html>.

16 Ibid.

17 Article 20(3) of the ICC Statute, *supra* n2, allows a second trial only if the initial proceedings were "for the purpose of shielding the person concerned from criminal responsibility" or were "not conducted independently or impartially in accordance with the norms of due process recognized by international law and were conducted in a manner which, in the circumstances, was inconsistent with an intent to bring the person concerned to justice." For a critique of this position, see Lee A. Casey, "Assessments of the United States Position: The Case against the International Criminal Court," *Fordham International Law Journal* 25, no. 3 (2002): 840–72, 843–8.

18 302 U.S. 319 (1937).

19 Based on the wording of the ICC Statute, the risk should be fairly small. See Jimmy Gurule, "United States Opposition to the 1998 Rome Statute Establishing an International Criminal Court: Is the Court's Jurisdiction Truly Complementary to National Criminal Jurisdiction?" *Cornell International Law Journal* 35, no. 1 (2002): 1–45. Gurule argues that the ICC would have to find willful obstruction of justice on the part of the US, not merely disagree with the outcome.

20 Steven R. Ratner and Jason S. Abrams make this point with regard to war crimes prosecutions. See their *Accountability for Human Rights Atrocities in International Law: Beyond the Nuremberg Legacy*, 2d ed. (Oxford: Oxford UP, 2001), 106–7.

21 Bernard Williams, "Persons, Character, and Morality," in *Moral Luck: Philosophical Papers: 1973–1980* (Cambridge: Cambridge UP, 1981), 18.
22 Michael Walzer, *Just and Unjust Wars: A Moral Argument with Historical Illustrations*, 2d ed. (New York: Basic Books, 1977), 251–63.
23 Rawls, *Law of Peoples, supra* n6, 98–9.
24 For a classic statement of this position as it applies to international relations that draws upon Hobbes, see Felix E. Oppenheim, "National Interest, Rationality, and Morality," *Political Theory* 15, no. 3 (1987): 369–89.
25 According to Howard Warrender's interpretation of Hobbes, Hobbes really does believe in binding moral principles, but he believes they are inoperative in a state of nature where persons' lives are endangered by trying to obey such principles. See *The Political Philosophy of Thomas Hobbes: His Theory of Obligation* (Oxford: Clarendon Press, 1966).
26 For a critique of the Hobbesian approach to international relations, see Charles R. Beitz, *Political Theory and International Relations* (Princeton: Princeton UP, 1979), 13–66.
27 These requirements are defended in more detail in Tuckness, *supra* n7, chap. 2.
28 This does not mean that the moral principle is completely set aside. It means that the principle is to be regarded as a principle of evaluation only, not a principle that can direct coercive actions. I have discussed the distinction between enforceable and non-enforceable moral principles elsewhere: Tuckness, *supra* n7, 41–4.
29 See article 16 of the ICC Statute, *supra* n2. For a discussion of this provision, see Schabas, *supra* n1, 82–5.
30 The recent disputes over those on death row cleared by DNA evidence should be a reminder of how imperfect the entire legal system is, not just with respect to capital punishment.
31 Lee A. Casey, *supra* n17, 840–8.
32 The John Birch Society is one example: see John F. McManus, "Unsafe in Any Form," on-line: John Birch Society <http://www.getusout.org/un/articles/icc_unsafe.htm>.
33 See Immanual Kant, "Perpetual Peace," in *Political Writings*, ed. Jans Reiss, 93–130 (Cambridge: Cambridge UP, 1991) and Rawls, *Law of Peoples, supra* n6, 36.
34 See Frederick Schauer, "Slippery Slopes," *Harvard Law Review* 99 (1985): 361–83; Wibren Van Der Burg, "The Slippery Slope Argument," *Ethics* 102 (1991): 42–65; and Richard Vernon, *The Career of Toleration: John Locke, Jonas Proast, and After* (Montreal: McGill-Queen's UP, 1997), 70–5.
35 Interestingly, the US has started to adopt an interpretation of international law that is much more protective of national sovereignty. See, for example,

Madeline Morris, "High Crimes and Misconceptions: The ICC and Non-Party States," *Law and Contemporary Problems* 64, no. 1 (2001): 13–66, who takes the position (also held by former Ambassador Scheffer) that the ICC could not exercise jurisdiction over nationals of a non-party state. Michael P. Scharf argues that this position is inconsistent with international law and with past US policy. See his "The ICC's Jurisdiction over the Nationals of Non-Party States: A Critique of the U.S. position," *Law and Contemporary Problems* 64, no. 1 (2001): 67–118.

36 On moral demands in contexts of noncompliance, see Liam B. Murphy, *Moral Demands in Nonideal Theory* (Oxford: Oxford UP, 2000).

6

Individual Responsibility for Collective Wrongs

TRACY ISAACS[*]

Genocide has a collective dimension both on the act side and the harm side.[1] An individual agent cannot, except in extraordinary circumstances, perpetrate a genocide single-handedly. It usually involves a number – and in some cases, such as the 1994 Rwandan genocide, an extraordinarily large number – of perpetrators. Thus, the act of perpetrating a genocide typically involves a collective agent. With respect to the harm, genocide is a harm against a group. In perpetrating a genocide, though individuals clearly are harmed as individuals, they are harmed because they are members of a group, and harmed with the intention of destroying the group. Thus, genocide typically involves a collective victim.

The collective elements of a genocide create special difficulties for the assignment of individual moral responsibility to perpetrators. In particular, if, in a specific genocide, the result would not have been achieved unless many participants acted in concert, then what may we accurately hold individual participants responsible *for*? Are they responsible for genocide or for murder? Are they responsible for genocide or for participating in genocide? Can we ever hold an individual responsible for genocide, while acknowledging that no individual's acts alone can be – or at least in the typical case, ever are – sufficient for genocide? Are there relevant or significant distinctions to be drawn here? I believe that there are.

This paper focuses on questions about moral responsibility that arise given the group dimension of genocide. The main difficulty that I explore is whether an individual can be held responsible for genocide when genocide is not perpetrated by an individual. Many of us want to be able to say that specific individuals are responsible for genocide – in the criminal courts we certainly want to be able to maintain this. Thus, it is necessary to explore the various possibilities for holding individuals responsible for acts which they did not perform on their own. I maintain that, since collective contexts make it possible for individuals to perform acts together that they would not be able to perform on their own, we need a framework for thinking about individual responsibility that takes this fact seriously. With respect to the issue at hand, I propose that we should consider individuals responsible for their part in collective efforts, and that it is important that their contributions be characterized in light of the collective actions and goals in which they take place. I explain the nature of this characterization in more detail later.

I consider three possibilities in addition to my own proposal. The first is that we consider individuals responsible only for their actions and the consequences of their actions. I present this proposal in two versions, endorsing the second. The first characterization does not fully capture the collective features of individual action. My amended version does. I also consider recent proposals by Larry May and by Christopher Kutz for holding individuals responsible for acts or consequences that could only be achieved by groups.[2] Each of these views has something to recommend it. Kutz's view, however, leaves some of the hard questions unresolved. May's proposal for holding heads of state responsible is useful for that limited range of cases, but, as he himself recognizes (and addresses), more than heads of state are often involved. What do we say about the others? I consider May's suggestions and conclude that in group wrongs involving large numbers of participants, each is responsible for her or his own contribution, but it is important that we understand the collective features of the circumstances in which the contribution takes place.

I have already pointed out that genocide has a group dimension both on the act side and on the harm side. This collective dimension can create difficulties for assigning responsibility to individuals for harms that can only come about through collective action. These sorts of difficulties can arise in cases far less extreme than genocide.

Consider, for example, the environmental harm of pollution. In the heat of July and August in southwestern Ontario, it is quite common to hear that Canada's national weather office, Environment Canada, has issued a "smog advisory" for a particular day. In issuing these alerts, Environment Canada warns people with respiratory problems to stay indoors and encourages people not to engage in strenuous physical activity out of doors. It also asks people not to turn on their air conditioning and to leave their cars at home. Operating air conditioners and automobiles will contribute to the smog, making it worse. From the point of view of an individual, however, running one air conditioner or driving a few kilometres to work is not going to make or break the problem. My leaving my car at home will not solve anything unless others also do so. Only one person running her air conditioning would not pose a problem. A singular contribution appears to be so minimal as to be of no consequence when considered in isolation. But our concern is not about acts in isolation. The pollution is the result of many individual actions taken together.

The most obvious difference between the case just described and the genocide case is that in the case just described we have no intention to contribute to smog. But the more important point in this discussion is that one person alone cannot produce this noxious smog. If we recognize that no one person's contribution amounts to the total harm, that each person only contributes a portion of the harm, then who is morally responsible?

If we are concerned only with causal responsibility, then it is easy to see that in neither the genocide case nor the pollution case is any one individual exclusively causally responsible for the total outcome. In these sorts of cases, full causal responsibility can only be attributed to groups. But moral responsibility is not the same thing as causal responsibility, for moral responsibility has a normative dimension that admits of praise and blame. When individuals are causally responsible for something, they are causally linked to that for which they are responsible. For example, I may be causally responsible for planting my garden. There is nothing morally salient about my actions. To say that I am causally responsible is simply to point out that my actions played a causally significant role in bringing about whatever I am causally responsible for. Causal responsibility is also something that we can attribute to nonmoral agents. A storm, for example, can be causally responsible for a power outage. An earthquake might be causally responsible for destroying a block of homes. In these examples, no moral agency is involved, but it still makes sense to attribute causal responsibility. When we consider agents to be morally responsible, we hold them responsible in a way that purely causal responsibility does not require. Only moral agents are morally responsible, that is, praiseworthy or blameworthy for what they do. Storms and earthquakes, though causally responsible, cannot be morally responsible. Moreover, it is not the case that every time moral agents are causally responsible, they must also be morally responsible. Even the most careful person might hurt someone by accident, for example. Furthermore, it is not the case that all moral responsibility requires that agents be causally responsible. It may be, for example, that through my negligence (my lack of causal involvement) someone comes to harm. So even if we establish that individuals are not themselves causally responsible for genocide, we have not ruled out that they may be morally responsible.

All three of the views that I consider have merits, but the amended version of the first is the most promising. The next section discusses the first possibility, namely, that individuals are morally responsible for their part in bringing about collective harms.

I

Recognizing that a lone individual cannot perpetrate a genocide, the proposal says that participants are responsible only for what they, as individuals, do. Thus, individual participants in genocide would be responsible for the killings that they perpetrated.

According to this view, individuals are not held responsible for anything that they did not do. Here, there is a direct relationship between the acts perpetrated by individuals and that for which they are held responsible. In this sense, the view is very individualistic.

Most of us think that murder is terrible, mass murder worse, and genocide worse still. But regardless of how we evaluate the three relative to each other, murder and mass murder are different from genocide. This observation might lead us to believe that the current proposal might be missing out on something, insofar as it does not capture this difference. For if we focus too narrowly on individuals, then we risk giving a distorted account of what the individuals do and what they take themselves to be doing. For example, if they are understanding their own acts as being part of a genocide, then our account of responsibility ought to take that seriously or it leaves something out of individuals' own conceptions of what they are doing. At the very least, then, we should be able to contextualize individual acts of murder within the broader context of genocide in order to be descriptively accurate.

This view still, however, only lets us attribute responsibility to individuals for their *part* in the genocide. Why might that be objectionable? The genocide example makes it difficult to see what the problem is because, even when not in the context of genocide, murder and mass murder still have a moral dimension – they are morally forbidden. But if we hold individuals responsible only for their parts, then no one – or only the collective entity as a whole – is responsible for the whole thing. Yet it is arguably the whole thing that, in the case of genocide, is especially troubling and wrong.

The point may be more easily grasped if we go back to the example of smog production. In that case, the acts of individuals do not appear to have moral relevance at all when they are taken in isolation. They take on moral significance when they are viewed in connection with the acts of others. And it is only the combined result, not the result of your act or my act of running the air conditioning or driving the car, that has a noticeably harmful impact. In this kind of case, when we hold each person responsible only for what she or he does, then no one appears to be doing anything objectionable. We are simply driving our cars and running our air conditioners, or at least that is how we understand and characterize our actions.

We could pass the moral objectionability in this kind of situation on to the group as a whole. But that seems not to satisfy our intuition that surely the individuals play some part for which they bear some responsibility as individuals. Given that smog is a preventable harm, it seems wrong to conclude that no one is doing anything objectionable, even as an individual, for that suggests that no one is morally obligated to act any differently. To attribute responsibility only to an artificial collective entity, and not to any of the participating individuals, seems not to capture responsibility where we want it to be situated, namely in the actions of individuals (regardless of whether we also want to hold collective entities morally responsible). In the genocide case, no less than in the smog case, if we cannot attribute responsibility to individuals for the genocide, but only for murder or mass murder, we similarly leave out something important. There is a difference, of course. For whereas an individual act of driving to work or running an air conditioner would not be morally wrong if it did not take place in the context of a smog advisory, an individual act of murder is morally wrong even if it is not performed in the context of a genocide. In both cases, however, we fail to capture the extent and nature of the wrong if we do not consider the individual act in the context of the acts of others.

A different way of thinking about this proposal allows us to implicate individuals in collective harms, and to characterize their individual contributions in the context of the collective action. I initially characterized individuals' contributions as murders or mass-murders. Instead, we should describe what they are responsible for not as "murders" or "mass-murders," but as "contributions to genocide" or "participation in genocide." It is similar for those of us who contribute to the smog. We are not simply running our air conditioners or driving our cars, we are contributing to the pollution of the environment. The case for this sort of description is somewhat stronger in the case of the genocide participants because, as we noted earlier, they understand themselves to be participating in genocide. That is what they intend to do. They share a collective goal with others, and they are acting in aid of that goal. Thus, understanding their actions as being subject to a description that makes reference to the collective context in which they take themselves to be acting provides a more ontologically accurate description of their actions as individuals. While it is true that the individuals may have committed murder or mass murder, it is also true that they did this as an intentional contribution to genocide. Understanding their individual acts in this broader collective context reveals more morally significant information about the act.

This way of understanding action is not original, but its applications to individual acts that take place in the context of collective acts has not been adequately appreciated.[3] Consider Donald Davidson's important work on individual action.[4] Among his many contributions, one of the most lasting and significant is his claim that the same act particular can have different levels of description.[5] Thus, to use Davidson's example, I may flip the light switch. But if, by doing so, I alert the burglar, turn on the light, open the electrical current, wake up the neighbours and so on, then my act may be re-described in these different ways. This is no different from the way that one person may be described in a number of ways – "the author of this paper," "the philosopher in room 435," "the former owner of the cats Moth and Storm." A given act may be described as "a switch-flipping," "an alerting of the burglar," "a moving of my index finger," or "a light-turning on."

Where the first account of this view falls short is in failing to acknowledge that the action of an individual may warrant descriptions beyond the ones that consider the act in isolation, focusing only on the individual. So a machete attack may also be a stabbing, a murder, a part of a mass murder, and a contribution to genocide. But these capture different features of the action. Which ways of describing the act are accurate will depend, in part, on an agent's intentions. For example, genocide, as defined by international law, requires the "intent to destroy, in whole or in part, a national, ethnical, racial, or religious group, as such."[6] This makes it different from atrocities against equally large numbers of people, but not performed with the specific intent. One can imagine, for example, indiscriminate killing with no larger purpose, but that still kills many, many people. We may not accurately describe such actions as genocide because the requisite intent is lacking. Thus, the acts of the individuals who participate could not be correctly described as "contributions to genocide." This is not, of course, to say that these agents would not be morally responsible for something. It is only to say that they would not be responsible for contributing to genocide.

The upshot of the foregoing discussion is that whether we are talking about individuals' acts in isolation or in collective contexts, what individuals are responsible for depends on which act descriptions it makes sense to use in describing their acts.[7] A wrong may be something for which an individual is solely responsible, or it may be something larger for which a group of people is responsible. But if we might describe individuals' acts as intentional (or perhaps negligent) contributions to the larger purpose, and particularly if the individuals understand themselves as acting intentionally in the service of that purpose, then we have a basis for holding them responsible. We still do not have a framework for holding an individual responsible for *the whole thing*, but we have gone beyond the initial proposal to the extent that when individuals' acts can be described in the context of collective harms, we have a morally significant understanding of their contributions.

Some might object that the genocide example and the smog examples are too different to warrant the same analysis.[8] The main difference, of course, is that in the smog case, but not the genocide case, there is no intention to participate in a group act. Clearly, contributing to smog and contributing to genocide are not on a moral par. However, once the moral relevance of a contribution to pollution is made clear, then it is irrelevant whether agents intend or merely foresee what they are actually doing when they turn on their air conditioners. Even if there are suitable applications of the doctrine of the double effect, this is not one of them.

Another way that these examples differ from one another is in the nature of the group. One reason that the presence of intention is so important in the genocide case is that it also points to a certain group solidarity. Not only is the participation of individuals intentional, but the intention highlights a joint goal around which the group members come together. The collective wrong is what the individual is committed to, and this is what makes the individual's act wrong in the way that I am claiming, and not just as an isolated individual act.[9] I have said that the individual's participation in the collective act of genocide is wrong because the individual takes her or himself to be participating in and intends to be participating in (and *is* participating in) genocide, and genocide is a collective wrong. In the smog case, however, there is no collective intention or joint goal, so the collectivity is much weaker. Indeed, there is also a third kind of case, midway between these two, in which there is a well-defined, cohesive group that harms without intending to. For such cases, we might ultimately need a different basis for responsibility, perhaps collective negligence. These differences are important, but they do not affect the point made with the smog example. The main reason for introducing the smog case is to illustrate that the collective context in which our actions take place contains morally relevant information, and that, when determining responsibility, it is important to take such information into account.

In the next section, I consider how Larry May justifies holding both collective entities and individual agents responsible for group crimes, such as genocide. According to his proposal, it is possible for individuals to be morally responsible for a genocide as a whole, not only for a part of it.

II

According to Larry May, there are two ways of holding individuals responsible for group crimes. The first is to establish that individuals acted with "discriminatory intent," which is, roughly, the intent to harm a group. The second way is to first establish that a collective entity such as a state is responsible, and to then turn our attention to the individuals who play the most significant role(s) in the collective or state structure.[10] In this section, I address his discussion of the second way.

May's focus is international crime, and he is specifically addressing when it is appropriate to prosecute individuals for international, group-based crimes, particularly crimes against humanity. In discussing the prosecution by the International Criminal Tribunal for the former Yugoslavia (ICTY) of "minor players" for crimes against humanity, May outlines a number of conceptual difficulties that arise in the attempt to establish discriminatory intent.[11] Recent international law requires discriminatory intent only for genocide, not for other crimes against humanity such as ethnic cleansing,[12] but May himself argues that in order to be fair to defendants discriminatory intent should be required.[13]

May's focus here is the legal case. We can, however, extrapolate a view about the moral case.[14] Is it possible for an individual to be morally responsible for a collective wrong?

May makes the point that the concept of international crime, under which the crimes of genocide and crimes against humanity fall, has a necessarily collective dimension. He notes that "crimes against humanity are crimes perpetrated by a state or state-like entity against a population or other group of people."[15] However, the sanctioning of states is not the approach taken in international criminal law since the Nuremberg trials. As in the moral case, rather than attribute responsibility to artificial collective entities such as states, we see a need to hold individuals responsible for such atrocities as genocide. Paraphrasing a famous statement about corporations, May notes that collective entities such as states or corporations "have neither pants to kick nor a soul to damn."[16]

The most straightforward cases of individual responsibility for collective crimes are those involving heads of state. In these cases, there is much less difficulty establishing a connection between the individual's purposes and acts and those of the collective entity.

May grounds the responsibility of individual leaders in "command responsibility." Leaders do not have to have ordered atrocities to be responsible for them. They simply have to have had knowledge that subordinates were engaged in such acts, "and failed to stop [them] or to punish those who so acted."[17] The failure to do anything about that criminal activity establishes a "constructive intention" that the atrocities be committed.

May proposes a very clever strategy for linking individuals such as heads of state to a group crime such as genocide. He suggests that the first task be to show that collective entities such as states can commit these crimes, and the second, to show that heads of state can be said to embody the *mens rea* of the state. He believes that in international tribunals the focus on the actions of individuals involves a significant oversight of the "conspiracy-like character of what often occurs in a state."[18] The main feature of the conspiracy model of responsibility that May emphasizes is that "each of the co-conspirators is treated as an agent of the others thereby allowing the imputation of the acts of one to the others."[19] In particular, once a conspiracy-like arrangement has been established, it makes sense to ask who played the most important role. That person does not have to have engaged in acts which, in isolation, are wrong. For example, the leader of a conspiracy to commit a robbery does not have to commit the robbery her or himself to be responsible for it. May believes that we think about the role of heads of state in criminal state actions similarly. He says that "while it is true that heads of state normally do not do the deeds of murder, rape, or torture [as crimes against humanity] themselves, these acts would not occur but for the direction of the leaders."[20] The subordinates are likely not to have engaged in crimes against humanity without the direction of leaders. Moreover, the leaders of states are normally the most responsible for what states do. It is rare for a state not to act in a way that is consistent with what the leader wants.

We can see from his account of the conspiracy model that May holds the responsibility of the collective entity to be, in an important sense, prior to that of the individual. The best way of thinking about the sorts of group acts that we are considering, such as genocide, is as intentional acts of the state.[21] Having established the collective responsibility of the state, we can move on to establish the individual responsibility of leaders. We do this because, as seen above, conceptually it makes sense to think of the leaders as "setting" the intentions of the state. They will be the easiest to implicate. Those who play a lesser role may also share some of the responsibility, but only the most powerful are in a position to set state intentions, and to ensure that they are carried out. As May points out, leaders are both natural and artificial persons. When they are acting in their leadership role as representatives of the state, their actions are the actions of the state. For example, when President Bush declares war on Iraq, then the United States of America declares war on Iraq. Bush's action may be re-described as an action of the state.

May's position allows us to do something that the previous alternative did not, namely, to hold an individual responsible for a wrong that a collective entity performed. Thus, the head of state and others in positions of sufficient power may be, according to this view, responsible for the group wrong of genocide, not just murder or even *participation* in genocide, but genocide itself. Thus, according to this view, individuals can be morally responsible for collective wrongs.

There are limitations, however, to deriving individual responsibility for group wrong from a prior attribution of collective responsibility to a collective entity. The first is that more loosely structured groups than states might perpetrate these sorts of wrongs. In Rwanda, for example, the genocide had a great deal of support from people in positions of power, but was not exactly "state-sanctioned." Indeed, by most accounts, it was set in motion by the shooting down of the president's plane. The proposal for holding heads of state responsible after establishing the state's responsibility requires a high level of structure in the relevant collective entity. The structure is necessary for clearly defining individuals' roles, and especially for highlighting who the likely candidates are for setting the group's intention.

In addition, this kind of proposal limits us in terms of who we can hold responsible, as individuals, for collective wrongs. Consider again the Rwandan genocide. Over 125,000 people were held to stand trial in connection with the genocide, and many are still being held. It might be desirable to implicate some people who do not hold positions in the power structure responsible for the genocide – the collective crime – not just for murder or even for participating in a genocide. May allows that "minor players" could act with the necessary intentions as well, and therefore be responsible, despite not being representatives of the state.[22] Thus, the mechanism through which they are responsible is different; it is through their own discriminatory intent. Is this sufficient for attributing responsibility for genocide even though, as individuals, they cannot perpetrate a genocide alone? May proposes that when such intent may be established, individuals are responsible for the group crime. He believes that it is important to require discriminatory intent for this kind of crime, while acknowledging that this requirement is difficult to establish in minor players who are not representatives of the state.[23] Where representatives of the state are concerned, there are fewer difficulties. For when we can establish the state's intention, the next step is to investigate who best captures or embodies the intent of the state. Usually, the heads of state will be the ones.

Because of the need for evidence, the legal case, especially the legal case for prosecuting someone for crimes against humanity, raises difficulties that the moral case does not. In some instances, the problems are practical and logistical. For instance, it is simply not possible for the International Criminal Tribunal for Rwanda to prosecute all 125,000 suspects for crimes against humanity. Thus, May's suggestion that an intention to participate in the group plan might be sufficient for establishing individual responsibility for a collective wrong raises fewer difficulties in the moral case than the legal one. Anyone who has the necessary intention will be morally implicated; it is not as important in the moral case as in the legal case to establish the intention.

Let us now turn to Christopher Kutz's proposal for understanding how individuals can be responsible for collective wrongs. According to his view, individual participants in collective wrongs are responsible not just for their contributions, but for the collective wrong itself.

III

Christopher Kutz develops a theory of complicit responsibility that captures the notion of individual responsibility for collective actions.[24] The central idea in his theory is participatory intention. A participatory intention is an intention to participate in a collective act, that is, to participate in bringing about a collective goal. In the Rwandan genocide, for example, the shared goal of the participants was the destruction of all Tutsis and Tutsi sympathizers. Anyone who participated in the genocide with this intention satisfies Kutz's requirement for the basis of responsibility.

Kutz's discussion takes place in the context of a problem very similar to the one under discussion here: the problem of attributing responsibility to individuals for collective wrongs, or more generally, the problem of attributing responsibility to individuals for what others do.[25] He believes that collective wrongs can be proper objects of individual responsibility, and participatory intentions provide the link by serving as the *basis* for responsibility. The basis is the ground for an ascription of responsibility. Kutz distinguishes between the *basis* for responsibility and the *object* of responsibility. The object is what an agent is held responsible for. In the cases under discussion, the object of responsibility is collective – the agents are responsible for the collective wrong. The basis on which they are responsible, the participatory intention, is individualistic, not collective. Kutz captures his idea of individual responsibility for collective harms in the following principle:

> The Complicity Principle: (Basis) I am accountable [responsible] for what others do when I intentionally participate in the wrong they do or harm they cause. (Object) I am accountable [responsible] for the harm or wrong we do together, independently of the actual difference I make.[26]

Now, despite maintaining that individuals can be responsible for collective wrongs in which they participated but to which they made no essential difference, Kutz does distinguish between different levels of responsibility. He does so by distinguishing between two kinds of "authorship." I may be an inclusive or an exclusive author of some act. Depending on which I am, I may be inclusively or exclusively responsible.

We are the exclusive authors of actions that we perform ourselves, and of events caused by those actions. We are the inclusive authors of actions of a group in which we participate. Exclusive authors can accurately say, "I did it." Inclusive authors can accurately say, "we did it," but not, "I did it." In the exclusive case, agents are connected directly, through a causal mechanism, to their actions. In the inclusive case, agents are connected indirectly, through a teleological mechanism that involves a shared goal, to the actions of others. In the case of collective action, this teleological aspect is fundamental. Collective actions essentially involve agents acting in concert to achieve shared goals.[27]

The inclusive author of an act is inclusively responsible for that act. A shared goal may explain why two people did what they did, but it also gives each person licence to think of the other's act as something that *they*, together, have done. To illustrate, let us consider one of Kutz's own examples. Suppose that you and I plan to go on a picnic. I buy the cheese and the bread; you buy the wine and the sparkling water. We are each the exclusive author of our respective acts; that relation holds directly and is causal (as well as teleologically oriented around our shared goal). But we can make the further claim that *we* bought the cheese, bread, wine, and sparkling water. Our joint goal binds our actions together so that they are not just mine and not just yours, but ours. Regardless of any causal relations between our individual acts and their outcomes, then, we are each inclusive authors of what we did together.[28]

Similarly, the responsibility link for inclusive responsibility is teleological rather than causal. To the extent that we share a goal, "we are properly held accountable for the actions of groups (and of individual group members) in which we participate because these actions represent our own conception of our agency and our project."[29] Our intentional acts reflect what we are willing and wanting to be doing. Once I join forces with others around a joint goal, my investment in that goal means that I can be properly held responsible for what we do to achieve it. And that means that I can be considered responsible, in an inclusive sense, for acts of which others are the exclusive authors. Thinking back to the picnic example, *we* bought the wine and sparkling water in preparation for the picnic, but only you can also say "*I* bought the wine and sparkling water." You are the exclusive author of that act; I am an inclusive author because that purchase takes place in the larger context of bringing about a goal that we share.

May's view concerning heads of state is most effective at attributing responsibility to individuals for collective wrongs such as genocide when those individuals can be considered representatives of the state. Kutz's notion of inclusive authorship and participatory intention makes it possible to link an individual to a collective wrong in much less structured circumstances. Let's consider it in the context of the Rwandan genocide as it will give us a way of considering many more than the sixty-five powerful suspects at the ICTR responsible for that genocide. For although the average perpetrators – in the year 2000 there were over 125,000 suspects awaiting trial in Rwanda – were not exclusive authors of the genocide, to the extent that they had a participatory intention to take part in it they were inclusive authors of the collective wrong. From the participants' perspective, it is accurate to think of the genocide as something that "we did." The actions of the group are, in a sense, representative of each participant's conception of her or his own agency. As Kutz points out, the individual's inclusive responsibility is independent of the difference that she or he makes to the outcome or the control that she or he has over the outcome.[30] According to Kutz, the relevant feature of responsibility is teleological, not causal. Agents are responsible, he argues, because they embrace the goal and act with the intention of helping the collective achieve the goal, even if they, as individuals, could not or did not achieve it on their own. No agent is wholly causally responsible for the collective act or outcome, but each is teleologically linked to that act or outcome through a commitment to the joint goal and to doing her or his part in aid of the goal.

The question that remains is this: Is there a morally relevant difference between inclusive and exclusive responsibility? After all, exclusive responsibility is established through a direct causal link together with a teleological link, whereas inclusive responsibility is only linked teleologically. If the addition of a causal link makes a moral difference at all, inclusive responsibility would likely be the less serious of the two. Kutz does not believe that we can establish, as a general rule, that one is more serious than the other. He cannot rest too heavily on the causal link, as he has already claimed that it is not necessary for responsibility. Instead, Kutz's short answer to the question of which is worse is that it depends entirely on the situation. He invokes, to illustrate, our reactions to the case of Othello. Othello, not Iago, is the exclusive author of the murder of Desdemona. In other words, in a direct causal sense, Othello kills her; she dies by his hand. However, argues Kutz, Iago, an inclusive author in the murder, is the greater villain because of his role in manipulating Othello. Kutz believes that though we think Othello guilty of murder, our reaction to him is tempered by the role Iago played; "Iago is the 'hellish villain' of the tragedy."[31] If a plausible case can be made for the claim that Iago is more deserving of contempt than Othello, then a direct causal link – that is, being the exclusive author – does not necessarily make someone more responsible.[32]

We can see something similar happening in cases of genocide. Kutz does not discuss the genocide example, or the role of leaders in this kind of case, but it is worth having a look at in the context of his distinction between inclusive and exclusive authorship and responsibility. Of particular import is the fact that genocide has a collective dimension, which entails that no individual agent is the exclusive author, and thus that no individual agent is exclusively responsible. As May points out, this gives it more the character of conspiracy. There are Iagos, but no Othello; that is, no single individual committed the whole genocide, as Othello committed the whole murder. All participants, from organizers, planners, and heads of states to minor players who did the actual deeds, are inclusive authors in these sorts of wrongs. I have maintained that genocide is something that only "we" can do (leaving aside extraordinary cases which would not raise the complicated questions that we are dealing with here). There is no "I did it" in the case of genocide, at least not in the terms of exclusive authorship set by Kutz. That is not necessarily a bad thing, but it is worth noting because it helps to reinforce the point that moral agents' level of moral responsibility for something need not be based on a direct causal connection between their actions and what they are responsible for.

The main appeal of Kutz's approach is precisely that he makes room for this less direct sort of responsibility and plausibly bases it in individuals' intentions. When, as an individual, you intend to participate in a group project, your intentional participation should implicate you in some way, regardless of the extent and nature of your actual contribution. As Kutz points out, your actual contribution might make a minimal difference to the outcome, yet still you are implicated in it as an agent. It is correct to consider you a member of a group who perpetrated the wrong as a group. Those who participated in the genocide cannot say "I did it," but they can certainly say "we did it," and they have no grounds on which to distance themselves from the "we."

What the inclusive/exclusive responsibility distinction does not do is give us grounds for distinguishing degrees of responsibility. As we have seen, there is no general rule that says that the responsibility of exclusive authors is necessarily more serious than that of inclusive authors. In genocide, major players no less than minor players are inclusive authors of the collective act. To determine degrees of responsibility we need to ask the same questions that May urged us to ask: Who planned, organized, and directed this collective action? Who played what role? Who was in charge?[33] There is, however, an important difference between May's view and Kutz's.

First, consider May. In his view, the responsibility of the heads of state is a function of the responsibility of the state itself and their role within the state structure. As he puts it, "if it is established that a state is responsible for various harms, then it makes sense to ask who in the state is the most responsible for what the state has done."[34] In most cases, that will be the leaders.[35]

Kutz's view makes it easier to implicate more people in the collective wrong because it does not rest as firmly on the responsibility of a collective entity. Instead, individuals are implicated if they consider themselves to be part of a group whose goals they share. By all accounts, the participants in the Rwandan genocide took themselves to be participating in a collective action, the goal of which was to destroy all Tutsis and their sympathizers. In Kutz's view, action with the intention to participate is sufficient for responsibility of a sort, namely, inclusive responsibility. This would not be sufficient for May because most of the participants, however they understood their actions, were not in a position to "set" the group's intentions. Within the group, they wielded insufficient power to control the group. Thus, whatever responsibility they have, it is for their individual contributions and not for the collective wrong. In Kutz's view, even if there are different degrees of responsibility among individuals, the object of responsibility is the same for all participants. Not only are they *all* responsible for genocide; they are also *each* responsible for genocide.

This paper began by asking whether individuals can ever be considered morally responsible for group wrong, such as genocide. If we accept Kutz's account of inclusive responsibility, the answer to this question is "yes." Each intentional participant is inclusively responsible for the collective action and its consequences. But a worry remains. Does the notion of inclusive responsibility tell us enough to be useful? Perhaps the idea of inclusive responsibility for a collective wrong, with participatory intention as the individualistic basis, dilutes responsibility so much that the real issues lie elsewhere and remain unresolved. It is a worry for Kutz's proposal, for example, that the basis for responsibility – the participatory intention – gives us no way of distinguishing degrees of responsibility. Anyone who has a participatory intention fulfills the same criterion for inclusive responsibility. Each is responsible for the collective wrong. This leaves us to wonder what the significance of being inclusively responsible is.

May addresses a related worry that could arise in regard to international law if the focus on intention in cases of genocide were to supersede all other considerations. He points out that unless an individual's actions were not just intended as contributions to genocide, but also did take place in the context of genocide, it would be very difficult to prosecute for genocide.[36] In other words, the mere existence of a participatory intention would not be enough for responsibility even if it resulted in action. With respect to moral, rather than legal, responsibility, I maintain that broader, collective features of acts make a difference to what it is appropriate to hold individuals responsible for. Though May is concerned most deeply with what could be proved in a criminal court, I believe that in the moral case, too, individuals' intentions to participate in a joint project are insufficient for responsibility if, in fact, no such joint project exists. One cannot be responsible, neither morally nor legally, neither partly nor wholly, for participating in a collective action that does not take place.

In the following section, I return to the view that individuals are responsible for their share of collective wrongs.

IV

If the revision of the first view that we considered has merit, then it may be good enough to think of individuals as responsible for their share. According to this view, their share is, after all, a share of genocide, and that is a morally significant fact about an agent's act. Returning to our question, then, we have a qualified answer. In certain cases – those well-articulated by May – in which an individual "sets" the relevant intentions of a collective entity, that individual may be considered responsible for the wrongs committed by that collective entity. But, I have maintained, in cases involving less formal structures, or involving agents who are not representatives of the collective in any formal and relevant way, the other participants are responsible, not for the collective wrong, but for their parts in it. Thus, the object of their responsibility is individualistic, not, as Kutz would have it, collective. The morally relevant description of their actions makes it clear that they are contributions to a collective wrong. In the most straightforward case, they are intentional contributions.

The main difference between my view and Kutz's is the nature of the object of responsibility. We agree that acting with the intention to participate is a sufficient basis for responsibility. But Kutz would press the point that individual contributions are frequently minimal; they seem not to make perceptible differences to the total harmful outcome. If they make little or no difference, then perhaps holding an individual responsible for them carries little normative weight. To respond, I maintain that the account I propose fares better than Kutz's in terms of the normative weight of moral responsibility. Kutz's view is subject to dilution because the significance of inclusive responsibility is unclear. In my view, the individual's act is described in the larger collective context as a contribution to the collective harm. Therefore, the individual contribution implicates the agent in the greater moral context, and cannot be ignored.

The main goal of this account is to capture the moral significance of the individual's action so that this significance does not fall by the wayside. In the initial version of the view outlined at the beginning of section I, the individual actions were not described as parts of a collective undertaking. Thus, their collective dimensions, from which we derive the full force of their moral significance, were not salient. Agents of course think of themselves as morally innocent if they are just driving to work. But once they begin to think of their actions as contributions to a serious health and environmental problem, the actions take on a moral dimension that they did not have before.

This recognition of the act's moral dimensions is not really different from any case in which the moral dimensions of actions are brought to an agent's attention. As agents, we can consider ourselves innocently engaged in activities whose wrong we fail, for whatever reason, to grasp. For example, many former veal-eaters stopped eating veal when they realized what calves have to go through before they become the most tender meat. Many people seek out "fair-trade" products in order not to participate in the exploitation of small farm owners. And most of us participated in the boycott of South African products during apartheid – drinking wine or sherry might be morally innocent, but supporting apartheid is not. These examples show that it is not unusual for actions that have the initial appearance of being morally neutral to take on moral qualities when seen in a broader context. But even acts that are not morally neutral in the first instance, such as murder, might have other morally relevant features when they are seen in broader contexts. I have argued that we may view murders that are contributions to genocide in this way.

CONCLUSION

In concentrating on moral responsibility, I have made few direct comments about the legal implications of my claims. In the legal case, particularly when individuals are charged with international crimes, such as crimes against humanity, and face international criminal tribunals, it matters a great deal what can be proved. The International Criminal Court has the best chance of successfully prosecuting representatives of states in the way suggested by May: once the ICC establishes that a collective entity such as a state has done wrong, it can turn to the heads of state and other political leaders as the most likely candidates for determining the state's plan and for being in a position to stop the plan from materializing. May has given a good account of how those in more minor roles could, if discriminatory intent is established, also be successfully prosecuted by international courts.[37] I have maintained that others, such as the 125,000 suspects in Rwanda, are responsible for their contributions, understood as contributions to genocide. Their contributions are likely to vary in severity, and so will their degree of responsibility. So also will the possibility of determining in a legally satisfactory way with what intentions they acted. As a case in point, the *gacaca* courts instituted in Rwanda to speed up the judicial process for the 125,000 suspects in the genocide have been criticized for their lack of rigour in dispensing justice.[38]

In conclusion, let me reiterate that my main concern is to address the question of whether individuals can ever be considered morally responsible for collective wrongs. I have claimed that sometimes this makes sense, but in most cases individuals are responsible only for their contributions. However, their contributions need to be understood in a particular way. For example, where genocide is concerned, it is important to bear in mind that while a given murder may well be a contribution to genocide, there is a descriptive difference between murder and genocide. Thus, when a murder is also a contribution to genocide, just as when eating a meal is also a contribution to animal suffering, we have additional, morally salient information about the act. This information implicates individual participants in collective wrongs, not by holding them responsible for collective wrongs, but by accurately characterizing their actions as contributions to collective wrongs. When genocide is an act of the state, and there is a representative of the state who sets the state's intentions, then, following May, we should consider that individual responsible for genocide. In the absence of such persons or such state action, there may not be one individual responsible for the collective wrong. But to the extent that individuals contribute to collective wrongs, they are morally implicated in those wrongs, and morally responsible for their contributions as contributions to collective wrongs.

NOTES

♣ Earlier versions of this chapter were presented at the conference "Bringing Power to Justice" held at the University of Western Ontario (UWO), March 2003, and at the Global Justice Seminar at the Watson Institute, Brown University, May 2003. Many thanks to audiences at those presentations for lively and helpful discussion. I would like to thank the UWO conference organizers Joanna Harrington, Michael Milde, and Richard Vernon, and Global Justice Seminar organizer Neta Crawford for their invitations to participate. I also received helpful comments from colleagues at the University of Western Ontario in moral, legal, and political philosophy at a meeting of the work-in-progress group. For those comments, I thank Robert Binkley, Samantha Brennan, Richard Bronaugh, Charles Jones, Dennis Klimchuk, Carolyn McLeod, Michael Milde, and Richard Vernon. Thanks to Larry May for helpful comments, and for sharing his in-progress manuscript *Crime and Humanity: Toward a Normative Account of International Criminal Law* (Cambridge: Cambridge UP, forthcoming) and for giving me permission to quote from it. Thanks also to my research assistant, Meena Krishnamurthy. This chapter was supported by a Social Sciences and Humanities Research Council of Canada Standard Research Grant.

1 According to international law, "genocide means any of the following acts committed with intent to destroy, in whole or in part, a national, ethnical, racial or religious group, as such:

(a) Killing members of the group;
(b) Causing serious bodily or mental harm to members of the group;
(c) Deliberately inflicting on the group conditions of life calculated to bring about its physical destruction in whole or in part;
(d) Imposing measures intended to prevent births within the group;
(e) Forcibly transferring children of the group to another group."

Convention for the Prevention and Punishment of the Crime of Genocide, 9 December 1948, 78 UNTS 277 [hereinafter Genocide Convention].

2 See Christopher Kutz, *Complicity: Ethics and Law for a Collective Age* (Cambridge: Cambridge UP, 2000); Larry May, *Crime and Humanity: Toward a Normative Account of International Criminal Law* (Cambridge UP, forthcoming).
3 See Donald Davidson, *Essays on Actions and Events* (Oxford: Clarendon Press, 1980); Joel Feinberg, "Action and Responsibility," *Philosophy in America*, ed. M. Black, 134–60 (Ithaca, NY: Cornell UP, 1965).
4 Ibid.
5 Donald Davidson, "Agency" and "The Individuation of Events" in *Essays on Actions and Events* (Oxford: Claredon Press, 1980).
6 Genocide Convention, *supra* n1.
7 Particular acts either do or do not admit of certain descriptions. Certain descriptions are morally relevant; others are not. We beg the question when we let a prior moral judgment about an action determine which description to use (as when we describe abortion as "murder," rather than the more neutral "killing," because we have already decided that it is wrong). For a more detailed defence of this view, see Tracy Isaacs "Moral Theory and Action Theory, Killing and Letting Die," *American Philosophical Quarterly* 32, no. 4 (1995): 355–68.
8 A number of people, including Michael Milde and Jeremy Bendik-Keymer, have raised this point.
9 I am grateful to Jeremy Bendik-Keymer and Virginia Held for drawing my attention to the significance of this feature of my view.
10 May, *supra* n2, chap. 6.
11 Ibid., chap. 7.
12 See the *Rome Statute of the International Criminal Court*, 17 July 1998, UN Doc. A/CONF. 183/9, 2187 UNTS 90, reprinted in *International Legal Materials* 37, no. 5 (1998): 1002, art. 5 [hereinafter ICC Statute]. Also, while the International Criminal Tribunal for the Former Yugoslavia Statute did not include the element of discriminatory intent, "the Trial Chamber has required discriminatory intent nonetheless, while the Appeals

Chamber rejected that element," May, *supra* n2, 202. ICTY Statute, Annex to SC Res. 827, UNSCOR, 48TH Sess., UN Doc. S/INF/49 (1993); *Prosecutor* v. *Dusko Tadic* (1997), Case No. IT-94-1-T, ICTY Trial Chamber, para. 652, on-line: United Nations <http://www.un.org/icty >.

13 May, *supra* n2, chap. 7. He reasons that without this element it is difficult to "distinguish isolated criminal acts from crimes against humanity" (202).

14 May has written about collective and shared responsibility in two previous works, *The Morality of Groups* (Notre Dame: Univ. of Notre Dame Press, 1987) and *Sharing Responsibility* (Chicago: Univ. of Chicago Press, 1992). In *The Morality of Groups*, he focuses on responsibility at the collective level, with the goal of establishing conditions under which it makes sense to hold groups responsible. He is not concerned in that work with individual moral responsibility. My question is whether individuals can ever be considered morally responsible for collective actions or harms that flow from them. In *Sharing Responsibility*, May defends the thesis that "people should see themselves as sharing moral responsibility for various harms perpetrated by, or occurring within, their communities" (1). This connection, though important, is weaker than the one that I am exploring. I am examining the potential for linking individuals to collective wrongs more through their contributions than through their association with a community. Thus, May's discussion in his forthcoming book is the most relevant to the range of questions under discussion here.

15 May, *supra* n2, 180.

16 Ibid., 236. The original quote, "Did you ever expect a corporation to have a conscience, when it has no soul to be damned, and no body to be kicked?", is attritubed to Edward, First Baron Thurlow (1731–1806), Lord Chancellor of England, in John C. Coffee, Jr., "'No Soul to Damn: No Body to Kick': An Unscandalized Inquiry into the Problem of Corporate Punishment," *Michigan Law Review* 79 (January 1981): 386.

17 May, *supra* n2, 231.

18 Ibid., 238.

19 Ibid., 239.

20 Ibid., 253.

21 Ibid., 226.

22 Ibid., chap. 7.

23 Ibid., 200–8, 225.

24 Kutz, *supra* n2, especially chaps 3, 4, and 5.

25 Kutz speaks of "accountability" rather than "responsibility," claiming that accountability is narrower in meaning than responsibility. Specifically, Kutz claims not to be as concerned with the internal conditions of responsibility

as a set of competencies, as he is with responsibility as a set of normative, relational duties that agents have to others. He maintains that "agents are accountable to others for a harm as a function of their relations to others, as well as of everyone's relation to the harm or the wrong" (18). I find Kutz's use of "accountability" at times inconsistent with understanding it as a set of normative duties, rather than as a way of evaluating agents morally – for praiseworthiness or blameworthiness – in light of their adherence to such a set. Since this is how I understand moral responsibility, I shall use "responsibility" interchangeably with Kutz's "accountability."

26 Kutz, *supra* n2, 122.

27 The concept of collective action has been discussed extensively by the following authors, and others: Michael E. Bratman, "Shared Cooperative Activity," *The Philosophical Review* 101, no. 2 (1992): 327–41; Margaret Gilbert, "Walking Together: A Paradigmatic Social Phenomenon," *Midwest Studies in Philosophy* 15 (1990): 1–14; Larry May, *The Morality of Groups* (Notre Dame: Univ. of Notre Dame Press, 1987); Raimo Tuomela and Maj Bonnevier-Tuomela, "From Social Imitation to Teamwork," *Contemporary Action Theory,* eds. Raimo Tuomela and Ghita Holmstrom-Hintikka, vol. 2, 1–47 (Boston: Kluwer Academic Publishers, 1997); Christopher Kutz, *Complicity: Ethics and Law for a Collective Age* (Cambridge: Cambridge UP, 2000).

28 Kutz, *supra* n2, 140.

29 Ibid., 141.

30 Ibid., 14.

31 Ibid., 151.

32 Ibid., 151–2.

33 In *Utilitarianism as a Public Philosophy* (Cambridge: Cambridge UP, 1995), Robert Goodin articulates a view of responsibility that he labels "Task-Responsibility" and distinguishes from "Blame-Responsibility." The main question in task responsibility is "Who was supposed to do what?" and responsibility is determined by task assignment. Goodin believes that this view is better than the "finger-pointing" purpose of blame-responsibility which, he argues, is ineffective when it comes to apportioning responsibility for group endeavours. See especially chap. 7, "Apportioning Responsibility."

34 May, *supra* n2, 253.

35 Ibid., 153.

36 Ibid., 279.

37 See ibid., chap. 7.

38 The Norwegian Helsinki Committee, "The Gacaca System and the International Criminal Tribunal for Rwanda: Prosecuting Genocide in Rwanda,", Report II/2002, on-line: <http://www.nhc.no/rapporter/landrapporter/rwandarap.PDF>.

7

The International Criminal Court as an Institution of Moral Regeneration: Problems and Prospects

CATHERINE LU

where th' offence is, let the great ax fall
King Claudius in *Hamlet*

Societies haunted by the legacies of violent communal conflict and atrocity confront the perilous task of moral regeneration. I understand the project of moral regeneration to involve establishing a new order of political, legal, and social relationships that affirms certain moral truths or principles denied by previous modes and orders, and which aims at preventing a recurrence of violations of those moral truths or principles.[1] The establishment of an International Criminal Court (ICC) represents the introduction of one international approach to the project of moral regeneration in the aftermath of communal violence and war. According to Amnesty International, "the struggle for international justice has taken a major stride forward" with the establishment of the ICC, a sentiment echoed by most human rights and humanitarian organizations, as well as by the UN Secretary General and numerous state leaders who endorsed the creation of the Court.[2]

In this chapter, I explore the different ways in which the ICC may be considered an institution of moral regeneration in international and domestic societies. Proponents of the ICC offer the following justifications for the creation of the Court: to achieve justice by ending impunity of violators; to strengthen the rule of law by remedying deficiencies of ad hoc tribunals and replacing national criminal justice systems when they are unwilling or unable to act; to deter future violators; and to help end conflicts.[3] While the purposes of the ICC can be captured by the concept of moral regeneration, its actual efficacy as an institution of moral regeneration will be measured not only, or even primarily, by its contributions to the development of international law but ultimately by the political and moral transformations its operation will be able to foster and support in international and domestic contexts. Although the declared legal, moral, political, and social objectives of the ICC are grand, it may be that acknowledging its limits as an institution of moral regeneration will be key to its success.

I. THE ICC AS A LEGAL, MORAL, AND POLITICAL INSTITUTION

The idea of an international criminal court has a long history, but until recently, it has largely been a history of missed opportunities.[4] To many international lawyers, the ICC represents a triumph of the rule of law over the rule of force in international society. The exercise of power according to rules consistently applied is the primary objective of the rule of law, and the ICC is, at least in part, an institutional embodiment of this legalistic objective.[5] In addition to furthering the rule of law in international and domestic societies, the substantive nature of the crimes addressed by the ICC gives prominence specifically to human rights and humanitarian law in contexts of war and peace. Given the tenuous hold of law in general in many domestic and international realms, and of humanitarian claims in particular, further entrenchment of the rule of law, and more specifically, of humanitarian principles, at the level of international governance can be seen to constitute not only a legal, but also a moral achievement in world politics.

At the same time, however, it is important to remember the mixed record of legal contributions to the development of international morality. Even in the face of the Holocaust, during the Nuremberg trials, the conservative tendencies of law exhibited themselves in jurists' concentration on the more conventional crimes against peace and war crimes, rather than the relatively newer charge of crimes against humanity. As Richard Vernon has observed, "the architects of the Nuremberg Charter, which introduced the offence of 'crime against humanity,' did what they could to conceal its novelty, and to render it organic with previous international law."[6] In domestic societies as well, "law and order" is a common slogan for those who seek to maintain the status quo, rather than those who seek to change it. While this might be comforting to conservative critics of the ICC, its advocates need to be mindful of the limits of law and legal mechanisms for engendering political, social, and moral change in international or domestic societies.

Indeed, the moral efficacy and practical impact of any system of law depend on the larger political, social, and moral contexts in which the system operates. The reliance of legal institutions on prior moral and political developments is abundantly evident in the history of the struggle to establish an international criminal court. From its inception, the idea of such a court itself sprang out of horrendous *political* developments that culminated in World War II and the Holocaust. The establishment of the ICC also required not only legal experts, but political and moral struggles between and within governments and civil society actors. In this sense, the establishment of legal norms and institutions is not something divorced from politics, nor is it superior to politics. Rather, as Judith Shklar has argued, "law is a form of political action, among others, which occasionally is applicable and effective and often is not. It is not an answer to politics, neither is it isolated from political purposes and struggles. ... The question is not, 'Is law political?' but 'What sort of politics can law maintain and reflect?'"[7]

Recognizing the interconnectedness of law, politics, and morality is one way to address realist worries that the ICC may be a misguided, ineffectual, or dangerous development based on idealism.[8] The concern is that in its commitment to legalistic justice, the ICC will marginalize or ignore other equally important moral and political values and goals. As Shklar warned: "In its exclusiveness, [legalistic] justice as a policy tends to ignore all other political ends and the very social circumstances which condition its effect and even its possibility. Formal justice depends for its social impact upon the total political environment in which juridical actions occur, and its functions cannot be understood in isolation."[9] Acknowledging the dynamic interrelatedness of law, politics, and morality allows us to see that the field of morally appropriate considerations and responses relating to acts of inhumanity is not as limited as strict legalists might claim, nor can the objectives of moral regeneration be reduced entirely to the achievement of legalistic justice. Realist criticisms may thus be valid warnings against an excessively legalistic interpretation of the criteria for moral regeneration. As an institution of moral regeneration, the ICC is more than a legal institution with legalistic objectives; its purpose and operation should also be understood in moral and political terms.

The framers of the ICC clearly acknowledge the larger moral and political justifications for its creation, which consist primarily in helping to end communal violent conflict and to prevent future violations. The preamble of the ICC Statute shows that state representatives understand the ICC to be an institution of moral accounting that expresses their determination "to put an end to impunity for the perpetrators of these crimes and thus to contribute to the prevention of such crimes."[10] The ultimate political objective underlying the creation of the Court is the prevention of future acts of atrocity. The wager is that the effective prevention of future atrocities and the establishment of an enduring peace may well require confronting issues of moral and political responsibility for past acts of atrocity, since failure to do so leaves the sources of violent conflict unexamined and unmitigated. The absence of an institutionalized mechanism of moral accounting leaves unresolved an explosive sense of injustice that can pave the way to repeated cycles of violence and instability.[11] In prudential terms, the ICC can help assuage and channel potentially destructive retributive emotions that often plague post-war and post-atrocity politics.

Acknowledging this underlying political objective of the ICC makes more intelligible and defensible certain political limits on its mandate and jurisdiction. From a legalistic perspective, article 16 of the ICC Statute, which grants the UN Security Council the power to prevent the Court from exercising its jurisdiction, might seem to be an intolerable compromise that implies the abdication of the rule of law to power politics. The fear of a legal purist is that prosecutions will be halted based on arbitrary political considerations, and this is indeed a plausible fear in the realm of world politics. Yet if we acknowledge the role of the ICC as a political institution charged with political objectives, article 16 cannot be objectionable just by virtue of setting political limits to the Court's jurisdiction. In this light, it is clear that the function of article 16 is to ensure that the ICC's pursuit of some of its objectives – to end impunity and vindicate the rule of law – is consistent with a primary political objective of international society, which is the maintenance of international peace and security. This rationale is evident in the article, which states that the Security Council can only suspend prosecutions after adopting a resolution under chapter VII of the UN Charter; this means that the suspension of prosecutions can only be justified on the ground that the pursuit of prosecutions would undermine directly and immediately sensitive political negotiations related to the promotion of international peace and security.[12] Thus, this political limit to the ICC's jurisdiction need not constitute an arbitrary or indefensible compromise between law and politics; rather it confirms that the pursuit of legal justice must ultimately be justified by its contribution to securing the political and social conditions for preventing future violations.

If we focus on the ultimate aim of moral regeneration, which is to prevent future violent conflicts and atrocities, three aspects of the ICC's mandate raise questions about its problems and prospects as an institution of moral regeneration. First, there may be potential tensions between the universalist presumptions of the ICC's mandate and the facts of political and cultural pluralism. Second, because the ICC focuses on individual accountability, other causal factors of violent conflict and atrocity may not receive enough attention. Third, its primary commitment to achieving accountability through punishment might conflict with measures required to form the social bases for reconciliation at international and domestic levels. The problems raised by these lines of inquiry are not fatal to the ICC, but they point to potential dangers that can undermine the moral efficacy of the ICC as an institution of moral regeneration.

II. MORAL UNIVERSALISM IN A PLURAL WORLD

The ICC constitutes a legal mechanism of accountability for the interstate and intrastate moral violations of genocide, crimes against humanity, war crimes, and aggression.[13] Some might see an inevitable conflict between the ICC's vindication of universalist humanitarian claims and the political order of sovereign states or international society itself. As Hedley Bull has put it: "Carried to its logical extreme, the doctrine of human rights and duties under international law is subversive of the whole principle that mankind should be organised as a society of sovereign states."[14] The worry is that the humanitarian mandate of the ICC will stand in normative conflict with the statist principles of international society; in simpler terms, the ICC's pursuit of justice for individuals threatens the stability of an international order designed for states.

The mandate of the ICC, however, points away from this radical conclusion. Although its ad hoc predecessors, the International Criminal Tribunals for the former Yugoslavia and Rwanda (ICTY and ICTR) enjoyed "primacy," the ICC's jurisdiction is limited by the concept of "complementarity." This means that the Court can only exercise jurisdiction when domestic courts fail to prosecute due to lack of will or incompetence. In reality, then, the ICC will simultaneously limit *and enhance* states' rights and responsibilities. As William Schabas has observed, the ratification of the ICC Statute took time partly because, in order to fulfill their responsibility arising from the notion of complementarity to prosecute suspects in their territorial jurisdiction, many states needed to "bring their substantive criminal law into line, enacting the offences of genocide, crimes against humanity and war crimes as defined in the Statute and ensuring that their courts can exercise universal jurisdiction over these crimes."[15] In validating universalist humanitarian principles, then, the ICC does not automatically undermine an international order of sovereign states.

Although the affirmation of humanitarian principles at the global level does not necessitate the elimination of states, it does require the gradual transformation of the moral basis of sovereigns' internal and external agency and accountability. This transformation of the normative basis of international order is now in progress, and has been spurred in part by recognition in the post–Cold War era that the moral legitimacy of the society of states was actually damaged by its failure to respond adequately to the political and humanitarian catastrophes produced by the Balkan wars and the 1994 Rwandan genocide. Bull noted in his discussion of the conflict between justice and order in world politics that "the proponent of order takes up his position partly because the existing order is, from his point of view, morally satisfactory, or not so unsatisfactory as to warrant its disturbance."[16] In the contemporary context, an international order that fails to halt, discipline, or condemn sovereigns that commit atrocities or genocide against their own populations is increasingly seen by member states to be morally unsatisfactory and, hence, unstable as well. One could argue that the ICTY and ICTR were created precisely to mark the moral regeneration of the international order itself. In other words, far from undermining international order, it could be argued that an institution such as the ICC is a necessary component of any legitimate and stable international order of sovereign states.

Even if the ICC's commitment to vindicating the rule of law and humanitarian law is consistent with the legitimacy and stability of international order, some might worry about the ability of the ICC to accommodate the fact of cultural pluralism. We need not entertain the argument that cultural distinctness can ever justify genocide, war crimes, and other crimes against humanity such as rape, disappearances, torture, and so on. Yet despite the universal condemnation of such acts, the fact of cultural pluralism may justify different kinds of responses to such acts. Critics might worry that an international legal mechanism of accountability would be an unjustifiable imposition on societies that have distinct cultural values pointing to alternative responses to atrocity. Shklar argued, for example, that the appeal to natural law during the Tokyo Trials after World War II seemed arbitrary "in a world society that is even more complex and pluralistic than the great nation-states of our time."[17]

Rwanda, after the 1994 genocide, is opting for a traditional mechanism of justice and reconciliation, called the *gacaca*, that emphasizes restitution and reparation over retribution. The main objective of the new *gacaca* courts "is not to determine guilt nor to apply state law ... but to restore harmony and social order in a given society, and to re-include the person who was the source of the disorder."[18] Similarly, Archbishop Desmond Tutu drew on the African concept of *ubuntu* ("humanity to others") to justify the South African Truth and Reconciliation Commission's mandate to grant amnesty to perpetrators of political violence in return for a truthful accounting.[19]

It is misleading, however, to attribute these different responses to differences in cultural values. Initially, the Rwandan government attempted the retributive route domestically; it is reviving the *gacaca* for reasons of moral and political expediency. Similarly, the amnesty provisions of the South African Truth and Reconciliation Commission were forged in the context of the political battle to effect a peaceful transition to democratic rule. Rwanda's former ambassador to the United States, Richard Sezibera, has argued that, after the genocide, "If we want to have justice and reconciliation in our country, we need to build our policy on four pillars. ... The first of these is that we need the deconstruction of the myths that have been built up, in order to help strengthen national unity and national reconciliation. Secondly, we need the punishment of the crimes committed. Third, we need the rehabilitation of those who were victims. And fourth, we need the construction of a new Rwandan national identity."[20] These tasks – truth, retribution, reparation, and transformation – constitute the project of regeneration that all societies dealing with the legacies of communal violence must confront. Differences in approaches to these tasks will likely depend more on distinct domestic and international political conditions and contexts, and the moral complexity of the issues, rather than on differences in cultural values.

This discussion does suggest that because it is faced with the morally complicated tasks of regeneration in a pluralistic world the ICC cannot meet its mandate through a blindly uniform application of legal rules. Rather, the moral efficacy of the ICC will clearly require a high degree of sensitivity to the unique histories and circumstances of each case. Insensitivity to context makes it less likely that the ICC will contribute positively to the project of moral regeneration. For example, Ian Buruma notes in his discussion of the Tokyo Trials that "instead of helping the Japanese to understand and accept their past, the trial left them with an attitude of cynicism and resentment."[21] His point is not that the project of moral regeneration was inapplicable to the case of Japan after World War II, but rather that in the Japanese context the Tokyo Trials proved to be an ineffectual and possibly counterproductive instrument for advancing the aims of that project. Critics of the ICC's moral and legal universalism may be assuaged if it is acknowledged that the validation of such universalism does not militate against contextualizing the project of moral regeneration.

III. INDIVIDUAL ACCOUNTABILITY AND THE PREVENTION OF FUTURE ATROCITIES

The ICC, with jurisdiction over "natural persons" above age eighteen, will be a mechanism for establishing *individual* accountability for various crimes against humanity, rather than state responsibility for crimes against states or individuals.[22] Other international courts, such as the International Court of Justice, the Inter-American Court of Human Rights, the European Court of Human Rights, and the

African Court of Human Rights, can only determine state accountability – not individual accountability – and therefore are only responsible for adjudicating "state (civil) responsibility for violations of international law."[23] In a political order of sovereign states, the moral agency and responsibility of states has thus been recognized by these courts that can be called upon by individuals or states to investigate and hold governments accountable for state violations of human rights and humanitarian law.[24] With the establishment of the ICC, the moral agency and responsibility of individuals to uphold international humanitarian law is affirmed; the message to those in positions of power is that their office, or status as agents of the state, does not absolve them of personal responsibility, at least in cases of war crimes, crimes against humanity, and genocide.

If the ultimate aim of moral regeneration is the prevention of future violence and atrocities, one might ask how the ICC's focus on individual accountability seeks to contribute to that goal. One argument holds that individuating guilt for atrocities can help promote social reconciliation. If specific individuals can be blamed and punished, their societies can be distanced from the moral stain of the atrocities, and need not bear the burden of collective guilt. The work of criminal trials, by holding individuals accountable, contributes to restoring the bases of social reconciliation by lessening inter-communal hostility.

As an empirical matter, it is not clear that this claim can work without some important conditions. Trials can actually exacerbate inter-communal tensions, especially when, in contexts of inter-communal war, they target individuals from only one community and are seen to be one-sided. The ICTR, for example, has focused on the prosecution of the anti-Tutsi *génocidaires*, but its failure to pursue the investigation and prosecution of indictable crimes committed during the genocide by members of the Tutsi-led group that now governs Rwanda has led to charges of "victor's justice." Helena Cobban argues that this apparent partiality, coupled with serious problems of maladministration, have undermined the ICTR's ability to support the process of national reconciliation in Rwanda.[25]

Yet even if we assume this lessening of inter-communal hostility to be empirically valid, this posited virtue of the ICC's work – achieved by containing responsibility for political violence and atrocities to individuals rather than their societies – may actually be a liability when one considers the complicated multiple roots of political violence, as such violence typically involves not only the actions of culpable individual agents but also the operation of defective or dysfunctional social, economic, and political structures of belief, authority, and power. Some might worry that in assigning responsibility to individual agents, the ICC's verdicts will only serve to obscure the institutional and structural roots of violent political conflict and atrocity.

Indeed, criminal trials render individuated justice that is based on a victim/perpetrator and guilt/innocence distinction. While they may be effective in establishing a moral accounting of those who gave the orders and committed the dirty deeds, they may be less capable of providing an accounting of the political, economic, and social ideologies, institutions, and structures that made the violations possible. As Buruma has put it, "trials are not up to dealing with collective responsibility and truth. The language is simply wrong."[26] If the ultimate aim of moral regeneration is to prevent future conflicts and atrocities, moral and legal condemnation and punishment of even the most culpable individual perpetrators may not be sufficient to effect the necessary political, social, and economic transformations.

With this concern in mind, advocates of truth commissions have argued that such commissions have been able to gather a fuller narrative of the conditions, ideologies, and institutions that perpetuated moral wrongs. As Elizabeth Kiss has noted, "most truth commissions prepare a report offering specific recommendations for legislative, political, institutional, educational, or other changes that are needed to ensure that abuses do not recur." They provide accountability by establishing "as a matter of public record the institutional mechanisms responsible for past abuses."[27]

The record of past international criminal tribunals shows that their participants were aware of the limits of focusing on individual guilt. For example, between 1946 and 1948, American military tribunals operating under Control Council Law No. 10, a modified version of the Charter of the International Military Tribunal that was responsible for prosecuting offences during World War II, sought to expose various levels of individual and institutional corruption by trying "groups of defendants, such as judges, doctors, bureaucrats and military leaders."[28] Cobban also notes that prosecutors of the

ICTR have chosen to emulate this strategy by trying "small numbers of high-level representatives of different sectors of society, ... including 'political leaders,' 'military leaders,' or 'church leaders' – and many of the trials have been designed and conducted using these same groupings."[29]

This prosecutorial strategy implies that the adjudication of individual moral agency and responsibility is related to an evaluation of social beliefs, institutions, and structures because individuals, in committing acts of genocide, war crimes, or crimes against humanity, are invariably acting within a context of social beliefs, roles, and identities. For example, an ICC verdict against members of a national army will likely reflect poorly on a country's military and political institutions. A judgment against Milosevic will likely contribute to the debate among Serbs about his political legacy and their collective identities and narratives.

Assigning individual responsibility, especially of leading political and military figures, is one way to start the process of moral accounting of the past. Under this view, the ICC's verdicts will affirm the crucial connection between individual agency and responsibility, especially of those in positions of power and authority, but they should not be read as the end of the accounting process. Rather, they should be seen as a beginning, opening the door to further avenues of investigation and reflection into the moral and causal responsibility of other individuals, and of institutions such as government agencies, banks, churches, militaries, judiciaries, media, international organizations, and other external parties. To the extent that violations are bound up with communal identities and narratives, the work of the ICC, in providing a well-documented record of violations, may also challenge the truthfulness and validity of these identities and narratives.

This discussion suggests that preventing future occurrences of war crimes, genocide, and crimes against humanity will likely entail a process of moral, political, and social metamorphosis that is long, painful, and conflictual for all involved. The project of moral regeneration is predicated on the assumption that failure to embark on such a process may make it too easy for the past politics of violence and atrocity to resurface in the future. Although the ICC's work of assigning individual responsibility may kick-start such a process, it cannot constitute the be-all and end-all of our understanding of moral and especially causal responsibility in contexts of political violence and atrocity. Without a complete account of causal factors, preventive strategies, although well-meaning, will likely be partial or misguided, and ineffectual.

IV. RETRIBUTION, REPARATION, AND RECONCILIATION

The decisions of the ICC, like those of all criminal courts, result in punishment of those deemed guilty. Practitioners of similar criminal courts have offered a variety of justifications for punishment that point to the main aims of the project of moral regeneration. Those who represent the ICTY, for example, have understood the purpose of punishment to include "deterrence, incapacitation of the dangerous and rehabilitation."[30] ICTR officials similarly have argued that holding individuals accountable by punishing them contributes to "deterrence, namely to dissuade for good, others who may be tempted in the future to perpetrate such atrocities by showing them that the international community shall not tolerate the serious violations of international humanitarian law and human rights."[31] If the posited connection between punishment and deterrence holds, then the retributive mandate of the ICC would clearly contribute to preventing the recurrence of atrocities.

In the contemporary international context, however, the retributive, and hence deterrent, capacity of the ICC is severely affected by its relative political weakness as an international institution. Given the lack of endorsement by some of the most powerful and populous states in the world, including the United States, China, and India, it is not at all clear that the ICC will be able to deliver on its promise to end the culture of impunity, since the effectiveness of its prosecutions and punitive authority will rely on the actual use of power by states to bring alleged perpetrators to the Court.[32] The ICC thus may not be able to wield effective punitive power, especially against the world's most powerful and potentially most egregious offenders. If punishment is necessary to effect deterrence, the ICC's restricted capacity to punish undermines its effectiveness as a deterrent of future violators.

There may, however, be other ways in which the work of the ICC can contribute to a general deterrence of atrocities. Indeed, the *moral* authority of the ICC is not necessarily undermined by its political weakness; the lack of endorsement by the world's most powerful states may even boost its moral legitimacy. In other words, critics might be right that the ICC will not be a highly effective punitive institution, but it may still have a significant moral and political impact. For example, despite their non-existent coercive powers, international non-governmental organizations such as Amnesty International and Médecins Sans Frontières have been able to command significant economic, political, and social resources in the service of their moral and political objectives. The existence of the ICC and its limited operation may therefore still contribute to a more general normative shift in international society towards greater political accountability and respect for human rights and humanitarian interests, and in the long run, this may even affect the conduct of powerful states.

In cases where the ICC can effectively exercise its punitive powers, the spirit with which it pursues its mandate should be informed by an awareness of the common human frailties that bind the judged and those who judge. As Shakespeare reminds us in *Hamlet*, it is unlikely that the political power that deals retribution can claim morally pure foundations. In this light, it would be wrong to view the ICC as an axe wielded by the morally pure against the irredeemably evil; rather, it will, at best, be a dramatic forum for the moral education of all of us who, by virtue of our human frailties, are ever in danger of similar moral defects and limits. This is not an argument to give up the task of assigning moral responsibility altogether, but it is a reminder to locate retribution in a human context of limited and defective moral knowledge, agency, and structures.

In addition, it will be important to acknowledge the limits of punishment as an instrument of moral regeneration. Indeed, the pursuit of prosecutions may not always be morally constructive in the complicated political and social environments produced by domestic or international violent conflict. In some cases, offering conditional amnesty may be more constructive in terms of securing the basic political or social conditions that are needed for moral regeneration.[33] This means that even when ICC prosecutors can effectively pursue a case, they should consider the impact of a prosecution on furthering the larger political and social objectives of moral regeneration. Furthermore, although it may be true that "punishment has a *telos*, ... not so much to produce good as ... to establish goodness,"[34] it would seem that punishment only serves to establish goodness in a rather negative way, since "all punishment is nothing but a form of rejection."[35] Punishment is, at best, a repudiation of moral falsehoods implied by moral wrongs or evil, but it does not positively establish goodness. To defeat evil and to promote goodness are related but distinct tasks.[36]

Recognition of the instrumental and intrinsic limits of punishment has spurred the development of notions of "restorative justice" in domestic contexts. In support of that development, the ICC does not focus only on punishing perpetrators, but also attempts to address the needs and concerns of victims. Most significantly, the ICC Statute empowers the Court to provide reparations to victims and their families for restitutive, compensatory, and rehabilitative purposes. The Court can do this by determining "the scope and extent of any damage, loss and injury to, or in respect of, victims," with a view to enabling reparative claims before national courts.[37] The Court can also provide reparations through a victims' Trust Fund that will consist of fines and assets seized or collected from convicted perpetrators.[38]

It is unfortunate that such a trust fund is likely to be small, and that international society is not more committed to providing additional resources to help rehabilitate victims of political violence and atrocity. Richard Sezibera has spoken of the need to construct "a new Rwandan national identity" as a basis for social reconciliation after the Rwandan genocide.[39] If social reconciliation is an important step towards preventing future violations, it is not only perpetrators whose identities need to change; victims also require assistance to transform the legacies of victimhood. Even if perpetrators are punished, the material impact of political violence and atrocity on the lives of victims will remain and can dominate their future, especially if communal resources are depleted and economically productive family members have been killed or injured. Without financial assistance at individual and communal levels to alter the material effects of political violence and atrocity, victims will likely have a hard time transforming their identities as victims, undermining prospects for social reconciliation. Given the limited financial commitment of international society to victims and their communities, the ICC might be considered a seriously misguided diversion of already scarce resources.[40] The inclusion in the ICC Statute of reparative measures for victims, however, raises the hope that the work of the ICC may result in greater financial commitments from international society for the project of moral regeneration in affected communities.

Helena Cobban has argued that in contexts of communal violence, victims, perpetrators, and bystanders can all be viewed as survivors who have been affected by the violence, and all require different forms of rehabilitation and healing.[41] Against retributivist logic, she notes that perpetrators of crimes against humanity are also corrupted, and ultimately perhaps even more thoroughly corrupted than their victims.[42] She thus argues for focusing our energies and resources more on healing the wounds of violence between and within communities, rather than on assigning criminal responsibility and punishment to individual perpetrators. In the end, the ICC's chief value to the project of moral regeneration may not lie in its punitive powers, but in its ability to establish an authoritative and truthful record of events and violations, to order and promote reparations for victims and the affected communities, and to encourage the self-reflection required for moral regeneration in all survivors of violence and atrocity.

CONCLUSION

In this essay, I have focused on the International Criminal Court as a legal, moral, and political institution that aims to serve the project of moral regeneration by affirming the rule of law and especially the significance of humanitarian law in domestic and international societies; by focusing on individual accountability in response to violations that constitute war crimes, genocide, and crimes against humanity; and by promoting deterrence through the punishment of perpetrators, and social reconciliation through reparations for victims. Although the jury must be out at this early stage in the life of the newly established ICC, we can draw some tentative conclusions from this discussion about how we might go about evaluating its performance. Clearly, it is not realistic or fair to expect the ICC to be able by itself to prevent genocide, war crimes, and other crimes against humanity, just as no domestic legal mechanism, by its mere existence, has been able to prevent war between states, civil wars, or even domestic familial and interpersonal violence. We ought, therefore, to be sceptical of international jurists' and human rights organizations' inflated appraisals of the capacity of the ICC to effect international or domestic moral regeneration.

Like all similar institutions, whether the ICC will serve or undermine the greater project of moral regeneration will depend on the moral, social, and political contexts in which it operates, and the spirit with which the Court pursues its mandate. I have argued that the ICC can be morally efficacious as an institution of moral regeneration if it can avoid the following dangers. First, it should be acknowledged that moral universalism does not entail a uniform application of legal rules. The ICC's affirmation of universalist humanitarian and legal principles will likely be more effective when it displays appropriate sensitivity to political and social contexts. Second, as a mechanism of moral accounting that focuses on individual agency and responsibility, the ICC will not be nearly sufficient by itself to address the institutional and structural roots of political violence and atrocity. The verdicts of the ICC therefore should not exhaust the search for moral and especially causal responsibility, which is crucial to the ultimate objective of prevention. Third, the instrumental and intrinsic limits of punishment for advancing the project of moral regeneration should be recognized. The moral utility of such measures as punishment, amnesty, and reparation depends on their contribution to the project of moral regeneration; that is, punishment, amnesty, and reparation make moral sense only if they do not undermine, but are consonant with, the *positive* promotion of respect for the humanitarian principles underlying the ICC's mandate.

These are not arguments against the creation of an institution such as the ICC, but they should remind its proponents that the work of the ICC alone cannot replace and should not displace the political, social, and moral struggles and transformations that are necessary for the effective prevention of future acts of inhumanity. If we return to the claim that an institution such as the ICC is a necessary component of a legitimate and stable international society, the preceding arguments should make it clear that the existence of the ICC alone is insufficient to legitimize or stabilize international order. Indeed, an international society that is quick to punish through the ICC, but slow to help empower the destitute and the marginalized, would constitute a perversion rather than a fulfillment of the universalist humanitarian ideals underlying the ICC's mandate. Paradoxically, the ICC's potential to support the project of moral regeneration in domestic societies that are haunted by the legacies of communal violence and atrocity may depend on further substantive transformations in the international economic and political context. In this sense, the quest for moral regeneration in domestic societies may be inextricably linked to the moral regeneration of international society itself.

NOTES

1 I first discussed the idea of moral regeneration in "Justice and Moral Regeneration: Lessons from the Treaty of Versailles," *International Studies Review* 4, no. 3 (2002): 3–25.

2 *The International Criminal Court*, on-line: Amnesty International <http://www.web.amnesty.org/web/web.nsf/pages/ICChome>.

3 See *Rome Statute of the International Criminal Court Overview*, on-line: United Nations <http://www.un.org/law/icc/general/overview.htm> [hereinafter ICC Statute Overview].

4 See William A. Schabas, *An Introduction to the International Criminal Court*, 2d ed. (Cambridge: Cambridge UP, 2004), 1–8; and the introduction to this volume.

5 According to Judith Shklar, legalism as an ideology privileges rule-following, and an understanding of moral relationships that consists of "duties and rights determined by rules." See Judith N. Shklar, *Legalism: Law, Morals and Political Trials* (1964; reprint, with a new introduction, Cambridge, Mass.: Harvard UP, 1986), 1.

6 Richard Vernon, "What Is Crime against Humanity?" *Journal of Political Philosophy* 10, 3 (2002): 231–49, 231–2. See also Shklar, *supra* n6, 146–7.

7 As Shklar cogently argues, adherents of legalism, whether they hold a positivist or natural conception of law, understand law and politics to be distinct spheres. Interestingly, international realists also understand the "rules" of politics to be distinct from the rules of morality or law. The autonomy of politics from law and morality is implicit, for example, in Machiavelli's argument that those who act according to moral rules while in the political sphere (where political rules apply) are only inviting ruin. See ibid., 143–4.

8 Stephen Krasner has voiced his opposition to the ICC, arguing that "the consequences of carrying out its mandate may in fact prove to be destructive." Stephen D. Krasner, "A World Court that Could Backfire," *The New York Times*, 15 January 2001, A15, final edition.

9 Shklar, *supra* n6, 146.

10 ICC Statute Overview, *supra* n4. See also the *Rome Statute of the International Criminal Court*, 17 July 1998, UN Doc. A/CONF. 183/9, 2187 UNTS 90, reprinted in *International Legal Materials* 37, no. 5 (1998): 1002 [hereinafter ICC Statute].

11 On the sense of injustice and the retributive emotions, see Melvin J. Lerner and Sally C. Lerner, eds., *The Justice Motive in Social Behavior: Adapting to Times of Scarcity and Change* (New York: Plenum Press, 1981).

12 The UN Security Council may "suspend prosecution but only by positive resolution, subject to annual renewal." See Schabas, *supra* n5, 83.

13 I am going to bracket the issue of "aggression" from the following discussion because states parties have not come to an agreement on how to define the term and the conditions for its application.

14 Hedley Bull, *The Anarchical Society: A Study of World Order in World Politics* (New York: Columbia UP, 1977), 152.

15 Schabas, *supra* n5, 19.

16 Bull, *supra* n15, 97.

17 Shklar, supra n6, 128.

18 Helena Cobban, "The Legacies of Collective Violence: The Rwandan Genocide and the Limits of Law," *Boston Review*, April/May 2002, on-line: Boston Review <http://www.bostonreview.net/BR27.2/cobban.html>.

19 Elizabeth Kiss, "Moral Ambition within and beyond Political Constraints: Reflections on Restorative Justice," in *Truth v. Justice: The Morality of Truth Commissions*, ed. Robert I. Rotberg and Dennis Thompson, 68–98 (Princeton: Princeton UP, 2000), 81.

20 Quoted in Cobban, *supra* n19.

21 Ian Buruma, *The Wages of Guilt: Memories of War in Germany and Japan* (London: Phoenix, 2002), 166.

22 ICC Statute, *supra* n11, art. 25. See further Schabas, *supra* n5.

23 Steven R. Ratner and Jason S. Abrams, *Accountability for Human Rights Atrocities in International Law: Beyond the Nuremberg Legacy*, 2d ed. (Oxford: Oxford UP, 2001), 225.

24 Ratner and Abrams view the bringing of a case by Bosnia and Herzegovina before the International Court of Justice in 1993 "to find the Federal Republic of Yugoslavia (Serbia-Montenegro) responsible for genocide and to order remedial measures" as the most significant example of a petition by a state calling upon an international court to determine a state's violation of its international humanitarian obligations (ibid.).

25 Helena Cobban, "Healing Rwanda: Can an International Court Deliver Justice?" *Boston Review*, December 2003/January 2004, on-line: Boston Review <http://bostonreview.net/BR28.6/cobban.html>.

26 Buruma, *supra* n22, 168.
27 Kiss, *supra* n20, 75.
28 Schabas, *supra* n5, 7.
29 Cobban, *supra* n26.
30 Quoted in Schabas, *supra* n5, 164.
31 Ibid., 164.
32 India and China have neither signed nor ratified the ICC Statute. Russia has signed but not yet ratified. The United States has renounced or "unsigned" the treaty. See Neil A. Lewis, "U.S. Is Set to Renounce Its Role in Pact for World Tribunal," *The New York Times*, 5 May 2002, 18, final edition.
33 On Mozambique's use of a general amnesty for "crimes against the state" after sixteen years of brutal war, see Priscilla B. Hayner, *Unspeakable Truths: Facing the Challenge of Truth Commissions* (New York: Routledge, 2002), 186–95.
34 Jean Hampton, "The Retributive Idea," in Jean Hampton and Jeffrie G. Murphy, *Forgiveness and Mercy*, 111–61 (Cambridge: Cambridge UP, 1988), 125–6. On the philosophical debates about the moral functions and justifications of punishment, see H.B. Acton, ed., *The Philosophy of Punishment* (London: Macmillan, 1969).
35 Daniel Cappon, "Punishment and the Person," *Ethics* 67, no. 3 (1957): 184–95, 188.
36 See Lu, *supra* n2; and Catherine Lu, "Victimhood, Retribution, and the International Criminal Court as an Institution of Moral Regeneration," in *La voie vers la Cour pénale internationale: tous les chemins mènent à Rome – The Highway to the International Criminal Court: All Roads Lead to Rome*, eds. Hélène Dumont and Anne-Marie Boisvert, (Montreal: Éditions Thémis, 2004), 363–72.
37 ICC Statute, *supra* n11, art. 75. See further Schabas, *supra* n5.
38 ICC Statute, *supra* n11, art. 79.
39 Quoted in Cobban, *supra* n19.
40 Cobban records that the ICTR's approved budget for the 2002–03 biennium period was $256.9 million US. She continues: "By comparison, $322 million was given in foreign aid in 2000 to Rwanda's 7.6 million people. Many extremely needy countries in Africa receive considerably less foreign aid than that." See Cobban, *supra* n26.
41 Cobban, *supra* n19.
42 This is a view articulated and endorsed by Socrates: "we ought not to retaliate or render evil for evil to any one, whatever evil we may have suffered from him." See Plato, *Crito*, 49, in *The Four Socratic Dialogues of Plato*, Benjamin Jowett trans. (Oxford: Clarendon Press, 1949); and *The Republic of Plato*, Allan Bloom trans. (United States: Basic Books, 1991).

8

Serving the Interests of Justice: Amnesties, Truth Commissions, and the International Criminal Court

DARRYL ROBINSON*

The entry into force of the ICC Statute of the International Criminal Court on 1 July 2002[1] means that many issues which were once of purely theoretical interest will soon arise in concrete form with very real legal and political ramifications. Prominent among these issues is the sensitive and controversial question of the relationship between the ICC and national reconciliation measures, such as truth commissions.

The ICC is a vital part of the international effort to eliminate the persistent climate of impunity which has so often sheltered those who commit serious international crimes. The ICC is a permanent international judicial institution designed to complement national judicial systems by prosecuting persons responsible for genocide, crimes against humanity, and war crimes where national judicial systems are unable or unwilling to do so. It is expected that the ICC will contribute to a climate of accountability not only through the demonstrative effect of its own prosecutions but, more importantly, through the "multiplier effect" of its complementary jurisdiction, as it encourages states to more diligently apprehend and prosecute international criminals.

While welcoming the creation of the ICC, some commentators have expressed concerns that its approach may prove to be too blunt in dealing with the varied and complex situations facing democracies in transition. For example, Charles Villa-Vicencio greets the ICC as "both morally impressive and legally a little frightening" because "it could be misinterpreted, albeit incorrectly, as foreclosing the use of truth commissions."[2] Similarly, Alex Boraine observes: "It is to be hoped ... that when the International Criminal Court comes into being, it will not, either by definition or by approach, discourage attempts by national states to come to terms with their past. ... It would be regrettable if the only approach to gross human rights violations comes in the form of trials and punishment. Every attempt should be made to assist countries to find their own solutions provided that there is no blatant disregard of fundamental human rights."[3] Other commentators, including strong supporters of the ICC and individual accountability, have suggested that there should be some scope for the ICC to defer to truth commission initiatives where such initiatives are legitimate and necessary mechanisms for a transition from repression or violence to a stable democracy.[4]

The issue of how to deal with national amnesties and national truth and reconciliation efforts was raised in the ICC negotiations,[5] but was not explicitly dealt with in the ICC Statute. Views on the matter clashed sharply, as many participants felt very strongly that prosecution is the sole appropriate response (and indeed an obligatory response), whereas others felt very strongly that alternative mechanisms were acceptable. Even among those delegations most committed to prosecution of all international crimes, many had misgivings about laying down an iron rule for all time mandating prosecution as the *only* acceptable response in all situations. On the other hand, creating an explicit exception allowing amnesties was equally untenable. Some delegations opposed any exceptions in principle, whereas others were concerned that any exception would be immediately exploited and abused. Indeed, the very purpose of the ICC was to ensure the investigation and punishment of serious international crimes, and to prompt states to overcome the considerations of expedience and *realpolitik* that had so often led them to trade away justice in the past.

The drafters of the ICC Statute wisely chose not to delve into these difficult questions. First of all, agreement would likely have been impossible, given the sharply clashing views on the matter. Second, even if there were agreement in principle, it would have been unwise to attempt to codify a comprehensive test to distinguish between acceptable and unacceptable reconciliation measures and to lock such a test into the statute.[6] Thus, the drafters turned to the faithful and familiar friend of diplomats, *ambiguity*, leaving a few small avenues open to the Court and allowing the Court to develop an appropriate approach when faced with concrete situations.

This chapter reviews some of the possible avenues available to the ICC and suggests possible interpretative approaches for the Court. The most likely point at which the ICC will determine whether to defer to national programs is pursuant to the discretion of its prosecutor to decline to prosecute where it would not be in the "interests of justice." The basic argument presented here is that the ICC, given its mandate, *must* generally insist on prosecution, but that there may be exceptional circumstances where it would not be in the interests of justice to interfere with a reconciliation mechanism, even though that mechanism falls short of prosecuting all offenders.

First, for transitional societies dealing with mass atrocities, a program of truth commissions and conditional amnesties for lower-level offenders, coupled with prosecution of the persons most responsible for such crimes, would likely be a sufficient response deserving deference from the ICC, especially where the number of offenders is prohibitive.

Second, if a state went further and allowed even the persons most responsible for international crimes to apply for conditional amnesties, this would be far more difficult to justify. This does not mean the door is completely closed, however, as the ICC may keep an open mind to creative and good faith alternatives to traditional models of prosecution. Still, in light of the ICC's mandate, the circumstances would have to be quite compelling, and one would require both pressing circumstances of necessity as well as an impressive non-prosecutorial approach which advances the objectives of accountability.

Third, a blanket amnesty for international crimes would be the antithesis of the purpose of the ICC and should never enjoy deference from the Court.

It is important to clarify at the outset that there is no inherent hostility or contradiction between the objectives of the International Criminal Court and truth and reconciliation efforts per se. Where they are used to *supplement* criminal investigations and prosecutions, truth commissions offer many important benefits that are not provided by prosecution alone. Criminal trials are a highly formalized process to determine the culpability of particular accused persons; they are not appropriate fora to deal with the greater context or root causes of a conflict or repressive regime, nor – in light of the rules of procedure and evidence – are they a welcoming forum for victims to share their experiences.[7] Truth commissions can supplement prosecutions as a valuable means to give a voice to victims; to build a comprehensive record of events, patterns, and causes; to provide meaningful official and societal acknowledgment; to promote reconciliation; to facilitate compensation of victims; to educate the public; and to make recommendations for the future.

Thus, prosecutions and truth commissions each serve valuable objectives which are not inherently in conflict.[8] The problem arises where truth commissions are accompanied by amnesties. The problem for the International Criminal Court is not the truth and reconciliation efforts, but rather the fact that serious international crimes are going unpunished. Indeed, the very raison d'être of the ICC is to help ensure that serious international crimes do not go unpunished.[9]

1. INTERPRETING THE ICC STATUTE

In determining an appropriate approach for the ICC with respect to national reconciliation efforts that fall short of full prosecution, it is useful to bear in mind several important features of the Court's jurisdiction.

The first point is that the jurisdiction of the ICC is limited to "the most serious crimes of concern to the international community as a whole," namely genocide, crimes against humanity, and war crimes.[10] These crimes are cautiously defined so as to focus on atrocities of particular scale and severity. Thus, these are the very crimes for which the imperative of punishment is greatest and for which amnesties are the most widely seen as inappropriate.[11]

The second point is that the purpose of the ICC is to ensure that violators do not escape punishment. The guiding philosophy is articulated in paragraphs three to five of the preamble of the ICC Statute, which read as follows (emphasis added):

Recognizing that such grave crimes threaten the peace, security and well-being of the world,

> Affirming that the most serious crimes of concern to the international community as a whole *must not go unpunished* and that their *effective prosecution must be ensured* by taking measures at the national level and by enhancing international cooperation,
>
> Determined to *put an end to impunity* for the perpetrators of these crimes and thus to contribute to the prevention of such crimes ...

These are the "marching orders" given by the international community to the ICC.

Third, it is important to bear in mind the narrow jurisdiction of the ICC and its basis in express state acceptance. This narrow jurisdictional regime militates against the argument that ICC insistence on prosecution would undermine either sovereignty or legitimate democratic decisions.[12] The ICC has jurisdiction only where the Security Council refers a matter, or where the state on whose territory the crime occurred or the state of nationality of the accused has accepted the jurisdiction of the ICC (such acceptance may be furnished by ratifying the ICC Statute or by submitting a declaration of acceptance to the Court).[13] In the case of a referral, special deference to the national choices of the state concerned is not necessary, since a Security Council decision under chapter VII of the UN Charter entails that the situation is a threat to international peace and security, and makes compliance by all states mandatory.[14] Without a Security Council referral, the ICC only has jurisdiction relating to civil conflict or repression within a state where that state has ratified the statute or expressly declared its willingness to have those crimes judged by the ICC.[15] In a sense, the state concerned has *entered into a compact with the ICC, specifically mandating the ICC to prosecute wherever the state itself fails to do so*.[16] Therefore, arguments that ICC insistence on prosecution may interfere with sovereignty or domestic democratic choices should not be given too much weight, since in reality the state has already specifically *contracted* with the ICC to perform precisely this function.

In light of the ICC's specific mandate and the compact which states have entered into with it, the ICC must be committed to prosecution and can defer to non-prosecutorial programs only in exceptional situations. Given the framework of the statute, there are three mechanisms by which deference is possible:

1 The ICC prosecutor may in some circumstances decline to prosecute on the grounds that it would not serve the *interests of justice* (article 53);

2 Where the alternative mechanisms being employed so closely meet the goals of accountability that they can be considered "*genuine" proceedings*, deference is possible under the "complementarity" regime (article 17);

3 Where the Security Council determines that investigation or prosecution would interfere with efforts to maintain or restore *international peace and security*, the Security Council may require the Court to suspend action (article 16).

II. THE INTERESTS OF JUSTICE: DISCRETION NOT TO PROCEED

A. The Structure of Article 53

The most likely point at which deference could be accorded to non-prosecutorial reconciliation measures would be when the prosecutor decides not to proceed with an investigation or prosecution. Article 53(1) of the ICC Statute governs the decision by the prosecutor on whether to launch an investigation once jurisdiction has been "triggered" by a referral from a state party or the Security Council.[17] Article 53 provides that the prosecutor *shall* initiate an investigation *unless* he or she determines that there is "no reasonable basis" to proceed. More specifically, article 53(1)(c) requires the prosecutor to consider whether, "taking into account the gravity of the crime and the interests of victims, there are nonetheless substantial reasons to believe that an investigation *would not serve the interests of justice*" (emphasis added).[18] This same consideration arises again under article 53(2), which governs the decision of the prosecutor, following the investigation, as to whether to continue to the next stage, namely, prosecution.[19]

This determination is not, however, purely a matter of prosecutorial discretion; the prosecutor is subjected to a significant degree of oversight by the Pre-Trial Chamber. With respect to decisions not to proceed based on the "interests of justice," article 53 allows for particularly careful scrutiny, and in two ways.

First, where the prosecutor's decision not to proceed is based on other grounds – e.g., lack of legal or factual basis, inadmissibility due to complementarity, or a crime of insufficient gravity to justify ICC action – the Pre-Trial Chamber can review the decision only upon request of the referring state party (or the Security Council in the case of a Security Council referral).[20] In contrast, where the decision not to proceed is based on the "interests of justice," the Pre-Trial Chamber may also initiate a review of that decision "on its own initiative."[21]

Second, where the prosecutor's decision not to proceed is based on other grounds, the Pre-Trial Chamber can only "*request* the prosecutor to reconsider" his or her decision.[22] In contrast, where the Pre-Trial Chamber decides of its own initiative to review a decision based on the "interests of justice," the prosecutor's decision requires the *approval* of the Pre-Trial Chamber.[23] Thus, the Pre-Trial Chamber can oblige the prosecutor to continue with the investigation or prosecution.[24]

As a result, in order for prosecution to be declined on the grounds of the "interests of justice," not only would the prosecutor have to be persuaded, but also very likely the Pre-Trial Chamber.

B. Interpretation of "Interests of Justice"

A fundamental first question is whether the notion of "interests of justice" is confined only to the interests of *retributive, criminal* justice, or whether broader considerations of "justice" can also be taken into account. The latter appears to be the only supportable interpretation. Article 53(2)(c) specifically contemplates that the prosecutor may take into account broader factors, including compassionate considerations such as the age or infirmity of the accused. Moreover, article 53(1)(b) specifically juxtaposes the traditional criminal justice considerations – the gravity of the crime and the interests of the victims – with the broader notion of "interests of justice" and clearly indicates that the latter might trump the former. Thus, the ordinary meaning of this text, examined in light of its object and purpose, suggests that "interests of justice" is a relatively broad concept.

Three "propositions" for interpreting the interests of justice in transitional situations are suggested here as one possible way for the Court to interpret and apply article 53.

C. Proposition One: The ICC must generally insist on prosecution of international crimes

As mentioned above, the mandate of the ICC is to promote effective prosecution of serious international crimes. Before considering possible exceptions in the pursuit of that mandate, it is necessary to examine some of the important reasons for having made the prosecution of international crimes a high priority.[25]

First, a central objective of accountability is to deter future violations and thereby help spare future victims.[26] For international crimes, this has an importance that extends beyond the borders of the state concerned: the granting of impunity sends a message to other regimes and other potential violators that they, too, may continue committing such crimes and hope for amnesty when their time comes.[27] One could understandably entertain doubts about the extent to which punishment has a deterrent effect in the context of entrenched regimes committing large-scale crimes, since they do not expect to lose power nor to be punished.[28] However, such a criticism is largely circular: it assumes a continued practice of allowing such regimes to enjoy impunity. The more the international community holds firm in apprehending and punishing those who commit international crimes, the more potential violators will be likely to consider the consequences and start to be dissuaded from launching criminal campaigns.

Second, although the pursuit of justice is often portrayed as conflicting with reconciliation, prosecution can facilitate reconciliation and nation-building in various ways. To begin, it can help expose violent extremists for what they are – criminals – thereby stigmatizing them, diminishing their influence, and removing them from power and society. Second, by providing survivors with a sense that justice has been done, it can help end cycles of revenge and vigilante justice, a precondition for real reconciliation. Third, by individualizing guilt and exposing the role of a leadership group in inciting hatred, prosecution helps a society overcome an "us" versus "them" outlook and demonstrate how opportunists manipulated sentiments for their own goals. Fourth, prosecution signifies a clean break with the regimes of the past and establishes the legitimacy of the new democratic government, demonstrating that it respects human rights and the rule of law.

Third, there is an important moral dimension. In discussions about amnesties, forgiveness, and truth commissions, there is sometimes a tendency to treat the crimes in a rather abstract manner, focusing on lesser crimes and overlooking serious international crimes. It is therefore vitally important to bear firmly in mind that the ICC deals only with the most serious international crimes, crimes which imply inconceivable horror and cruelty. These are situations of mass murder, gang rape, and torture. There is a profoundly important deontological basis for punishing of such atrocious crimes: as a moral obligation to the victims, and to denounce and repudiate the violations, and re-assert basic moral values.[29] The intensity of the natural need for justice – not only truth – should not be underestimated. This is why victims' groups have continued to press vigorously for justice even when truth has been uncovered and acknowledged through a truth commission process.[30]

Fourth, there is also an important question of international legal *obligations*. This chapter will not attempt an exhaustive enquiry into the issue of the duty to bring to justice perpetrators of certain crimes, because the responsibility of the ICC to prosecute flows not from any breach of duty by the state,[31] but rather from the mandate given to the ICC by the accepting state or by the Security Council.[32] Nevertheless, the question of whether a state is or is not breaching a duty to prosecute would certainly be a factor for consideration in the exercise of discretion, so the matter needs to be touched on here. Moreover, the literature on possible limitations to the duty suggests useful principles that could be adopted by the ICC.

Even among international lawyers who argue that prosecution should sometimes give way to alternative means of dealing with the past, many or most would also allow that there are exceptionally serious crimes for which prosecution may be required under international law.[33] The first pertinent question is which crimes are covered by the duty. To summarize very briefly, it is relatively clear that states are under a duty to bring to justice those responsible for genocide, acts of torture, and grave breaches of the Geneva Conventions of 1949. These obligations are derived from treaties,[34] but are now widely considered to be reinforced by equivalent customary international law obligations.[35]

With respect to the other crimes in the ICC Statute (crimes against humanity and serious violations of the laws of armed conflict), the situation is less clear. There is no treaty expressly imposing a duty to prosecute such crimes, and the state of customary international law on the point is controversial. In fact, it has often been noted that actual state practice has traditionally been distinctively unsupportive of such a duty, and tended in the past to condone the granting of amnesties.[36] Nevertheless, there are convincing reasons to suggest that under current or emerging customary international law there is a duty to bring to justice[37] perpetrators of genocide, crimes against humanity, and war crimes, at least with respect to crimes committed on the state's territory or by its nationals.[38] First, there has been a marked revolution in state practice, decisively shifting from history's tacit endorsement of amnesties to today's consistent rejection of them for serious international crimes. This is illustrated by the disclaimer attached by the UN to the 1999 Lomé peace accord[39] and the subsequent rejection of amnesties,[40] and the exclusion of international crimes from the community reconciliation process in East Timor.[41] Second, this practice is accompanied by numerous declarations affirming a duty to prosecute, in resolutions (such as the Resolution on Impunity adopted by the Commission on Human Rights),[42] declarations (such as the Vienna Declaration and Programme of Action),[43] and even the preamble of the ICC Statute.[44] Without overstating the weight to be given to "paper practice," these declarations are relevant as in combination with the actual practice of states they show that the practice of rejecting amnesties is accompanied by a sense of legal obligation. Third, a growing body of jurisprudence – generated by the Inter-American human rights system,[45] the UN human rights system,[46] and other national and international bodies[47] – is affirming that amnesties for serious violations also are incompatible with a state's basic human rights obligations. Fourth, given that the ICC crimes are equally considered "the most serious crimes of concern to the international community as a whole," it would seem incongruous and convoluted to recognize a duty for some ICC Statute crimes (e.g., an isolated war crime of torture) but not for equally serious or more serious ICC Statute crimes (e.g., crimes against humanity of murder, extermination, or sexual violence). Thus, there are persuasive reasons to conclude that there is a duty, or at least an emerging duty, to bring to justice those responsible for genocide, crimes against humanity, or war crimes, at least where the crimes are committed on a state's territory or by its nationals.[48]

The other major question is the *extent* of that duty. Those who are critical of the idea of a duty to prosecute have argued that it does not take into account the potentially precarious position of new, fragile democracies, that it would be reckless to require fragile democracies to proceed with a course that may lead to their destruction, and in addition, that in situations involving thousands of perpetrators, prosecuting everyone may be logistically impossible, financially ruinous, and socially divisive.[49]

In response, many advocates of the duty have recognized two limitations. First, the duty does not necessarily require a transitional government to prosecute *all* offenders; the duty may be satisfied by prosecuting the ringleaders and persons most responsible.[50] Second, the duty may be subject to an exception of "necessity" in situations of a "grave and imminent threat," such that governments would not be required "to press prosecution to the point of provoking their own collapse."[51] Such an exception is not to be invoked lightly; the international duty is intended as a counterweight to pressure from groups seeking impunity and it should thus help embolden fragile democracies to carry out prosecutions rather than seek an "easy escape route."[52] It is suggested below that these two suggested limitations provide a useful frame of reference for the ICC in deciding whether to defer to a national program that falls short of full prosecution.

D. Proposition Two: In transitional situations following mass violence, a targeted program prosecuting only those most responsible may be appropriate

Transitional societies may be faced with extraordinary situations where prosecution of all offenders is simply not possible nor even desirable. In such cases, it may be useful to draw a distinction between those persons most responsible for international crimes and lesser offenders. There can be practical, legal, and moral grounds to deal with lesser offenders through truth commissions and conditional amnesties, whereas the persons most responsible – planners, leaders, and those committing the most notorious crimes – should still be held criminally accountable.

First, on a practical level, prosecution of thousands of perpetrators may be financially and logistically completely impossible. In addition, to deal with a significant portion of the population through criminal proceedings and incarceration may not be the best approach to rebuilding a traumatized society.

Second, on a legal level, the duty to bring perpetrators to justice in transitional situations arguably extends only to those persons most responsible. As Diane Orentlicher concludes, "customary law would ... not require prosecution of every person. ... Prosecution of those who were most responsible for designing and implementing a system of human rights atrocities or for especially notorious crimes that were emblematic of past violations would seemingly discharge governments' customary law obligation ... provided the criteria used to select potential defendants did not appear to condone or tolerate past abuses."[53] Given that the ICC will generally focus only on the persons most responsible, domestic prosecution of such persons will prevent most potential jurisdictional conflicts with the ICC.[54] Moreover, the fact that a state would be satisfying its international legal obligations is a factor weighing against ICC interference.

Third, and most importantly, on a moral level there is a significant difference between the situation of the low-level perpetrator and those who orchestrate the crimes or who distinguish themselves with their sadistic enthusiasm. There is a greater case for deference to the judgment of a democratic society as to how to deal with those individuals who were manipulated by propaganda and swept up in a tide of evil. For low-level perpetrators, one can imagine the value of sincere repentance and forgiveness, and should not preclude creative and good faith experiments with community-rooted alternatives.

The situation is quite different with respect to those persons "most responsible" for serious international crimes. This includes the individuals who plan, foment, and orchestrate international crimes, as well as those individuals who enthusiastically embrace the policies of terror, and who take advantage of a context of lawlessness to indulge their own sadistic tendencies. For these architects and enthusiasts, the idea of granting amnesty is particularly problematic. These are individuals who may be responsible for hundreds, thousands, or even hundreds of thousands of deaths. Punishment of such individuals is essential to honour the victims, to uphold basic values, and to send a message of deterrence to other potential ringleaders.

E. Proposition Three: It is conceivable that even more drastic situations of necessity could justify making non-prosecutorial alternatives available even to the persons most responsible for international crimes; any such exception would have to be very stringently justified

It is often argued that amnesties are a practical necessity to stop a conflict or to secure and maintain a transition from a military regime to a democratic government.[55] Groups responsible for international crimes may not be willing to cease hostilities or cede power "if they or their close associates will face life imprisonment as a result."[56] In such situations, amnesties might be regarded as "the price for getting rid of tyrants and their associates," and they have therefore been considered "one of the techniques for ending civil wars or enabling transitions from authoritarian to democratic governments."[57] Similarly, where a new democracy has a fragile hold on power, and the former military is still intact and threatened, launching prosecutions may amount to "political suicide."[58]

Many advocates of prosecuting all international crimes have conceded a potential exception in situations where insistence on prosecution would compel a fragile democracy to bring about its destruction or would trigger further conflict and violence.[59] José Zalaquett has argued that "political leaders cannot afford to be moved only by their convictions, oblivious to real-life constraints," and that although "ideological purists" would say "it is preferable to suffer longer under tyranny ... than to make progress through untidy compromises," such a position reflects an arrogant disdain for the "dreadful costs of such a cavalier gamble."[60] As has been argued by Carlos Nino, "Though it is true that many people approach the issue of human rights violations with a strong retributive impulse, almost all who think momentarily about the issue are not prepared to defend a policy of punishing those abuses once it becomes clear that such a policy would probably provoke, by a causal chain, similar or even worse abuses."[61]

However, any "necessity" exception should be very carefully and narrowly construed.

First, granting for the sake of argument that a "necessity" exception is justified on consequentialist grounds, it is appropriate to weigh *all* of the consequences, including the long-term global consequences of granting impunity to violators.[62] If governments adopt a general approach that "impunity may be granted whenever expedient," the consequence of giving into expediency in case after case will be impunity in case after case, thus reinforcing expectations of impunity and encouraging future violators. There must therefore be serious scrutiny of the claims of "necessity," as this will help ensure that decision-makers do not give in to the easy temptation of concluding that an amnesty is unavoidable in their specific circumstances. As Méndez argues, "it is important to assess the threats before the new government realistically, to take into consideration the countervailing strength of democratic forces in society."[63]

Indeed, recent experience has tended to contradict the supposedly "pragmatic" view that prosecution is destabilizing and that amnesties are necessary for peace. The very opposite propositions have in fact been recently borne out. For example, in Sierra Leone, blanket amnesties were granted for horrific crimes against humanity in the belief that this was necessary for peace and reconciliation; this instead merely reinforced a culture of impunity in which brutal acts of mutilation and lawlessness continued. After more conflict and more atrocities, the policy was reversed in favour of prosecution and punishment of those bearing the greatest responsibility for international crimes.[64] Likewise, many argued that the indictment of Slobodan Milosevic by the ICTY during the Kosovo conflict would only stiffen his resolve and prolong the conflict, and yet a peace agreement was reached shortly after the indictment, and Mr Milosevic is now in The Hague facing trial.[65] These and other cases cast considerable doubt on the received wisdom that peace and justice are somehow at odds.

Second, any necessity "exception" should not be an excuse to completely abdicate the duty to deal with such crimes. An automatic amnesty for all perpetrators, including ringleaders, would be entirely contrary to the emerging principles in this area and would properly invite condemnation. The international community has a significant stake in deterring such sweeping amnesty agreements due to the message such agreements send to other regimes and other potential violators that they, too, may unleash large scale brutality against human beings and then make an amnesty deal if and when necessary. Moreover, blanket amnesties are the *precise antithesis* of the purpose of the ICC.[66] For the ICC to defer to a blanket amnesty for fear that those responsible will resort to violence would be for the ICC to capitulate to blackmail. Moreover, ICC jurisdiction arises because the state concerned has accepted the Court's jurisdiction – and therefore "contracted" with the ICC to prosecute where the state fails to do so – or because the Security Council has determined under chapter VII that impunity is a threat to international peace and security. Accordingly, the ICC should probably consider itself institutionally incapable of deferring to blanket amnesties under any circumstances.

Acknowledging the possibility of a necessity exception should be seen not as an invitation to condone blanket amnesties, but rather as a means for the international community to keep an open mind about good faith creative alternatives to prosecution, which might include truth commissions granting conditional amnesties. As was discussed above, such alternative approaches are easiest to accept with respect to low-level offenders following situations of mass atrocities. Where even the persons most responsible are entitled to apply for amnesties under a national reconciliation mechanism, far more careful scrutiny is needed.

I would suggest that, in deciding whether a "necessity exception" might apply, one should consider the balance between the extent of the departure from full prosecution – that is, the *quality of the measures taken* and *the severity of the factors necessitating a deviation* – to decide whether the society has done all possible to advance accountability-related goals. Different authors have suggested different lists of criteria or factors to consider,[67] but the following seem generally recognized as relevant:

- Was the measure adopted by democratic will?
- Is the departure from the standard of criminal prosecution of all offenders based on necessity, that is irresistible social, economic, or political realities?
- Is there a full and effective investigation into the facts?
- Does the fact-finding inquiry provide the names of perpetrators?
- Is the relevant commission or body independent and suitably resourced?
- Is there at least some form of punishment of perpetrators: are they identified, required to come forward, required to do community service, subject to lustration? Is some form of remedy or compensation provided to victims?
- Does the national approach provide a sense of closure or justice to victims?
- Is there a commitment to comply with other human rights obligations?

In light of the core purpose of the ICC and its prior compact with the state concerned, a program where even the persons most responsible may apply for amnesties should receive deference "only in the most compelling of cases."[68]

III. GENUINE PROCEEDINGS: COMPLEMENTARITY

If article 53 offers a small opening for non-prosecutorial reconciliation programs, article 17 offers only a needle's eye. Whereas article 53 deals with the rather ambiguous notion of the interests of justice, article 17 is much more narrowly focused on the question of whether there is or has been a genuine national proceeding to investigate and prosecute the accused. This is the principle of "complementarity": states are given the first opportunity to prosecute, and a case will be inadmissible before the ICC if a state with jurisdiction genuinely investigates or prosecutes the matter.[69] Article 17 provides as follows:

> 1. Having regard to paragraph 10 of the Preamble and article 1, the Court shall determine that a case is inadmissible where:
> (a) The case is being investigated or prosecuted by a State which has jurisdiction over it, unless the State is unwilling or unable genuinely to carry out the investigation or prosecution;
> (b) The case has been investigated by a State which has jurisdiction over it and the State has decided not to prosecute the person concerned, unless the decision resulted from the unwillingness or inability of the State genuinely to prosecute;
> (c) The person concerned has already been tried for conduct which is the subject of the complaint, and a trial by the Court is not permitted under article 20, paragraph 3;[70]
> ...[71]
> 2. In order to determine unwillingness in a particular case, the Court shall consider, having regard to the principles of due process recognized by international law, whether one or more of the following exist, as applicable:
> (a) The proceedings were or are being undertaken or the national decision was made for the purpose of shielding the person concerned from criminal responsibility for crimes within the jurisdiction of the Court referred to in article 5;

(b) There has been an unjustified delay in the proceedings which in the circumstances is inconsistent with an intent to bring the person concerned to justice;
(c) The proceedings were not or are not being conducted independently or impartially, and they were or are being conducted in a manner which, in the circumstances, is inconsistent with an intent to bring the person concerned to justice.
3. In order to determine inability in a particular case, the Court shall consider whether, due to a total or substantial collapse or unavailability of its national judicial system, the State is unable to obtain the accused or the necessary evidence and testimony or otherwise unable to carry out its proceedings.

During the negotiations, some delegations (most importantly, the delegation of South Africa) sought explicit recognition of truth and reconciliation commissions in article 17. Other delegations, as well as NGOS, resisted any such provision. Due to the politically controversial and philosophically difficult nature of any such provision, the issue was deliberately sidestepped in article 17, although a narrow doorway was left for the Court to consider whether such a procedure was indeed a "genuine" effort to do justice.

This doorway is presented in article 17(1)(b). Article 17(1)(a) deals with situations of ongoing investigations and prosecutions, and thus does not provide a durable solution where a state does not proceed with prosecutions. Article 17(1)(c), read in conjunction with article 20 (*ne bis in idem* – or "double jeopardy"), is applicable only where there has been a "trial" by a "court,"[72] and thus is not relevant to non-prosecution situations. Thus, article 17(1)(b) is the only feasible avenue.[73] In order to satisfy the terms of article 17(1)(b), it would have to be possible to say, first, that the truth commission or other body "investigated" the matter; second, that it "decided" not to prosecute; and third, that the decision did not result from the unwillingness or inability of the state to genuinely prosecute.

The first critical issue is the meaning of the term "investigation."[74] The Court could interpret the term as referring only to a criminal investigation, which will mean that deference to truth and reconciliation efforts would only be possible under article 53. It is also open to the Court to adopt a slightly broader approach. For example, the Court could determine that the term "investigation" also comprises a diligent, methodical effort to gather the evidence and ascertain the facts relating to the conduct in question, in order to make an objective determination in accordance with pertinent criteria (e.g., sufficiency of evidence, seriousness of the conduct, role of the perpetrator). These criteria are consistent with typical criminal investigations but might also be satisfied by other forms of investigation, such as those carried out in fulfillment of the "right to know" (i.e., to uncover the truth and determine who was responsible).[75]

The second issue will be the meaning of the term "decision" in regard to a decision to not prosecute. It is suggested here that the term "decision" can only have meaning where there is more than one option available to the purported decision-maker. Thus, there must at least be a possibility of prosecution. Where a body cannot choose prosecution because prosecution is already barred by legislation, it would be disingenuous to refer to a "decision" to not prosecute.

The third issue is whether a decision resulted from an unwillingness or inability to carry out a genuine prosecution. In making this determination, the Court will be guided *inter alia* by the considerations appearing in article 17(2) and (3), such as whether there was an intent to shield perpetrators from justice. The test arising from those provisions is a rigorous one, although the list of criteria should not be interpreted as a closed list: the open-ended wording "shall *consider* ... whether" was deliberately chosen, as opposed to language imposing a fixed requirement (e.g., "means" or "must conclude that"), thus indicating that terms such as "intent to shield" are illustrative.

Some examples will illustrate how these tests might be applied.

Scenario one: targeted prosecution. In this scenario, assume that a state decides to only prosecute those most responsible, and to deal with lower-level perpetrators by non-prosecutorial methods. Assume further that the number of persons selected for prosecution is not so small that it is evidently a gesture to avoid real prosecutions. In such a case, if there were a credible effort to gather the facts and select the most responsible offenders, and a particular offender of interest to the ICC was in good faith not selected for prosecution, it could still be said that the case has been "investigated" by the screening body, and that there was "a decision not to prosecute," thus satisfying the criteria of article 17(1)(b). Moreover, it could not be said that the decision flowed from a desire to "shield" the person from prosecution or an unwillingness or inability to genuinely prosecute; on the contrary, it flowed from objective and reasonable criteria, such as the evidence available and the role of the perpetrator. Thus, a credible procedure to assess all the information and select persons most responsible for prosecution could arguably satisfy article 17 even with respect to those not selected for prosecution.

Scenario two: blanket amnesties. The bestowal of blanket amnesties could never satisfy the complementarity test. First, there would likely be no investigation. Second, even if there were an "investigation," for example by a truth commission, it could hardly be said that there was a "decision" to not prosecute, since prosecution was not even an option, as it was barred by legislation. Even if one attempted to characterize the adoption of the amnesty legislation as the decision, that legislative act would be a decision resulting from an unwillingness or inability to carry out genuine prosecutions, with a patent objective of shielding perpetrators from justice. One could argue that the primary intent was to promote reconciliation and not to shield perpetrators, but it would still be undeniable that the means was chosen in part to shield perpetrators. Thus, there would clearly be an intent – a substantial even if not primary intent – to shield perpetrators.

Scenario three: conditional amnesties. A third example would be a truth and reconciliation commission authorized to grant amnesties on a case-by-case basis. In principle, it would likely be very difficult for a truth commission bestowing conditional amnesties to satisfy the complementarity regime, although it is at least conceivable.

The first question would be whether there had been an investigation. If the term "investigation" were interpreted in the broad manner suggested above, a detailed and rigorous inquiry by a truth commission could suffice.

With respect to the second requirement, a decision to not prosecute, it was suggested above that the term "decision" requires that prosecution at least be an option. Thus, the granting of amnesty would have to be conditional on meeting certain criteria, rather than something automatic; the truth commission would have to have the power to deny amnesty. The South African model could satisfy this requirement.[76]

The third step, the assessment of whether the decision to not prosecute resulted from an "unwillingness" or "inability" to genuinely prosecute, is the most philosophically challenging question. The ICC would have to decide whether the system established was a system to shield perpetrators or whether it could be said to be a "genuine" proceeding aimed at providing justice, given all of the relevant circumstances. These relevant circumstances would likely include the nature and credibility of the commission and the extent to which any departures from the normal model of prosecution are justified by necessity. Given the focus of article 17 on procedures designed "to bring the person concerned to justice," the Court would probably look for prosecution-like hallmarks, such as the following:

- *Quasi-judicial character*: Does the decision-making body determine the facts and assess those facts in accordance with objective criteria? Is the person concerned required to appear before the decision-making body?
- *Independence*: Is the decision-making body independent, and seen to be independent, of political influence? Is it an impartial decision-maker?
- *Effectiveness*: Is the decision-making body equipped with sufficient resources and the powers necessary to carry out its mandate? Does it have the powers needed to determine the truth, including obtaining testimony and documents and obtaining compliance with its orders?
- *The article 17 objective of "bringing to justice"*: To what extent is the procedure aimed at providing justice? Where prosecution is denied, are there other forms of significant sanction or punishment: public naming, lustration, obligations of reparation, public service to help repair the harm done?
- *Necessity*: Is the departure from classical prosecution necessitated by compelling political, social, and economic constraints? Is this a genuine effort to do justice? Is the measure democratically adopted and supported by majority will as a necessary and appropriate measure?

Overall, it will be important to assess the extent to which a procedure that is similar in quality to prosecution is genuinely implemented. It is suggested here that the door is not entirely closed to alternative methods of providing justice, and that there is room for the Court to consider other approaches. However, given the *teleos* of article 17, the grounds for flexibility are quite narrow, especially in comparison with article 53.

IV. MAINTENANCE OF PEACE AND SECURITY: SECURITY COUNCIL DEFERRAL

A third mechanism which the ICC might use to defer to national reconciliation efforts is article 16. It states: "No investigation or prosecution may be commenced or proceeded with under this Statute for a period of 12 months after the Security Council, in a resolution adopted under Chapter VII of the Charter of the United Nations, has requested the Court to that effect; that request may be renewed by the Security Council under the same conditions." This provision reflects a compromise between those who sought complete Security Council control over the ICC docket and those who thought any Security Council role would be an inappropriate political interference.[77] The resulting provision is rather akin to the discretionary power of the executive branch in many countries to issue a "stay of proceedings." Given the need for a Security Council majority (and unanimity of the five permanent members), and the anticipated hesitance of states to frustrate accountability for international crimes, it was thought that this provision was unlikely to be abused,[78] although the council's startling actions on 12 July 2002 cast the gravest doubt on this.[79]

Such a request can only be issued by the Security Council acting under chapter VII of the UN Charter, which deals with the maintenance of international peace and security. It is possible that the Security Council might request deferral from the ICC where a delicate non-prosecutorial truth and reconciliation process is underway. For the council, the determining considerations will relate to the promotion of international peace and security, which could involve many considerations similar to those canvassed in this chapter, such as necessity, peace-building, reconciliation, conflict prevention, threats to democracy, and risks of future mass atrocities.

V. PROSECUTION BY OTHER STATES

Finally, it should also be recalled that the International Criminal Court is not the only stakeholder in upholding the principle of accountability. Many other states will be in a position to exercise jurisdiction over genocide, crimes against humanity, and war crimes, on such grounds as passive nationality jurisdiction (jurisdiction based on the nationality of the victim) and universal jurisdiction (jurisdiction based on the seriousness of the offence against international law). These states are not bound by the amnesty deals struck within a particular society,[80] nor are they restricted by any principle of complementarity requiring them to defer to the prosecutorial efforts of others. Moreover, even if the ICC declines to prosecute, on the view that doing so would not serve the interests of justice, nothing in the ICC Statute or in international law would preclude other states from exercising extra-territorial jurisdiction in accordance with their own laws.

Nevertheless, it is likely that states will also choose to take into account factors similar to those discussed in this chapter. In accordance with their own domestic legislation and interests, states would generally not choose to initiate prosecution of international crimes in another state where they conclude that doing so would be contrary to the interests of justice.[81] This supposition is already borne out in practice. For example, the Spanish request for the extradition of Senator Pinochet reflected a dissatisfaction with the sweeping self-amnesty granted in Chile.[82] On the other hand, up to the present date, states have declined to initiate prosecutions for crimes against humanity committed under the apartheid regime in South Africa, which likely reflects the higher level of international regard for the reconciliation measures adopted in the unique circumstances of South Africa.[83]

CONCLUSION

There is no intrinsic tension between the goals of the ICC – accountability and deterrence through punishment of offenders – and the goals of truth and reconciliation commissions – to heal societies, expose the past, and facilitate reconciliation. There is, however, a difficulty when truth commissions are combined with amnesties for serious international crimes, because the very purpose of the International Criminal Court is to ensure that perpetrators of genocide, crimes against humanity, and war crimes do not escape prosecution for their crimes.

As an institution, it is absolutely appropriate and necessary for the ICC to maintain a narrow focus on the objective of prosecution and punishment of those responsible for these serious international crimes. This does not mean, however, that the ICC must be absolutely closed-minded toward alternative experiments in dealing with the past which are genuine and democratic efforts advancing the goals of accountability. There may be exceptional circumstances in which a rigid approach by the ICC would be irresponsible. The most significant mechanism by which deference is possible will be under the discretion not to proceed where prosecution would not serve "the interests of justice." The complementarity regime presents another possible means of deference, but this is much narrower due to its specific focus on genuine proceedings. If it were possible for an alternative procedure to meet this test, it would have to be a very sophisticated process providing many of the same features and benefits of prosecution.

Developing appropriate standards for assessing transitional justice mechanisms will be an extremely challenging exercise for the ICC, both politically and philosophically. This chapter suggests some possible considerations. Any approach will likely involve an assessment of the extent of the departure from the ideal of prosecution, as well as the reasons for that departure. First, where there are no prosecutions at all – particularly if this is due to a blanket amnesty – deference would in any circumstance be contrary to the letter and spirit of the statute. Second, where a transitional society is unable to prosecute all offenders, but has established a program to prosecute those most responsible for the most serious international crimes, deference will likely be granted in the interests of justice. Third, a particularly challenging scenario would be where even those persons most responsible for international crimes are able to apply for conditional amnesties. The design of the ICC is such that it should generally not defer to such an arrangement, but its door is not necessarily completely closed. In situations of grave necessity, a thoughtful assessment of all relevant circumstances, including the criteria applied and the nature of the decision-making body, would be necessary to determine whether ICC action was in the interests of justice.

NOTES

♣ The opinions expressed in this chapter are the author's own and do not necessarily reflect the views of the ICC, nor the Government of Canada. The author is very grateful to the NYU Hauser Global Scholars Program and to the participants in the NYU School of Law Seminar for Hauser Scholars for their helpful comments on an earlier draft.

1 *Rome Statute of the International Criminal Court*, 17 July 1998, UN Doc. A/CONF. 183/9, 2187 UNTS 90, reprinted in International Legal Materials 37, no. 5 (1998): 1002 [hereinafter ICC Statute]. The sixtieth instrument of ratification was deposited on 11 April 2002, and therefore, in accordance with article 126 of the ICC Statute, the statute entered into force on 1 July 2002.

2 Charles Villa-Vicencio, "Why Perpetrators Should Not Always Be Prosecuted: Where the International Criminal Court and Truth Commissions Meet," *Emory Law Journal* 49, no. 1 (2000): 205–22, 205.

3 Alex Boraine, *A Country Unmasked: South Africa's Truth and Reconciliation Commission* (Cape Town, NY: Oxford UP, 2000).

4 See, for example, Mahnoush H. Arsanjani, "The International Criminal Court and National Amnesty Laws," *ASIL Proceedings* 93 (1999): 65–8; and Michael Scharf, "The Amnesty Exception to the Jurisdiction of the International Criminal Court," *Cornell International Law Journal* 32, no. 1 (1999): 507–27. UN Secretary General Kofi Annan has suggested that it would be "inconceivable" for the ICC to set aside an approach like that adopted in the South African situation: Kofi Annan, Speech at the Witwatersrand University Graduation Ceremony (1 September 1998), quoted in Villa-Vicencio, *supra* n2, 222.

5 For example, an informal discussion paper circulated by the United States is still available at <http://www.iccnow.org/romearchive/documentsreports/4PrepCmt/USDraftonAmnestiesPardons.doc>.

6 See, for example, Madeline Morris, "Foreword," *Law and Contemporary Problems* 59, no. 4 (1996): 1–4.

7 See, for example, Martha Minow, "The Hope for Healing: What Can Truth Commissions Do?" in *Truth v. Justice: The Morality of Truth Commissions*, ed. Robert Rotberg and Dennis Thompson, 235–60 (Princeton: Princeton UP, 2000), 235.

8 It is true that the simultaneous functioning of a national or international prosecution effort and a truth and reconciliation effort can raise significant technical or practical complications. For example, a truth commission may complicate prosecution efforts when hearing statements from victims who would also be excellent witnesses for a prosecution, because it creates a record that might be used for cross-examination. There are also questions of whether a truth commission should share evidence with the international criminal proceeding (as this might impair the willingness to give information to the commission). In addition, the overlapping efforts of two investigative bodies can cause "witness fatigue" within a population. These are important questions, but they do not represent fundamental conflicts and are beyond the scope of this paper.

9 ICC Statute, *supra* n1, preamble, para. 4.

10 Ibid., arts 5 to 8. The crime of aggression may also be added to the Court's jurisdiction in the future, once a suitable definition is developed and adopted. Arts 5(2), 121, and 123 of the ICC Statute.

11 Amnesties may even be impermissible under international law. See the discussion below of the duty to bring perpetrators to justice, section II, part C.

12 This argument has been raised, for example, by Marc Grossman, US under secretary for Political Affairs, in "American Foreign Policy and the International Criminal Court," Remarks to the Center for Strategic and International Studies, Washington DC, (6 May 2002), on-line: US Department of State <www.state.gov/p/9949.htm>.

13 ICC Statute, *supra* n1, arts 12 and 13.

14 Ibid., articles 12 and 13; and arts 25, 48, and 103 of the UN Charter.

15 A very interesting exception to this proposition would occur in cases where members of one state carry out international crimes on the territory of another state, and that victim state has accepted the Court's jurisdiction. In such a case, it would be highly dubious for the offending society to carry out non-prosecutorial means of "forgiving" itself and its nationals for the crimes committed against nationals of another state. Another variation would be a situation of international armed conflict, which could theoretically end with a peace accord providing, on a mutual basis, for some form of amnesties. In such a case, the considerations articulated below for deferring in appropriate cases to such a mechanism would likely be equally pertinent. Note, however, the Geneva Convention Relative to the Protection of Civilian Persons in Time of War, 12 August 1949, 75 UNTS 287-417 (1950), art. 148 (non-absolution of liability for war crimes).

16 See, for example, ICC Statute, *supra* n1, art. 17, and preamble, paras 4 to 7.

17 Ibid., arts 13(c) and 14. Where the prosecutor initiates an investigation at his own initiative, the logical interpretation is that the prosecutor would already consider the interests of justice in making his or her determination that there is a "reasonable basis to proceed" under article 15(3). This interpretation has now been confirmed in rule 48 of the ICC Rules of Procedure and Evidence, Doc. ICC-ASP/1/3, on-line: International Criminal Court <http://www.icc-cpi.int/library/officialjournal/Rules_of_Proc_and_Evid_070704-EN.pdf> [hereinafter ICC RPE]. Rule 48 states: "In determining whether there is a reasonable basis to proceed under Article 15, paragraph 3, the Prosecutor shall consider the factors set out in Article 53, paragraph 1(a) to (c)." See also Håkan Friman, "Investigation and Prosecution" in *The International Criminal Court: Elements of Crimes and Rules of Procedure and Evidence*, ed. Roy S. Lee et al., 493–538 (Ardsley, NY: Transnational Publishers, 2001), 495–8.

18 ICC Statute, *supra* n1, art. 53(1)(c).

19 The same "interest of justice" test is mentioned in article 53(2)(c) of the ICC Statute, but this article also refers to "the age or infirmity of the alleged perpetrator and his or her role in the alleged crime," since at the prosecution stage the prosecutor will have particular suspects in mind and be able to consider personal factors. See Morten Bergsmo and Pieter Kruger, "Article 53"

in *Commentary on the Rome Statute of the International Criminal Court*, ed. Otto Triffterer (Baden-Baden: Nomos, 1999).

20 ICC Statute, *supra* n1, art. 53(3)(a).

21 Ibid., art. 53(3)(b). See also rule 109 of the ICC RPE, *supra* n17.

22 ICC Statute, *supra* n1, art. 53(3)(a) (emphasis added). The Rules of Procedure and Evidence make clear that this is indeed only a "reconsideration" and not an obligation to reach a different decision. The obligation on the prosecutor is to "reconsider that decision as soon as possible" (rule 108), and then to notify the Pre-Trial Chamber and other participants of his or her "final decision" (rule 109), ICC RPE *supra* n17.

23 ICC Statute, *supra* n1, art. 53(3)(b).

24 This interpretation is confirmed in rule 110 of the ICC RPE, *supra* n17. This approach could lead to the unusual prospect of a prosecutor being forced to carry out an investigation that the prosecutor does not believe is in the interests of justice. One may legitimately wonder about the efficacy of such a requirement, and one can wonder how vigorous the investigation might be in such a situation.

25 The reasons for prosecution are canvassed in the groundbreaking article by Diane Orentlicher, "Settling Accounts: The Duty to Prosecute Human Rights Violations of a Prior Regime," *Yale Law Journal* 100, no. 8 (1991): 2537–615; as well as in Juan E. Méndez, "Accountability for the Past," *Human Rights Quarterly* 19, no. 2 (1997): 255–82; M. Cherif Bassiouni, "Searching for Peace and Achieving Justice: The Need for Accountability," *Law and Contemporary Problems* 59, no. 4 (1996): 9–28; W. Michael Reisman, "Legal Responses to Genocide and Other Massive Violations of Human Rights," *Law and Contemporary Problems* 59, no. 4 (1996): 75–80; Stephan Landsman, "Alternative Responses to Serious Human Rights Abuses: Of Prosecutions and Truth Commissions," *Law and Contemporary Problems* 59, no. 4 (1996): 81–92; Luc Huyse, "Justice after Transition: On the Choices Successor Elites Make in Dealing with the Past," in *Transitional Justice: How Emerging Democracies Reckon with Former Regimes*, ed. Neil J. Kritz, 1.104–15 (Washington, DC: US Institute of Peace Press, 1995); Samuel P. Huntington, "The Third Wave: Democratization in the Late Twentieth Century," in Kritz, ed., ibid., 1.65–6; Jamel Benomar, "Justice After Transition," in Kritz, ed., ibid., 1.32–41; and Jo M. Pasqualucci, "The Whole Truth and Nothing But the Truth: Truth Commissions, Impunity and the Inter-American Human Rights System," *Boston University International Law Journal* 12, no. 2 (1994): 321–70.

26 See, *for example,* the findings of the Working Group on Enforced or Involuntary Disappearance, expressing concern about amnesty laws that grant

impunity to alleged violators of human rights (para. 23), which state that "perhaps the single most important factor contributing to the phenomenon of disappearances may be that of impunity. The Working Group's experience over the past 10 years has confirmed the age-old adage that impunity breeds contempt for the law. Perpetrators of human rights violations, whether civilian or military, will become all the more brazen when they are not held to account before a court of law": "Report of the Working Group on Enforced or Involuntary Disappearances, 46th Session," reproduced in *Kritz*, ed., *supra* n25, 3.473–5, 474.

27 See, for example, Reisman, *supra* n25; and Scharf, *supra* n4.

28 See, for example, Villa-Vicencio, *supra* n2, 210; and Immi Tallgren, "The Sensibility and Sense of International Criminal Law," *European Journal of International Law* 13, no. 3 (2002): 561–96.

29 See, for example, Immanuel Kant, *Groundwork of the Metaphysics of Morals* (1785); see also Naomi Roht-Arriaza, "Punishment, Redress and Pardon: Theoretical and Psychological Approaches" in *Impunity and Human Rights in International Law and Practice*, 13–23 (New York: Oxford UP, 1995).

30 "Those who posited that truth could substitute for justice ... are now seeing that even almost twenty years later the thirst for justice is there even after at least a good part of the truth has been officially acknowledged," Naomi Roht-Arriaza, "Truth Commissions and Amnesties in Latin America: The Second Generation," ASIL *Proceedings* (1998): 313, referring to, among other things, the efforts to bring Pinochet to justice. This basic fact can also be seen in the repeated national and international challenges brought against amnesty laws even where truth commissions have been provided (for example, the challenges in El Salvador, Argentina, Uruguay, and South Africa). See also Henry Rousso, *The Vichy Syndrome: History and Memory in France Since 1944* (Cambridge, Mass.: Harvard UP, 1991), 215: "Nothing but a trial could satisfy the victims' need for justice, however. And their statements after the trial made it clear that this was what they felt too, far more than they cared about participating in any educational process." See also John Dugard, "Retrospective Justice: International Law and the South African Model" in *Transitional Justice and the Rule of Law in New Democracies*, ed. A. James McAdams, 269–90 (Notre Dame, Ind.: Univ. of Notre Dame Press, 1997), 284.

31 Even if a state were not obliged to prosecute particular offenders, the ICC would not necessarily defer to an amnesty: the ICC would nevertheless be mandated under its statute to investigate and prosecute such crimes, unless one of the statute's conditions for non-action were met. Conversely, even if a state were breaching its duty to prosecute certain offenders, this would not

mean that the ICC was *obliged* to prosecute: the ICC might decide not to prosecute after considering all the relevant factors. Thus, this issue of a duty to prosecute relates to the *state's* obligations, and is relevant to but not determinative of the stance of the ICC in carrying out its mandate. See Garth Meintjes, "Domestic Amnesties and International Accountability" in *International Crimes, Peace and Human Rights: The Role of the International Criminal Court*, ed. Dinah Shelton, 83–91 (Ardsley, NY: Transnational Publishers, 2000), esp. 90.

32 See section I above.

33 See, for example, Ruti J. Teitel, *Transitional Justice* (Oxford UP, 2000), 60–2, arguing that crimes against humanity pose a limit on considerations of clemency and political restraints, "a limit that appears to be largely immune to national politics" (60). See also Stephan Landsman, *supra* n25; and Douglas Cassel, "Lessons from the Americas: Guidelines for the International Response to Amnesties for Atrocities," *Law and Contemporary Problems* 59, no. 4 (1996): 197–230.

34 *Convention on the Prevention and Punishment of the Crime of Genocide*, 1948, 78 UNTS 277, art. 4; *Convention against Torture and Other Cruel, Inhuman or Degrading Treatment or Punishment*, 1984, 85 UNTS 1465, art. 7, reprinted in *International Legal Materials* 23, no. 5 (1984): 1027; and *Geneva Convention relative to the Protection of Civilian Persons in Times of War*, 1948, 75 UNTS 287, arts 146–7.

35 See, for example, *Reservations to the Convention on the Prevention and Punishment of Genocide* (28 May 1951), Advisory Opinion, [1957] ICJ Reports, 15; *Prosecutor* v. *Anto Furundzija* (2001), Case No. IT-95-17/1-7 (International Criminal Tribunal for the Former Yugoslavia), paras 137–48 and 155, on-line: United Nations <http://www.un.org/icty/judgement.htm>; and for further analysis see Christopher Joyner, "Redressing Impunity for Human Rights Violations," *Denver Journal of International Law and Policy* 26, no. 4 (1998): 591–624; Carla Edelenbos, "Human Rights Violations: A Duty to Prosecute?" *Leiden Journal of International Law* 7, no. 2 (1994): 5–21; Naomi Roht-Arianna, "Nontreaty Sources of the Obligation to Investigate and Prosecute," in Roht-Arianne, ed., *Impunity and Human Rights*, *supra* n29, 39–56; and Orentlicher, *supra* n25.

36 See Scharf, *supra* n4, 521, noting that with respect to crimes against humanity the most common state practice traditionally has been to grant amnesties or de facto impunity. See also Michael Scharf, "The Letter of the Law: The Scope of the International Legal Obligation to Prosecute Human Rights Crimes," *Law and Contemporary Problems* 59, no. 4 (1996): 41–62; John Dugard, "Possible Conflicts of Jurisdiction with Truth Commissions,"

in *The Rome Statute of the International Criminal Court: A Commentary*, eds. Antonio Cassese et al., 693–704 (Oxford: Oxford UP, 2002); and Emily Schabacker, "Reconciliation or Justice and Ashes: Amnesty Commissions and the Duty to Punish Human Rights Offences," *New York International Law Review* 12, no. 2 (1999): 1–54, reviewing the state practice on this matter.

37 The phrase "duty to prosecute" may be somewhat misleading, as it may be misunderstood as implying that *domestic* prosecution is the only acceptable response. In fact, the duty *aut dedere aut judicare* ("prosecute or extradite") can be satisfied through national prosecution, extradition to another willing state, or surrender to an international court or tribunal for prosecution. Thus, the phrase "bring to justice" is used wherever possible in this chapter.

38 The following observations relate only to a state's obligation with respect to crimes committed on its territory or by its nationals because that is all that is relevant in the context of concurring jurisdiction of the ICC.

39 The disclaimer asserted that the amnesty did not include genocide, crimes against humanity, and war crimes. See *Seventh Progress Report of the Secretary-General on the UN Observer Mission in Sierra Leone*, 30 June 1999, UN Doc. S/1999/836, para. 7.

40 See *Agreement between the United Nations and the Government of Sierra Leone on the Establishment of a Special Court for Sierra Leone*, 16 January 2002, on-line: Sierra Leone Web <http://www.sierra-leone.org/specialcourtagreement.html>; and *Statute of the Special Court of Sierra Leone*, especially article 10 (amnesties no bar to prosecution), on-line: Sierra Leone Web <http://www.sierra-leone.org/specialcourtstatute.html>.

41 "Serious criminal offences" are excluded from the Community Reconciliation Process; see Schedule 1 to *Regulation 2001/10 on the Establishment of a Commission for Reception, Truth and Reconciliation in East Timor*, 13 July 2000, UNTAET/REG/2001/10. "Serious criminal offence" includes genocide, crimes against humanity, war crimes, murder, sexual offences and torture: see Section 1.3 of UNTAET/REG/2000/15 of 6 June 2000.

42 *CHR Resolution on Impunity*, 25 April 2001, UN Doc. E/CN.4/RES/2001/70.

43 *Vienna Declaration and Programme of Action*, adopted 25 June 1993, UN Doc. A/CONF.157/23, para. 60: "States should abrogate legislation leading to impunity for those responsible for grave violations of human rights such as torture and prosecute such violations, thereby providing a firm basis for the rule of law."

44 Paragraph 6 of the preamble to the ICC Statute, *supra* n1, recalls "that it is the duty of every State to exercise its criminal jurisdiction over those responsible for international crimes." However, in fairness it must also be recalled

that this provision appears in the preamble because states could not accept such a provision in the operative text.

45 See for example the conclusion of the Inter-American Court of Human Rights in *Velásquez-Rodríguez* that the state "has a legal duty ... to use the means at its disposal to carry out a serious investigation of violations committed within its jurisdiction, to identify those responsible, to impose the appropriate punishment and to ensure the victim adequate compensation." *Velásquez-Rodríguez*, 1988 Annual Report of the Inter-American Court of Human Rights, 35, para. 174. See also the *Barrios Altos Case*, (14 March 2001), Inter-Am. Ct. HR (Ser. C) No. 75, paras 41–5 (declaring two 1995 amnesty laws incompatible with the American Convention on Human Rights, and hence without legal effect). For further analysis, see Douglas Cassel, *supra* n33 and Pasqualucci, *supra* n25.

46 For example, the Human Rights Committee has held that amnesties for torture are incompatible with the ICCPR: General Comment No. 20 (44) (Art. 7), 1992, UN Doc. CCPR/C21/Rev.1/Add.3, para. 15. See also the review of several relevant decisions in "Study Concerning the Right to Restitution, Compensation and Rehabilitation for Victims of Gross Violations of Human Rights and Fundamental Freedoms, Final Report Submitted by Mr. Theo van Boven, Special Rapporteur," reproduced in *Law and Contemporary Problems* 59, no. 4 (1996): 284.

47 See for example the review in Naomi Roht-Arriaza and Lauren Gibson, "The Developing Jurisprudence on Amnesty," *Human Rights Quarterly* 20, no. 4 (1998): 843–85; Orentlicher, *supra* n25; Scharf, "The Letter of the Law," *supra* n36; Schabacker, *supra* n36; and van Boven, *supra* n46.

48 See, for example, "Question of the Impunity of Perpetrators of Human Rights Violations (Civil and Political), Final Report Prepared by Mr. Joinet Pursuant to Sub-Commission Decision 1996/119," reproduced in *Law and Contemporary Problems* 59, no. 4 (1996): 250–81.

49 See Carlos Nino, "The Duty to Punish Past Abuses of Human Rights Put into Context: The Case of Argentina," *Yale Law Journal* 100, no. 8 (1991): 2619–40; and see José Zalaquett, "Balancing Ethical Imperatives and Political Constraints: The Dilemma of New Democracies Confronting Past Human Rights Violations," *Hastings Law Journal* 43, no. 6 (1992): 1425–38.

50 This is discussed in more detail below, section II, part D.

51 Orentlicher, *supra* n25, 2548. This necessity exception is not to be invoked lightly; it refers to situations of real necessity, and a state cannot evade its duty simply to appease the powerful or because it is politically inexpedient (ibid., 2595). See also, for example, Juan Méndez, "In Defence of Transitional Justice," in McAdams, ed., *supra* n30, 1–26, 4: "Just as it makes no sense

to exaggerate the political obstacles, it is equally wrong to postulate an obligation to punish the perpetrators of past offences without regard to the potential consequences for the future enjoyment of rights by all others."

52 Orentlicher, *supra* n25, 2549; see also Landsman, *supra* n25, 89.

53 Orentlicher, *supra* n25, 2599. Likewise, Neil J. Kritz, "Coming to Terms With Atrocities: A Review of Accountability Mechanisms for Mass Violations of Human Rights," *Law and Contemporary Problems* 59, no. 4 (1996): 127–52, 134 notes that "international law does not, however, demand the prosecution of every individual implicated in the atrocities. A symbolic or representative number of prosecutions of those most culpable may satisfy international obligations, especially where an overly extensive trial program will threaten the stability of the country." See also Madeleine Morris, "International Guidelines against Impunity: Facilitating Accountability," *Law and Contemporary Problems* 59, no. 4 (1996): 29–39; and Pasqualucci, *supra* n25, 334.

54 Provided that the state's efforts to select the most serious crimes for prosecution were based on objective criteria and carried out in good faith, it would be appropriate for the prosecutor to defer to the national program, even if the rosecutor would have made a few different choices in selecting perpetrators. A more activist, interventionist stance on the part of the prosecutor would be justified where there was reason to believe that the omission to prosecute particular persons was more than a simple "difference in judgment" but rather a politically-motivated decision.

55 For a thorough review of the various policy arguments, see the works cited *supra* n25, as well as José Zalaquett, "Confronting Human Rights Violations Committed by Former Governments: Principles Applicable and Political Constraints," in Kritz, ed., *supra* n25, 3–31; Villa-Vicencio, *supra* n2; Arsanjani, *supra* n4; and Scharf, *supra* n4.

56 Scharf, *supra* n4, 508.

57 Arsanjani, *supra* n4, 65.

58 See Benomar, *supra* n25, and Schabacker, *supra* n36.

59 Orentlicher, *supra* n25, 2548; Mendez, *supra* n51, 4.

60 Zalaquett, *supra* n49.

61 Nino, *supra* n49, 2620.

62 See, for example, John Dugard, *supra* n30.

63 Ibid., 9.

64 See UN SC Res. 1315 (2000), 14 August 2000; and *Report of the Secretary-General on the Establishment of a Special Court for Sierra Leone*, 4 October 2000, UN Doc. S/2000/915.

65 For example, "Milosevic Indicted," ABC *News*, 27 May 1999, on-line: <http://abcnews.go.com/sections/world/DailyNews/milosevic990527.html#sidebar>.

66 Blanket amnesties bestowed by a regime for its own benefit ("self-amnesties") have been singled out for particular criticism, as they purport to allow a regime to unilaterally protect itself from the consequences of its own wrongdoing. See, for example, Méndez, *supra* n25; and Pasqualucci, *supra* n25, 344.

67 See John Dugard, "Dealing with Crimes of a Past Regime: Is Amnesty Still an Option?" *Leiden Journal of International Law* 12, no. 4 (1999): 1001–15; Arsanjani, *supra* n4, Landsman, *supra* n25, Zalaquett, *supra* n49, Cassel, *supra* n33, Villa-Vicencio, *supra* n2, and Paul Van Zyl, "Justice without Punishment: Guaranteeing Human Rights in Transitional Societies," in *Looking Back/Reaching Forward: Reflections on the Truth and Reconciliation Commission of South Africa*, eds. Charles Villa-Vicencio and Wilhelm Verwoerd, 42–57 (Cape Town, South Africa: Univ. of Cape Town Press, 2000).

68 Scharf, *supra* n4, 527.

69 John T. Holmes, "Complementarity: National Courts *versus* the ICC," in Antonio Cassese et al., *supra* n36, 667–86; John T. Holmes, "The Principle of Complementarity" in *The International Criminal Court: The Making of the Rome Statute: Issues, Negotiations, Results*, ed. Roy S. Lee, 41–78 (The Hague: Kluwer Law International, 1999); Sharon Williams, "Article 17: Issues of Admissibility" in Triffterer, ed., *supra* n19, 383–94.

70 ICC Statute, *supra* n1, art. 20(3) deals with the principle *ne bis in idem.*

71 Ibid., art. 17(1)(d) adds: "The case is not of sufficient gravity to justify further action by the Court." This criterion addresses not complementarity but rather the separate issue of gravity, a criterion included to reflect the intention that the ICC will focus its limited resources on the gravest crimes falling within its jurisdiction.

72 See ibid., art. 17(1)(c) and art. 20 (*ne bis in idem*).

73 "It is also conceivable that an amnesty granted in the context of a 'truth commission' process could be considered an 'investigation' followed by a *bona fide* decision not to proceed for purposes of Art. 17(1)(b)." Bruce Broomhall, "The International Criminal Court: A Checklist for National Implementation," in *ICC Ratification and National Implementing Legislation*, ed. M.C. Bassiouni, 113–59 (Paris: Association Internationale de Droit Pénal, 1999), 144.

74 Indeed, a critical and often overlooked point with respect to article 17 is that, to fall even prima facie within any of the headings (a) to (c), there

must at minimum be an "*investigation*" by the State. Where no investigation has been initiated at all, none of the grounds of article 17(1)(a) to (c) are applicable, and thus one cannot even turn to an assessment of the "genuineness" of the state's proceedings.

75 See the review of Inter-American and Human Rights Committee jurisprudence on the right to know and the duty to investigate in Cassel, *supra* n33, esp. 208–19; as well as Joinet, *supra* n48 and the *CHR Resolution on Impunity*, *supra* n42, para. 8.

76 See sections 16–21 of the Promotion of National Unity and Reconciliation Act, 1995, Republic of South Africa Government Gazette, vol. 361, No. 16579, 26 July 1995.

77 See Lionel Yee, "The International Criminal Court and the Security Council: Articles 13(b) and 16" in Lee, ed., *supra* n69, 143–52; and Morten Bergsmo and Jelena Pejić, "Article 16: Deferral of Investigation or Prosecution" in Triffterer, ed., *supra* n19, 373–82.

78 As has been observed by Naomi Roht-Arriaza, "there would be a political cost to the Security Council in detailing its reasons for invoking its right to deferral." "Amnesty and the International Criminal Court" in *International Crimes, Peace and Human Rights: The Role of the International Criminal Court*, ed. Dinah Shelton, 77–82 (Ardsley, NY: Transnational Publishers, 2000). See also Philippe Kirsch, QC, and Darryl Robinson, "Reaching Agreement at the Rome Conference," in Cassese *et al.*, eds., *supra* n36, 67–91.

79 On 12 July 2002, the council adopted (or *purported* to adopt, given the absence of even a pretext of a threat to international peace and security) Resolution 1422, requesting a deferral for any ICC investigation of any peacekeeper who is a national of a non-state party to the ICC Statute. The resolution was resoundingly condemned by numerous UN member states addressing the council on 10 July 2002, but was eventually adopted at the insistence of the US, which threatened to veto all UN peacekeeping mandate renewals until its demands were met. For commentary on resolution 1422, see, for example, Carsten Stahn, "The Ambiguities of Security Council Resolution 1422 (2002)," *European Journal of International Law* 14, no. 1 (2003): 85–104.

80 See the observations in *Prosecutor* v. *Furundzija* (10 December 1998), Case No. IT-95-17/1, (International Criminal Tribunal for the Former Yugoslavia, Trial Chamber II), para. 155, on-line: United Nations, <http://www.un.org/icty/judgement.htm>.

81 In this connection, a "rule of reasonableness" has been suggested in deciding whether to respect national amnesties: Roman Boed, "The Effect of a Domestic Amnesty on the Ability of Foreign States to Prosecute Alleged

Perpetrators of Serious Human Rights Violations," *Cornell International Law Journal* 33, no. 2 (2000): 297–330, 325. See also Dugard, *supra* n67, 1009.

82 See, for example, International Commission of Jurists, *Crimes Against Humanity: Pinochet Faces Justice* (1999), 20–3 and 98.

83 See, for example, John Dugard, "Reconciliation and Justice: The South African Experience," *Transnational Law and Contemporary Problems* 8, no. 2 (1998): 277–311, 301.

9

Global(izing) Justice? The International Criminal Court

ANTONIO FRANCESCHET

Global justice is a moral ideal. It is also the subject of ethical discourse about the organization of political, economic, and social affairs on this planet.[1] Globalization refers to a constellation of processes that effectively de-territorialize much of the political, economic, and social affairs on this planet.[2] These processes have, to date, encouraged and promoted an intensification of global inequalities, poverty, and economic stratification.[3] The International Criminal Court (ICC) is a new institution yet one that has been sought by many states, international lawyers, and human rights activists since at least the mid-twentieth century. With the adoption of the ICC Statute in 1998,[4] and its subsequent ratification by a sufficient number of signatory states in 2002, a supranational and global court now exists, one with jurisdiction over the most serious violations of human rights and humanitarian law.[5] This chapter analyses the likely contributions of the ICC to global justice – in a context of globalization.

The apparently strong endorsement of the ICC by a wide variety of states suggests that a reasonably wide consensus is now available on the "rule of law" globally.[6] The ICC is a particularly significant achievement because traditional international law has applied (with very few exceptions) to states; there have been hardly any effective and certainly no permanent legal instruments to prosecute and punish individuals across territorial frontiers. By the same token, there have been few truly supranational legal means to vindicate the rights of victims of gross human rights violations. The ad hoc tribunals set up by the UN Security Council for the former Yugoslavia, Rwanda, and, most recently, Sierra Leone, are exceptional cases. Building upon these institutional precedents, the ICC is aimed at ensuring that universal human rights standards are not subordinated to, and sacrificed by, state sovereignty, thus giving individuals – no matter where they live – access to the protection of a legal order. However, an exclusive focus on globalizing the rule of law has, perhaps conveniently, eclipsed global dialogue, action, and responsiveness on the other central problems of global justice, namely, increased poverty and inequality. Therefore, although the ICC is a moral and political accomplishment – a step in the right direction for progressive internationalists – it may also reflect profound moral and political *detachment* on the part of many of its state signatories.[7] Simply put, even though the ICC and the general aim of a global rule of law are extremely important, they can at best only partially fulfill any generally conceived duty to promote and protect the basic rights and autonomy of much of the world's inhabitants in an era of globalization.

This chapter examines both the *potential limits* and the *limited potential* of the ICC as an institution promoting global justice. The potential limits of the ICC emerge from its narrow, legalistic mandate. As a worst-case scenario, the ICC is likely to be a band-aid solution to global injustice. Sadly, this is how the ICC will be viewed by many in the world who, although in (sometimes desperate) need of protection from gross violations of human rights and humanitarian law, are too enmeshed in the daily struggle for survival in an increasingly stratified global order. Perhaps worse, the ICC will suffer from a more general crisis of legitimacy that all international and global governing bodies face in an era of greater substantive injustices within and across states and societies.[8] Nonetheless, the limited potential of the ICC must be recognized, promoted, and cautiously celebrated. If, under a best-case scenario, the ICC succeeds in promoting a global rule of law in a way that directly protects and promotes human rights – and not just, as under traditional international law, the rights of sovereign states – there is the reasonable hope that the most disadvantaged individuals in today's global order will be empowered to make their demands for greater substantive justice on the more powerful and advantaged segments of both national and global societies.

I. GLOBAL JUSTICE, LEGITIMACY, AND THE LIMITS OF THE ICC

What is meant by "global justice"? To start with the "global" part, there is some disagreement. For some it is merely a synonym for international or, more precisely, inter-state relations. In this sense, global justice means, or ought only to mean, the procedural rules, norms, and practices of a society of independent sovereign *states*, a society that – after decolonization – spans all the way across the globe.[9] These rules, norms, and practices allow states (as representatives of certain peoples or groups of individuals) to co-exist and, if possible, minimize unnecessary harm to each other.[10] For others, however, "global" means going somewhat beyond a society of currently recognized states to embrace the vital interests, needs, and basic rights of all *individuals* directly.[11] In other words, inter-state boundaries, state sovereignty, and territoriality are, if not morally irrelevant, then morally contingent upon how well they serve and promote human interests and rights. In this chapter, it is this second, more cosmopolitan, conception of global justice that is assumed – but not explicitly or directly defended. From this vantage point, discourse about global "justice" concerns a substantive purpose: the autonomy of individuals and the conditions required to protect and promote it. I also take for granted that human rights and, more specifically, attention to the most fundamental of these – that is, "basic rights" such as and including those found in the Universal Declaration of Human Rights[12] and UN Covenants[13] – form the core concern of global justice. Justice thus entails *responsibilities* by sovereign states to promote and protect the human rights of the members of each national community. However, it also entails global or cosmopolitan accountability and duties on the part of outside agents and authorities, especially where there is failure or incapacity within sovereign states. As Jones explains it, "global justice include[s] various positive actions aimed at protecting the vital interests of everyone, regardless of their location, nationality, or citizenship."[14]

What is the potential contribution of an institution like the ICC to global justice in the cosmopolitan sense described above? There seem to be at least three distinct responses: the first is to claim that global justice is *directly* served by an ICC. Rather than sovereign immunity and individual impunity – the kind of things claimed by the Pinochets of the world and recently denied to Milosevic – the ICC will institutionalize a permanent, supranational legal regime of punishment, individual accountability, and, it is hoped, deterrence. Thus, the basic rights of individuals – as victims and potential victims – within and across inter-state boundaries will be safeguarded. Compared with the statist International Court of Justice, for example, the ICC puts the basic rights of individuals at the centre of legitimate international concern and responsibility. As Schabas states, "not only does the ICC provide for prosecution and punishment of individuals, it also recognizes a legitimate participation for the individual victim."[15] Some international lawyers and human rights activists will speak of global justice almost exclusively in these terms,[16] and are accused of paying insufficient attention to the wider global political, social, and economic context in which the ICC will operate.[17] Divorced from such contextual factors, there is a mistaken assumption that the rule of law can by itself ensure basic rights, provided that the politicians do not get in the way and compromise legal principle for politically or economically expedient goals.

For some, global justice is not primarily about the appropriate distribution of punishments for crimes, but rather the fair (re)distribution of material and social goods required to fulfill the vital interests or basic rights of individuals, especially the poorest. For example, Jones's recent defence of cosmopolitanism states that punishment, prosecution, and individual accountability for the "core" crimes are not a central concern in his theory of global justice.[18] The assumption here is that legal instruments aimed only at dealing with the most violent atrocities do little to positively fulfill vital interests and basic rights. Rather than focusing on narrow and specific legal instruments for individual crimes, the focus should be, in this view, on adapting and transforming the political and especially economic institutions (states, markets, intergovernmental institutions, etc.) to make the distribution of a much wider array of economic and social goods fairer. Indeed, global poverty and inequality are treated as a form of structural violence in that they are preventable harms that are tolerated, if not actively reinforced by, the wealthy and powerful in global society. As Pogge writes:

> People can kill one another with bombs and machetes. But economic arrangements are quite as effective. Millions were killed in the Irish potato famine, in Stalin's forced collectivization, in Mao's Great Leap Forward,

> in contemporary North Korea, as well as in many other human-made disasters. The ongoing catastrophe of world hunger is of the same kind. But it is also different: by being less confined in space and time, even more devastating, and less recognized. It claims a third of all human deaths. But these deaths happen far away, to people we never encounter. They happen in social contexts whose dependence on the existing global order we do not understand. And they happen in areas where we assume people have always been desperately poor. It seems unlikely, then, that the citizens and governments of developed countries will be struck by the problem enough to recognize their responsibility.[19]

Extending the global rule of law for so-called core crimes like genocide – a crime that requires deliberate, calculated acts to destroy a people – in a global order that also legally permits the systemic destruction of people through starvation would seem to be perverse.

One might ask, however, whether tackling distributive global injustices like poverty cannot be met with simultaneous action on strengthening the rule of law? In other words, individual criminal accountability, while retributive, is ideally an essential *part* of a more holistic strategy to fulfill basic rights. In other words, both the retributive rule of law issues *and* welfare or social entitlement issues are *inter-related*. The "rule of law," *if pursued in the right social and political context*, can also support and promote the basic rights of people. This third response is one to which the present chapter contributes, primarily by investigating the limits and possibilities of a supranational criminal court in a context of globalization.

Certainly the ICC is an important step in the project to civilize world order by strengthening human rights. This is reflected in the statements of many of its strongest advocates, such as UN Secretary General, Kofi Annan: "In the prospect of an international criminal court lies the promise of universal justice. That is the simple and soaring hope of this vision ... [it will] ensure that no ruler, no State, no junta and no army anywhere can abuse human rights with impunity. Only then will the innocents of distant wars and conflicts know that they, too, may sleep under the cover of justice; that they, too, have rights, and that those who violate those rights will be punished."[20] However, the rule of law can and has historically coexisted in societies with tremendously perverse inequality and poverty suffered by the "innocents." Does the recent pledge by a majority of the international community to create, support, and abide by the ICC simply create an institution to co-exist alongside political, economic, and social conditions that essentially violate basic rights? Presently there seems little to indicate otherwise. The implications of this moral failure should concern the Court's greatest advocates. If, as Annan's remarks indicate, the ICC is justified by a moral good of universal or global justice, the rule of law is a necessary but, ultimately, insufficient guiding principle. Punishment (retribution) can at best partially uphold basic rights, not least because it is backward-looking. Also, the forward-looking goal of deterrence has limited value in that it may eliminate potential incidence of crime, but does not positively contribute to fulfilling material requirements that permit people to exercise their basic rights.

Nonetheless, the ICC promises to be a significant achievement if it "works" as intended. The punishment of those who believe they can victimize with impunity will be guided by due process rather than by self-help or vengeance. However, there are many forces and factors that will impede this progress; not least is the uncertain commitment of states (even states parties) to the execution of the ICC Statute. In light of the fact that negotiations were difficult and essentially a decades long process, it is worth asking why, finally, there has been sufficient state consensus to create the ICC (albeit without the current support of the US)? Certainly the end of the Cold War helped to create new, perhaps less ideological space for consensus. Additionally, the terrible inaction in response to crimes against humanity and genocide in the former Yugoslavia and Rwanda gave some urgency to the issue. However, these factors are insufficient to explain state commitments. A more potent explanation has to do with the ideational power of the rule of law as a point of consensus and legitimating factor in any social order, not least an evolving society of states. The Hague Conventions, the Geneva Conventions, human rights treaties and, now, the ICC Statute, manifest the growing commitment to the rule of law internationally. The ICC is part of the long evolution of customary and treaty law, an evolution that recognizes state interests in protecting human dignity and punishing egregious affronts to this value.

But human dignity as an international human right is also a more specific product of liberalism and, more particularly, the liberal conception of political legitimacy. Stanley Hoffmann argues that "the international dimension of liberalism ... [is] little more than the projection of domestic liberalism on a world scale."[21] In this spirit, Gary Jonathan Bass's recent historical analysis of five earlier attempts to create international criminal legal institutions provides compelling evidence for Hoffmann's assertion.[22] Bass shows that liberal states have been both genuinely "principled" and predictably "selfish" (or non-cosmopolitan) in their attempts to prosecute violent acts that have shocked the conscience of humankind. Liberal states, as he defines them, have sought to promote the rule of law even when successful prosecutions were extremely unpredictable, difficult to achieve, and sometimes impossible. This is "principled" because the outcome of "fair trials" cannot be politically predetermined. However, these same liberal states have demonstrated inconsistency, hypocrisy, and unwillingness to adhere to the international rule of law under certain conditions. In particular, when the soldiers and citizens of a liberal state are exposed to harm or, worse, subject to prosecution for their own war crimes, the global projection of the rule of law has been ignored. (The current rejection of and hostility towards the ICC by the US government appears only to confirm Bass's analysis.) The general lesson Bass draws from the five historic cases he analyses – Napoleon, the genocide in Armenia, both World Wars, and Yugoslavia – is that liberal states, *like all states*, are imperfect when judged against the standard of global "legality." However, Bass adds that liberal states are still *better* actors for the cause of global justice than are other kinds of regimes.

Another finding, one to which the author does not give sufficient attention, is as follows: the *project* of rendering global politics more consistent with the rule of law, while led by liberal states, often attracts the support of other states – or at least may not meet strong opposition from non-liberal states. For example, the Soviet Union, in spite of its propensity for show trials, grudgingly participated in the precedent-setting Nuremberg experiment after World War II (for ostensibly less principled reasons). Recently, China did not use its veto on the UN Security Council to prevent the ad hoc tribunals for Yugoslavia and Rwanda in the 1990s. In other words, non-liberal states might "tag along for the ride" for a variety of reasons, including gaining an international stamp of legitimacy. When liberal ideals like the rule of law become accepted by the plurality of states into customary and treaty law, the nature of international legitimacy changes.

The politics behind the pre-history of the ICC have exhibited many of these dynamics: the principled efforts of many states, both liberal and liberalizing; hypocrisy and/or a lack of commitment on the part of states that fear harm to military personnel (the US foremost); and the desire by many states, both liberal and liberalizing, to gain legitimacy "by association" (with the rule of law).[23] However, the ICC is far more ambitious and potentially significant than previous efforts to domesticate and civilize international order through the rule of law. It will be a permanent and semi-autonomous court (on paper it has substantial independence, although an effective veto of the Security Council is a limit). For this reason, it has a far greater potential to contribute to global justice. However, it also has a far greater potential to *fail* in meeting lofty expectations promised to the "innocents" to whom Annan asserts that all states and societies have fundamental duties.

The main focus in the literature on the ICC has been on how legitimate it will be without greater state commitment and consent. However, comparatively little has been done to analyse the potential damage to the ICC's future legitimacy created by other, structural issues in an era of globalization, particularly growing poverty and inequality. This problem is related to, yet analytically separable from, the uneven and often weak commitments of states – liberal and illiberal – to a strong global rule of law. Certainly, as Bass would argue, weak and uneven rule of law is preferable to nothing, especially when it comes to systematic and widespread abuse involving ethnic cleansing and genocide. For "nothing," here, may in practice mean the perpetuation of violence or revenge, summary executions, or impunity. However, it still needs to be considered whether a weak and uneven pursuit of the rule of law is especially problematic when it is the *only* goal pursued with (occasional) zeal by states. This problem is also one of legitimacy.

If global justice is narrowly construed in terms of trials, criminal statutes, punishment, and so on, rather than greater distributive equality and human well-being, the rule of law itself is potentially weakened. The rule of law will be attacked and undermined if the global societal context continues to permit, if not create, widespread poverty, inequality, and thereby, the systematic violation of basic rights. In other words, the ICC can do little to challenge – and can only suffer from – a prevailing suspicion that the rule of law benefits the privileged and powerful actors in any social order.

This point can be made with some effectiveness by referring to the evolution of liberalism *within* the domestic societies of the West. The rule of law was initially a radical doctrine that early liberals employed to criticize the monopoly of social and political power held by a privileged aristocratic class. Liberals argued that mere lawfulness was insufficient if the political and social institutions through which law functioned did not adhere to certain formal principles like due process, impartiality, individual rights, judicial independence, and fair trials. But the rule of law was arguably never an end in itself for liberalism but rather a means to guarantee a higher goal: *freedom* or more positively, *autonomy*.

However, the rule of law has also functioned in liberal society as a "conservative," rather than radical, ideal. That is, the gains made for certain classes in market society became entrenched by a legal sphere focused on protecting formal equality (and private property), not on promoting and helping to fulfill the needs of the poor, unemployed, and socially marginalized. The rule of law thus soon became viewed simply as part of the "superstructure" by Marx and a rival socialist ideology rather than as an authentic way of protecting individual autonomy. Subsequently, the liberal defence of the rule of law splintered into two: the "classical" liberals defended dogmatically the rule of law as a sacrosanct end in itself; but the "new," or welfare, liberals argued that the rule of law should be viewed as a *means* having autonomy as its end. If the rule of law did not contribute to this higher goal, then liberal society would lose its primary justification and hence, also, its social legitimacy. If liberal society was to *legitimize* itself, the rule of law would have to be matched with compensating mechanisms to redistribute social goods or equalize welfare. The twentieth-century welfare state is thus explainable by, among other things, the recognition by some liberals that the legitimacy of the rule of law (something that protects property rights) would increasingly depend on greater distributive justice and social entitlements.[24]

Undeniably, the rule of law has had an even more problematic relationship to distributive justice and welfare issues in global politics. Nardin and Jackson, two "classical" liberal international theorists, insist that the most legitimate moral customs in global politics are essentially divorced from distributive or substantive justice.[25] From this vantage point, international law and morality are inherently supportive of sovereignty, non-aggression, and non-intervention.

Although less robust than its domestic analogue, certainly the international rule of law has incorporated human rights and humanitarian law, each of which concern human dignity, and, therefore, autonomy. But Nardin asserts these largely twentieth-century innovations are consistent with the purely *formal* logic of the rule of law. These laws do not – with the exception of some weakly enforced international commitments to social, economic, and cultural rights – legally require redistribution.[26] Nardin's reading of international liberalism, then, is essentially a "conservative" interpretation of the rule of law in a society of states: the norm constrains actors from doing harm, but it does not redistribute goods or address substantive injustices.

Will the ICC simply extend the rule of law in an essentially "conservative" way? If so, is it enmeshed in a larger legitimacy problem in today's era of globalization? Are the ICC's potential legitimacy problems compounded by the effects of neoliberal economic practices that have become the orthodoxy in the past generation? It is impossible to predict precisely, but if existing structural conditions in global society persist, we should expect at least three particular and more specific problems that the ICC will encounter. All three problems have already shown themselves to be present in the case of the ad hoc tribunals created by the UN in the 1990s to deal with the former Yugoslavia (ICTY) and Rwanda (ICTR). They also point to the importance of a larger socio-economic and political context in which the ICC will have the burden of trying to operate effectively.

The first problem is that of the Court's perceived irrelevance and distance from societal concerns. In societies where economic, social, and other crises are severe, the ICC will be too far removed from the day-to-day struggles for survival. Perhaps unreasonably, the social legitimacy of a legal institution is connected to its perceived practical (ir)relevance in society. As an example, the ICTR is not just physically removed from Rwanda, with the court in Tanzania and the chief prosecutor until recently headquartered in The Hague; it could also be on the moon for all the ordinary Rwandans trying to cope with the skyrocketing incidence of AIDS, poverty, post-genocide psychological traumas, and the fear of renewed civil war. In this environment, the ICTR does not evoke much interest among Rwandans.[27] As Gérald Ghima, a chief prosecutor in Rwanda claims, "the societies against whom the crimes were committed know little about the Tribunal's work and care even less about it. Any court that lacks contact with the victims of the crimes it is trying will always lack legitimacy."[28]

The second problem is that of political elites and perpetrators exploiting difficult economic and social conditions. It is not hard to imagine that political elites in countries in which gross violations of human rights occur will attempt to deflect from their own role in contributing to the economic, social, and other crises by attacking the ICC. Certainly crises like ethnic cleansing in the former Yugoslavia and the genocide in Rwanda were orchestrated and executed by internal agents. However, if economic crises and poverty are perpetuated by external economic policies, and if little is done by outside actors to address the deleterious effects of such policies, elites and perpetrators are better positioned to manipulate public antipathy against all outside, Western-linked institutions. Whether Milosevic was president or simply an indignant defendant on the dock, he has been able to exploit – with diminishing success – the perception that the West is just using the rule of law to attack the weak, persecuted Serbs. Although conditions may differ greatly in future cases where the ICC tries to prosecute and punish offenders, the economic crises and deprivations allowed to flourish in today's globalizing order will give ammunition to those wishing to discredit the institution. Arguments about the sovereignty of the nation – as an excuse to deny the legitimate jurisdiction of the ICC – are much easier to make when the nation is viewed as being made vulnerable and undermined economically by outside forces. Additionally, harsh and harmful neoliberal market discipline tied to structural adjustment programs – much like punitive sanctions from the UN Security Council – can be linked, whether fairly or not, by elites and/or perpetrators to attempts by the ICC to impose a global rule of law.

The third and perhaps most serious foreseeable problem concerns the weak capacities of states and societies to participate as equals in executing and implementing the global rule of law. Developing countries are tremendously disadvantaged in terms of capacity and resources relative to countries in the global North. Invariably, developing states and societies are (ideally, at least) concerned with putting limited and stretched resources into meeting basic needs. It is therefore unlikely they will be able to contribute a commensurate share of the ICC's financing, staff, or other resources. The international legal presumption of sovereign equality means that each state signatory needs to amend its criminal code and domestic legislation in line with the ICC Statute prior to ratification. However, this domestic convergence with international standards, while important, will not lead to greater equality or the enhanced participation of developing countries. Of particular significance is the principle of "complementarity" used to describe the ICC's jurisdictional powers. This principle means that if a state is either "unwilling" or "unable" to investigate and prosecute a crime that falls under the ICC Statute, the ICC can legally step in. In a context of global inequality, where not all states possess the capacities and resources to meet international standards, complementarity may simply reinforce power inequalities. Interestingly, a former chief prosecutor of the ad hoc tribunals has been particularly critical: "Louise Arbour argued essentially that the regime would work in favour of rich, developed countries and against poor countries. Although the Court's Prosecutor might easily make the claim that a justice system in an underdeveloped country was ineffective and therefore 'unable' to proceed, essentially for reasons of poverty, the difficulties involved in challenging a State with a sophisticated and functional justice system would be virtually insurmountable."[29] Arbour, who had to deal with the sense by many Rwandans that the ICTR was a foreign instrument to assuage Western guilt, no doubt based her concerns on difficult professional experiences. Unless the institutional and administrative capacity of developing countries is improved – and this seems difficult under conditions of contemporary globalization – the ICC will likely lack the relevance and legitimacy in many of the states that have gone to the trouble of ratifying the treaty and amending domestic legislation.

A dominant critical assumption about the ICC has been that it will lack in legitimacy because powerful states will jealously protect their domestic jurisdiction or sovereignty. This is certainly a bias in the American literature, given the domestic political debates between so-called internationalists and unilateralists. However, for most of the world the sovereignty preoccupation of states will be connected to continuing realities of global inequality and poverty. Sovereignty will, as it has in the past, become a convenient and popular normative device to defend the interests of societies from outside, Western powers. The ICC will exist in this context and it will be increasingly difficult territory in which to attempt to build its own putatively supranational capacity and global legitimacy. Extending the rule of law globally thus very much depends on how much progress can be made in tackling other global political, economic, and social disparities.

II. POTENTIAL CONTRIBUTIONS OF THE ICC TO GLOBAL JUSTICE

The Canadian diplomat, and now president of the ICC, Philippe Kirsch, who chaired the difficult negotiations to produce the ICC Statute in Rome, has written that the effectiveness of international tribunals "must be placed in a longer-term perspective."[30] The legitimacy problem that the ICC will likely face in light of growing global poverty and inequality is serious and, in any worst-case scenario, debilitating. However, the potential of the ICC to *indirectly* promote a wider and more substantive kind of global justice deserves consideration. If, in a best-case scenario, the application of a global rule of law on core crimes is done with relative success and with minimal geopolitical interference, the ICC can have broader salutary effects. A humane world order requires the rule of law as a context to strengthen efforts to create fairer political, social, and economic conditions.

The ICC Statute pushes forward the international customary and treaty law rules with respect to human rights. Thus, the ICC is yet another limit on state sovereignty as a device to shield the perpetrators of human rights abuse. The treaty to which signatories have agreed means that states now cede jurisdiction if they fail to prosecute suspected perpetrators, thus obviously including the state's leaders and military personnel. As Giulio M. Gallarotti and Arik Y. Preis write, "the creation of a permanent international criminal court after so many years of failure stands as a testament to the resilience of principles in the community of states. The compelling principles in this case emanate from a belief that national boundaries should not determine the scope and practice of justice, but that such things must be defined by the world at large."[31] The ICC will be a relatively independent body in prosecuting and punishing, thanks mainly to civil society groups committed to universal basic rights. Civil society movements and NGOs kept the ICC on the agenda and pushed it forward in the opportune context of the post–Cold War era.[32] These civil society actors forged a strategic coalition with a broad and influential bloc of "like-minded" states to keep the process moving and to resist the tendency of some states, mainly the US, to demand a very small degree of independence for the court in addition to a truncated jurisdiction and list of admissible crimes.[33]

Unfortunately, the ICC will at first have very limited authority over vast portions of the planet in light of the absence of the US and China as states parties. Additionally, it will have to rely on a tenuous and no doubt rocky relationship with existing states parties to build up competence. However, there is a hope that the global extension of the rule of law can, if not *directly* lead to a consensus on global duties with respect to substantive and redistributive issues, at least *indirectly* improve the relevant conditions. If the rule of law can be extended, and with a larger measure of consistency than it is currently under simply UN Security Council agreements and the occasional exercise of "universal jurisdiction" by states, the increased freedom of individuals and groups to push for changes is ideally created. In other words, if the ICC can actually do what its advocates hope, and if geopolitics can be tamed somewhat from impeding its progress, then the potential freedom from atrocities committed in certain countries can likely promote individuals and groups to organize and improve their circumstances. When the rule of law is enhanced in societies, so too is the social space for organizing civil society for demands on states and other social institutions.

The ICC indicates some normative movement towards a post-Westphalian or de-territorialized constitutional order along the lines described recently by Andrew Linklater: "Extending the rule of law so that all individuals including fellow-nationals can be brought before international courts of law when they are suspected of human rights violations marks the transition from … sovereignty, to a post-Westphalian global order in which significant national powers are transferred to international legal authorities."[34] Significantly, Linklater notes that the rule of law and constitutionalism were first used "in the struggle against absolutism" in European feudal times but that, initially at least, the "right of protection under the law" had "little significance for the mass of population which lacked for real economic and political power."[35] While certainly not inevitable, the normative demands of legal equality created "forward momentum" in the context of subsequent social struggles within liberal states for social and welfare rights.[36] "The right of protection under the law was deemed incomplete without the additional right of participation in the law-making process ... [so that] weaker members of society could fully exercise their civic rights."[37] To the extent that globalization is encouraging a de-territorialization of politics, these constitutional dynamics are likely encouraged and globalized by the ICC.

Assuming that states parties are truly committed to upholding a future "atrocities regime" and accepting a responsibility to protect individuals globally, then, at the very least, societal groups will be able to risk greater efforts for social justice.[38] Additionally, if the ICC succeeds on its own limited terms, efforts to foster reconciliation in post-conflict societies will be strengthened, thus freeing up state and societal resources to meeting basic rights.[39] Certainly these ifs (as part of a best-case scenario) are not guaranteed and are therefore problematic: the worst thing for the future legitimacy of the ICC could be a future broken promise of protection to civil populations – the "victims," in Kofi Annan's words.

Finally, the ICC encourages states that are currently under transition to democracy to adjust further the essential purposes of governance in favour of upholding basic rights. As noted above, signatories must amend domestic legislation and recognize as legitimate the customary and treaty law on the core crimes. This contributes to further normative change at the state and international levels to the effect that institutions have a *responsibility* to defend and protect the vital interests and basic rights of all peoples. However, the question of state institutional capacity and capability to promote such rights is also currently challenged by global economic conditions. Global social movements that have pushed for the ICC arguably have an opportunity now to forge strategic alliances with those seeking a fairer global economy, and for conditions that would positively enable states to meet the basic rights of citizens. Reducing crippling debt loads, and adopting more favourable terms of trade and more sensitive lending practices should be linked more directly by global civil society actors to improving the ICC's future legitimacy.

How realistic is such a linking strategy? For those who are interested in progressive change, the importance of global civil society at this historic juncture has been a growing theme. The ICC Statute, like the Ottawa Convention on Anti-personnel Mines,[40] is a case of transnational social activists co-opting and shaming states in order to bring about change. The states that have been receptive to this social activism have sought to gain legitimacy through commitment to a humane world order. Anti-personnel mines have been stigmatized as contrary to "civilized" standards; and genocide, war crimes, and crimes against humanity have, since the 1990s, become the focus of renewed approbation in light of the atrocities in the former Yugoslavia and Rwanda. The making of the ICC is thus linked to a particular receptivity by states to the pressures by global civil society actors to "do something" to protect human dignity and put aside the traditional geopolitical reasons of state.[41]

Can the same kind of dynamics that led to the creation of humane, global moral commitments by states in the case of the ICC be channelled to support a broader conception of justice that includes substantive or redistributive issues? There appears to be little at this point to suggest that states are willing to make any strong *direct* connection between a civilized world order based on the rule of law and the prevailing neoliberal economic model. For example, although Canada has played the "good international citizen" on the landmines and ICC files, it has arguably not gone beyond a mere rhetorical concern for global poverty and inequality, and certainly does not view these problems as connected to neoliberal globalization. The ICC may thus in fact be a legitimizing device for a hegemonic ideological construct that separates economic globalization from moral and political scrutiny and contestation.[42] Paradoxically, then, Bass's concept of "selfishness" obstructing the commitment of liberal states to the global rule of law can be extended to explain why they commit to the rule of law in the first place. That is, the ICC allows states to express concern and commitment to individual dignity and justice, without being fundamentally concerned with these moral goals *if* they happen to have been the result of structural conditions in the global economy. Direct, personal violence and not so-called structural violence is the only thing states seem willing or capable of making commitments to in an era of neoliberal globalization.

The ICC can indirectly contribute to a more substantive fulfillment of global justice. However, this contribution is best realized under scenarios that clash with structural realities. If the ICC can fulfill its expectations, increased social and political space can potentially be created for struggles in states and societies for greater distributive justice. Free from the threats of violence, progressive elements in civil society can push states on other, positive actions to improve basic rights. Additionally, the ICC encourages existing changes in state purposes and responsibilities, adding further to the weight of human rights conventions globally. However, it is ultimately up to civil society actors globally and domestically to push state institutions to live up to such purposes and in more substantive ways. It should be underlined, however, that these *indirect* potential contributions by the ICC depend on the Court successfully resisting the geopolitical interests of great powers. In other words, all salutary effects require the institution being able to live up to its original mandate reached at Rome.

CONCLUSION

The limits of the ICC emerge from its specific mandate, namely the prosecution and punishment of individuals suspected and found guilty of genocide, crimes against humanity, and war crimes. This narrowness is not by itself a surprise or even a problem for the operation of the Court; legal instruments need to be restricted and extremely specific in order to function effectively, efficiently, and in accord with the ideal of the rule of law. There is thus perhaps little point in complaining that the ICC should be able to do more than this or be something different. However, not unlike courts within most liberal domestic societies, the ICC is most promisingly conceived as a "progressive conservative" institution: while it will *not* directly challenge the substantive and distributive injustices in globalization – injustices that may preclude individuals from enjoying their full human rights – it will be empowered to directly protect individuals from certain violations. To the extent that individuals are freed from the most serious and violent threats to their autonomy, at least the space for them to organize and struggle for greater rights and justice is then opened. Thus, the ICC may *indirectly* contribute to more socially progressive outcomes that fundamentally alter the structures that produce global inequality and poverty.

Ideally the rule of law is supportive of efforts to achieve greater social justice, both nationally and globally. However, states are often committed to the rule of law while showing little concern for substantive justice claims. Commitments to an enhanced legal order can be made simply to distract attention from power inequalities in society: the rule of law thus becomes an ideological veil masking hegemony in an era of globalization. A blind commitment to the rule of law can even result in pathological consequences that violate basic rights. An important recent example is the case of multinational drug companies hiding behind patent protection legislation and global trade laws to prevent developing countries from creating generic anti-retroviral drugs for those with AIDS. Unlike trade and patent laws – which protect the rights of firms and investor – the ICC appears to have the more virtuous purpose of protecting all people globally from gross violations of human rights and humanitarian law. However, the legitimacy and thus capacity of the ICC to reach this goal is likely to be weakened if inequality and poverty are not also tackled. Nonetheless, it is significant that the ICC came into being because of a concern by states for their legitimacy in world order, in addition to the successful efforts of civil society actors to exploit this concern. It is too early to predict the future of the ICC, but if – under the best-case scenarios – it enjoys success in establishing a global rule of law, the hope remains that space will appear for peoples to demand the fulfillment of the conditions that are necessary to the full exercise of basic rights.

NOTES

1 Charles Jones, *Global Justice: Defending Cosmopolitanism* (Oxford: Oxford UP, 1999); Thomas W. Pogge, ed., *Global Justice* (Oxford, UK: Blackwell Publishers, 2001); Pablo De Grieff and Ciaran Cronin, eds., *Global Justice and Transnational Politics: Essays on the Moral and Political Challenges of Globalization* (Cambridge, Mass.: MIT Press, 2002).

2 Jan Aart Scholte, *Globalization: a Critical Introduction* (Basingstoke, UK: Palgrave Macmillan, 2000); David Held, Anthony McGrew, et al., *Global Transformations: Politics, Economics, and Culture* (Stanford: Stanford UP, 1999).

3 Andrew Hurrell and Ngaire Woods, eds., *Inequality, Globalization, and World Politics* (Oxford: Oxford UP, 1999).

4 *Rome Statute of the International Criminal Court*, 17 July 1998, UN Doc. A/CONF. 183/9, 2187 UNTS 90, reprinted in *International Legal Materials* 37, no. 5 (1998): 1002, art. 5 [hereinafter ICC Statute].

5 These serious violations are referred to as "core crimes" in the ICC Statute: crimes against humanity, war crimes, and genocide. The ICC Statute builds upon existing international legal definitions from such sources as the Nuremberg judgments, the Geneva Conventions, and the Genocide Convention. States parties have yet to agree on definitions of "aggression"

for the purposes of the ICC Statute. On the long history of efforts to bring about an ICC, see G.M. Gallarotti and A.Y. Preis, "Toward Universal Human Rights and the Rule of Law: the Permanent International Criminal Court," *Australian Journal of International Affairs* 53, no. 1 (1999): 95–111; F. Benedetti and J.L. Washburn, "Drafting the International Criminal Court Treaty: Two Years to Rome and an Afterword on the Rome Diplomatic Conference," *Global Governance: A Review of Multilateralism and International Organizations* 5, 1 (1999): 1–37; William Schabas, *An Introduction to the International Criminal Court*, 2d ed. (Cambridge: Cambridge UP, 2004); and V.P. Nanda, "The Establishment of a Permanent International Criminal Court: Challenges Ahead," *Human Rights Quarterly* 20, no. 2 (1998): 413–28.

6 The ICC Statute was signed by 120 states on 18 July 1998 despite the strong objections of the US, which did not sign until December 1999. Sixty signatories were required to ratify the ICC Statute to make the treaty a binding instrument under international law. This was achieved on 11 April 2002 and, at the time of writing, there are ninety-five states parties. See on-line: International Criminal Court <http://www.icc-cpi.int/home.html&l=en>. Although it was widely hoped that the US would one day ratify the ICC Statute (once its particular objections could be met through negotiations), the administration of George W. Bush announced on 6 May 2002 that it would renounce the signature made by the Clinton administration. For a general analysis of politics behind the American position on the ICC, see Bartram S. Brown, "Unilateralism, Multilateralism and the International Criminal Court," in *Multilateralism and United States Foreign Policy: Ambivalent Engagement*, ed. S. Patrick (Boulder, Colo.: Lynne Rienner Publishers, 2001), 323–44. In this chapter, the rule of law is synonymous with a principle of "legality." This principle means more than "the laws will be applied"; it is a standard of legitimate political order. Derived from liberal ideology and practice, the rule of law has typically meant, among other things, constitutional divisions of powers and an independent judiciary capable of protecting citizens and minorities from arbitrary abuses of power; that no person (e.g., leader) is above the law; and that the legal system is impartial and respectful of individual rights, including both the accused and the victims of criminal actions. When considering the rule of law internationally, there are some obvious differences and arguably shortcomings, namely, the lack of a single constitution and a specified division of powers and authority. However, a weak set of judicial institutions has existed and enforcement powers have been institutionalized in the UN Security Council. Nonetheless, the rule

of law has been an important normative ideal in international politics, one that accounts in part for the development of the ICC.

7 See David Rieff, "Court of Dreams," *The New Republic*, 7 September 1998, 17; and Thomas W. Smith, "Moral Hazard and Humanitarian Law: The International Criminal Court and the Limits of Legalism," *International Politics* 39 (2002): 175–92.

8 Craig N. Murphy, "Global Governance: Poorly Done, Poorly Understood," *International Affairs* 76, no. 4 (2000): 789–803.

9 Robert Jackson, *The Global Covenant: Human Conduct in a World of States* (Oxford: Oxford UP, 2000).

10 Terry Nardin, *Law, Morality, and the Relations of States* (Princeton: Princeton UP, 1983); John Rawls, *The Law of Peoples* (Cambridge, Mass.: Harvard UP, 1999).

11 See Jones, *supra* n1; Thomas W. Pogge, "The Moral Demands of Global Justice," *Dissent* 47, 4 (2000): 37–43; and K.-C. Tan, *Toleration, Diversity, and Global Justice* (University Park, Pa.: Univ. of Pennsylvania State Press, 2000).

12 GA Res. 217A (III), UN Doc. A/810 (1948) 71.

13 *International Covenant on Civil and Political Rights*, 19 December 1966, 999 UNTS 171 (entered into force 23 March 1976); and *International Covenant on Economic, Social and Cultural Rights*, 16 December 1966, 993 UNTS 3 (entered into force 3 January 1976).

14 Jones, *supra* n1, 22.

15 Schabas, *supra* n5, x.

16 See G. Robertson, *Crimes against Humanity: The Struggle for Global Justice* (New York: Free Press, 1999).

17 See R.W. Tucker, "The International Criminal Court Controversy," *World Policy Journal* 18, no. 2 (2001): 75–81; and Gary Jonathan Bass, *Stay the Hand of Vengeance: The Politics of War Crimes Tribunals* (Princeton: Princeton UP, 2000), 80.

18 Jones, *supra* n1, 2.

19 Pogge, *supra* n11, 41.

20 *Rome Statute of the International Criminal Court, Overview*, 1999, on-line: United Nations *<http://www.un.org/law/icc/general/overview.htm>*.

21 Stanley Hoffmann, "The Crisis of Liberal Internationalism," *Foreign Policy* 98 (1995): 159–77, 161.

22 Bass, *supra* n17.

23 This is not something explicitly tested by Bass in his five cases. Certainly his assertion that nineteenth-century Britain is akin to a "liberalizing" state is compelling when explaining why early attempts at war crimes tribunals were

not fully imbued with the spirit of legality. However, there were arguably no global (or external) standards by which to judge and criticize Britain at the time, as there are for today's democratizing and liberalizing states. What is striking about the ICC is the impressive number of states in transition (particularly Southern Cone Latin American and East Central European states) that signed the ICC Statute. Even Zimbabwe signed the statute, although admittedly this falls short of ratification.

24 The above paragraph draws inspiration from Antonio Franceschet and David Long, "Taking Liberalism Seriously: Liberal International Theory in an Age of Globalization," a paper presented at the International Studies Association Annual Convention, Los Angeles, 14–18 March 2000.

25 Nardin, *supra* n10; Jackson, *supra* n9.

26 Nardin, *supra* n10, 275. See also Jackson, *supra* n9.

27 C. Rudolph, "Constructing an Atrocities Regime: The Politics of War Crimes Tribunals," *International Organization* 55, no. 3 (2001): 655–91, 670.

28 International Crisis Group, *International Criminal Tribunal for Rwanda: Justice Delayed*, Africa Report, no. 30 (Nairobi/Arusha/Brussels), 7 June 2001, 24, on-line: International Crisis Group <http://www. crisisgroup.org >.

29 Schabas, *supra* n5, 86.

30 Philippe Kirsch, "The International Criminal Court: Current Issues and Perspectives," *Law and Contemporary Problems* 64, no. 1 (2001): 3–11, 4.

31 Gallarotti and Preis, *supra* n5, 110.

32 Michael J. Struett, "The Politics of Constructing an International Criminal Court," a paper presented at the International Studies Association Meetings, New Orleans, 24–27 March 2002.

33 See Benedetti and Washburn, *supra* n5. For an analysis of Canada's leading role in the "like-minded" group of states, see Antonio Franceschet and W. Andy Knight, "International(ist) Citizenship: Canada and the International Criminal Court," *Canadian Foreign Policy* 8, no. 2 (2001): 51–74.

34 Andrew Linklater, *The Transformation of Community: Ethical Foundations of the Post-Westphalian Era* (Cambridge, UK: Polity Press, 1998), 171.

35 Ibid., 184.

36 Ibid., 185.

37 Ibid.

38 The phrase "atrocities regime" comes from Rudolph, *supra* n27.

39 Jennifer Widner, "Courts and Democracy in Postconflict Transitions: A Social Scientist's Perspective on the African Case," *American Journal of* International Law 95, no. 1 (2001): 64–75.

40 *Convention on the Prohibition of the Use, Stockpiling, Production and Transfer of Anti-Personnel Mines and on their Destruction*, 18 September 1997, reprinted in *International Legal Materials* 36, no. 6 (1997): 1507.

41 Michael J. Struett, "NGOs, the International Criminal Court, and the Politics of Writing International Law," a paper presented at the Roundtable on the ICC, University of Utrecht, Netherlands, 4–6 July 2002.

42 See James L. Richardson, *Contending Liberalisms in World Politics: Ideology and Power* (Boulder, Colo.: Lynne Rienner Publishers, 2001).

Contributors

DAPO AKANDE is a lecturer in public international law at the University of Oxford and the Yamani Fellow and Tutor in Law at St Peters College. He was previously a lecturer in International Law at the University of Durham in the United Kingdom and has been a visiting professor at the University of Miami School of Law. His interests include the law and procedure of international tribunals, the law relating to international organizations, and international criminal law; he has published on these topics in leading international law journals. He is a member of the International Law Association's Committee on Accountability of International Organizations and he has advised and assisted counsel in cases before the International Court of Justice and the International Tribunal for the Law of the Sea, and before WTO and NAFTA dispute settlement panels. He has also provided advice on international law issues arising in domestic proceedings in several countries.

ANTONIO FRANCESCHET is an assistant professor of political science at Acadia University in Wolfville, Nova Scotia. He has published *Kant and Liberal Internationalism: Sovereignty, Justice, and Global Reform* (New York: Palgrave Macmillan, 2002), in addition to articles on international theory and ethics in *Global Governance*, *Canadian Foreign Policy*, *Review of International Studies*, *European Journal of International Relations*, and *International Journal*. He is currently editing a book entitled *The Ethics of Global Governance*.

JOANNA HARRINGTON is an associate professor at the Faculty of Law at the University of Alberta. She previously held appointments at the University of Western Ontario and the University of Nottingham, and visiting appointments at the University of Puerto Rico and the University of New South Wales. Her primary area of interest is the domestic application of international law, including international human rights law – an interest that builds on her experience as the Legal Officer to Lord Lester of Herne Hill, QC, during the incorporation of the European Convention on Human Rights into British law. Her recent publications have appeared in the *American Journal of International Law*, the *McGill Law Journal*, and the *Supreme Court Law Review*.

TRACY ISAACS is an associate professor in the Department of Philosophy at the University of Western Ontario. She has published articles on moral philosophy, feminist ethics, and action theory, and has a particular interest in philosophical questions about moral responsibility. Her contribution to this volume takes up some of the themes in her book-in-progress, *Individual Responsibility in Collective Contexts*. Her published articles have appeared in the journals *Ethics*, *Criminal Justice Ethics*, *The Southern Journal of Philosophy*, *Dialogue*, and *American Philosophical Quarterly*, and she is co-editor of the volume *A Question of Values: New Canadian Perspectives in Ethics and Political Philosophy* (Amsterdam: Rodopi Press, 1997) with Samantha Brennan and Michael Milde. Her next major research project will address issues of identity and agency under oppression.

CATHERINE LU is an assistant professor of political science at McGill University. Her work has included studies on the concept of justice, cosmopolitanism as a moral perspective, the ethics of humanitarian intervention, and moral regeneration after war, oppression, and atrocity. She has published articles in *The Journal of Political Philosophy*, *International Studies Review*, *Ethics and International Affairs*, *International Relations*, and *Review of International Studies*. For the 2004–05 academic year, she was on a faculty fellowship at the Edmond J. Safra Foundation Center for Ethics at Harvard University. Her forthcoming book is called *Just and Unjust Interventions in Word Politics: Public and Private* (London: Palgrave Macmillan, 2006).

MICHAEL MILDE is an associate professor in the Department of Philosophy and is associate dean (academic) of the Faculty of Arts and Humanities at the University of Western Ontario. He has published primarily in the area of legal and political philosophy, with a particular interest in social contract theory and constitutionalism. He is a consulting editor for the *Canadian Journal of Law and Jurisprudence*.

DARRYL ROBINSON currently serves in the ICC Office of the Prosecutor as a legal adviser on issues of jurisdiction, complementarity, and cooperation. From 1997 to 2003, he was a legal officer in the Human Rights and Humanitarian Law Section of the Canadian Department of Foreign Affairs and International Trade, responsible for international criminal justice issues. He was a member of the Canadian delegation to the ICC Preparatory Committee, Diplomatic Conference, Preparatory Commission, and Assembly of States Parties. He also taught international human rights law at the University of Ottawa from 1999 to 2003. Prior to that, he was a law clerk at the Supreme Court of Canada. Robinson obtained his LL.M at New York University School of Law, where he was a Hauser Global Scholar. He has numerous publications in the field of international criminal law.

MICHAEL SCHARF is a professor of law and the director of the Frederick K. Cox International Law Center at Case Western Reserve University School of Law. During the first Bush administration and Clinton administrations, Scharf served in the Office of the Legal Adviser of the US Department of State, where he held the positions of Counsel to the Counter-Terrorism Bureau, Attorney-Advisor for Law Enforcement and Intelligence, Attorney-Adviser for United Nations Affairs, and delegate to the United Nations General Assembly and to the United Nations Human Rights Commission. He is the author of over forty scholarly articles and seven books, including *Balkan Justice*, which was nominated for the Pulitzer Prize in 1998, *The International Criminal Tribunal for Rwanda*, which was awarded the American Society of International Law's Certificate of Merit for the Outstanding Book in International Law in 1999, *Peace with Justice*, which won the International Association of Penal Law's book of the year award for 2003, and casebooks on *The Law of International Organizations* and *International Criminal Law.*

ALEX TUCKNESS is an assistant professor of political science at Iowa State University and a former faculty fellow in ethics at Harvard University. He received his Ph.D. from Princeton University in political theory. He is the author of *Locke and the Legislative Point of View: Toleration, Contested Principles, and the Law* (Princeton: Princeton University Press, 2002). His articles have appeared in the *Journal of the History of Philosophy*, the *Journal of Political Philosophy*, the *American Journal of Political Science*, and the *Journal of the History of Ideas*.

RICHARD VERNON is a professor of political science at the University of Western Ontario. His publications include *Political Morality: A Theory of Liberal Democracy* (London: Continuum, 2001). He is currently working on issues of international justice.

DAVID WIPPMAN is a professor of law at Cornell University Law School. He has been teaching public international law, human rights, and international criminal law at Cornell since 1992. Before joining the faculty at Cornell, Wippman spent ten years in private practice. As a partner in the law firm of Reichler, Appelbaum & Wippman, he represented a number of foreign governments in litigation before US courts and international tribunals, as well as in legislative lobbying and political consulting on public and private international law issues. In 1998–99, Wippman served as a director in the Office of Multilateral and Humanitarian Affairs at the US National Security Council. In that capacity, he worked on war crimes issues, the International Criminal Court, economic sanctions, and UN political issues. Wippman is a graduate of Princeton University and Yale Law School, where he served as the editor-in-chief of the *Yale Law Journal*.